Marianne Bøe is a post-doctoral research associate at the Department of Archaeology, History, Cultural Studies and Religion, University of Bergen. She is an historian of religions who holds a PhD from the Centre for Women's and Gender Studies, University of Bergen. She has published widely on women's issues and religion, as well as on Muslim family law and Islam in Iran and in Europe.

FAMILY LAW IN CONTEMPORARY IRAN

Women's Rights Activism and Shari'a

Marianne Bøe

I.B. TAURIS
LONDON · NEW YORK

First published in 2015 by I.B.Tauris & Co. Ltd
www.ibtauris.com

International Library of Iranian Studies 54

ISBN: 978 1 78076 900 4
eISBN: 978 0 85773 763 2

A full CIP record for this book is available from the British Library
A full CIP record is available from the Library of Congress

Library of Congress Catalog Card Number: available

Typeset in Garamond Three by OKS Prepress Services, Chennai, India

For Liv

CONTENTS

ABBREVIATIONS

CEDAW	Convention on the Elimination of all forms of Discrimination Against Women
FPB	Family Protection Bill (*Layehe-ye Hemayat-e az Khanevadeh*)
FPL	Family Protection Law (*Qanun-e Hemayat-e Khanevadeh*)
ILNA	Iranian Labour News Agency
IRNA	Islamic Republic News Agency
NRK	Norwegian Broadcasting Association (Norsk rikskringkasting AS)
OMSC	One Million Signatures Campaign (*Yek Milyun Emza-ye Baraye Taghir-e Qavanin-e Tab'iz Amiz*)
SIS	Sisters in Islam
WLUML	Women Living Under Muslim Laws
WOI	Women's Organisation of Iran (*Sazeman-e Zanan-e Iran*)
WSIR	Women's Society of the Islamic Revolution (*Jam'e-ye Zanan-e Enghelab-e Eslami*)

TRANSLITERATION AND TRANSLATION

In the text, both standard Arabic and standard Persian terms are used. The transliteration is based on a simplified version of the IJMES transliteration guide.[1] In the text, the letters ع (*'ayn*) and ء (*hamza*) are marked respectively ' and ', but diacritical characters and markers showing length of vowels are disregarded. In addition, the letter ی is denoted by either y or i. Regular English spelling for words commonly translated from Arabic or Persian, such as Qur'an and Shah, is employed. Arabic and Persian words not commonly used in English are italicised. Unless otherwise mentioned, all translations from Persian and Arabic are by the present author.

ACKNOWLEDGEMENTS

The research that forms the basis of this book was originally conducted as a PhD project at the University of Bergen, Norway, from 2008 until 2012. Many people have guided and supported me through the project. First and foremost, I am grateful to all the interviewees who have given of their time and knowledge. Without their contribution, there would have been no book. I also want to thank Laleh and Mahta for the help, love and care they have provided during my stays in Tehran. *Daste shoma dard nakone!* I would like to offer a special thanks to my main supervisor Richard J. Natvig, and to the two co-supervisors I have had in this process, Knut S. Vikør and Ellen Mortensen. I am indebted to colleagues at the Centre for Women's and Gender Research (SKOK), the Department of Archaeology, History, Culture, and Religion (AHKR), and those affiliated with the Centre for Middle Eastern and Islamic Studies (SMI), who have given of their time to read and discuss my work, both in academic and social settings. I particularly want to mention Anders Bjørkelo, Ingvild Flaskerud, Eirik Hovden, Kari Jegerstedt, Lisbeth Mikaelsson, Ziba Mir-Hosseini, Valentine M. Moghadam, Gaudencia Mutema, Catharina Raudvere, Håkan Rydving, Mahmoud Salih, Gilda Seddighi, David Thurfjell, Liv Tønnessen and Hans Geir Aasmundsen. I would also like to give a special thanks to Virginia Myers for her assistance as copy-editor, and to Alan Qaderi for patiently reading and translating Persian texts with me. Finally,

I want to express gratitude to family and friends for always taking an interest in my work, and to my mother Eli and father Arnt Even for all the love and support. Most of all, I thank Kevin for being my biggest fan throughout it all.

INTRODUCTION

Family law has been a divisive and ongoing issue of debate in Iran since the early 1900s. Throughout different periods, various forms of codification have been launched seeking to fulfil a dual purpose of implementing both Shari'a and women's rights. The most recent initiative came in 2007, when the Family Protection Bill (*Layehe-ye Hemayat-e az Khanevadeh*) was introduced. With this bill, family law once again emerged as a contentious issue, to which women's rights activists have offered significant contributions.[1] This book deals with the discussion that evolved over the Family Protection Bill in Iran between 2007 and 2011. Mainly, the debate is presented from the perspectives of Iranian women's rights activists. Those included in the book represent highly diverse ideas and opinions on the bill. Still, the various conceptions of family law that the activists use are all rooted in the discursive tradition of Islam and the history of Iran – although in different ways. The activists in this book make references to principles of Islamic jurisprudence (*usul al-fiqh*), CEDAW,[2] Ayatollah Khomeini, 'Ali Shari'ati, Forough Farrokhzad and Mehrangiz Manoochehrian, to mention a few. Accordingly, they offer a vivid glimpse into the ideas of Shari'a and women's rights at play in contemporary Iranian society.

The quest for a family law code in Iran

Discussions on family law legislation are not new to Iran. The quest for a designated Iranian family law code has been persistent throughout the state's modern history. In terms of legal codifications, the development of family law can be summarised in three main waves. The Iranian Civil Code from 1928 represented the first designated family law codification, and a second initiative was enacted in the Family Protection Law in 1967. In 1979, with the establishment of the Islamic Republic of Iran, the 1967 Act was officially denounced. Since then only isolated reforms have been passed in family law, and together with the 1928 Iranian Civil Code they have served as the legal basis for family law rulings since 1979. However, a substitute codification of family law was lacking until 2007, when the so-called Family Protection Bill was introduced. In effect, this bill was the first official draft of an Iranian family law code in 40 years.

The Family Protection Bill represents a comprehensive draft of family law legislation, and with it the debate on family law once again emerged as a divisive public issue. The government of President Mahmoud Ahmadinejad (2005–13) initially introduced the bill in 2007, although the first preparations are said to date further back. How to regulate Shari'a in a contemporary Islamic state, and in particular the practices of polygyny (*chandhamsari*), dower (*mehrieh*) and temporary marriage (*sighe/mut'a*), were among the most conflict-ridden topics. One of the more contentious issues has been whether a man has an unlimited right to take more than one wife, or if he is dependent on his first wife's consent. In addition, the limits of state or private regulation of temporary marriage and dower have been discussed. Mainly, three articles of the bill were the subject of public debate:

1. Article 22 dealing with rules on temporary marriage (*mut'a* or *sighe*),
2. Article 23 proposing new regulations on polygyny (*chandzani*),[3]
3. Article 25/24 addressing restrictions in terms of dower (*mehrieh*).

These three articles have caused widespread disagreements over the bill and have led to three revisions of it between 2007 and 2011. In 2012 the debate over the content of the bill was put on hold.

Its future is now dependent on how larger internal and external conflicts in Iran play out. It is, however, expected that the bill will re-emerge in one form or another. Although its final fate remains to be seen, one thing is certain: the quest for an Iranian family law code has not yet reached its end and will continue in the years to come.

Family law and women's rights activism in Iran

A major concern in this book is to analyse the Family Protection Bill as a contemporary debate on Islam engaged in by a selection of women's rights activists.[4] Although there are connections to be traced between women's rights activism and family law debates in Iran, the context of the present Islamic Republic provides a special case for their study. In Iran – a state in which Shari'a is said to govern the legal system and which has also been proclaimed as an Islamic Republic – Islam and Shari'a hold a preferential place. Only in countries such as Sudan and Saudi Arabia has the official call for a return to Shari'a been made so explicitly. Concurrently, women's and gender issues in Islam have been high on the official agenda. Still, Iran is not a country that tends to be associated with open public debate, as the government carefully controls debates, especially on religion and gender.

In particular, the high level of censorship has risen since the demonstrations that followed the 2009 presidential election. Among other groups, women's rights activists have been targeted with increasing control and surveillance; many have been threatened, imprisoned, or forced to leave the country because of their opinions. Speaking up against state-defined concepts of Shari'a and women's rights is associated not only with being against the Islamic Republic, but also with being an enemy of God (*mohareb*). In such an authoritarian and dictatorial setting, the restrictions are beyond what is commonly associated with a vibrant public debate as defined, for example, by Jürgen Habermas (1991). Despite these enforced limitations and the lack of an open democracy, however, it seems striking that family law is a topic of public discussion in which not only politicians and religious scholars (*ulama*) engage, but also members of the wider society such as women's rights activists. This book will show that within the limited framework permitted for public debate in the Islamic Republic, the issue of family law legislation remains highly contentious.

The dual call for safeguarding both Shari'a prescriptions and women's rights has been intrinsic to the different attempts at family law reforms in Iran. Although the importance and emphasis of these demands has shifted over time, the need for implementing both Shari'a and women's rights has been reflected in family law reforms and debates to some degree ever since the early 1900s. Various actors debating elements of family law reform today continue to stress these two requirements, although with different emphases. Women's rights activists who oppose the Family Protection Bill, as well as those of them who defend it, refer to principles of Shari'a and women's rights alike in support of their arguments. The relationship between these two poles signifies ongoing efforts to define 'authentic' models of gender in Islam.

Dissemination of religious knowledge

In recent years, an interesting shift has come to the fore in terms of producing religious knowledge in Islam. An increasing number of Muslims no longer accept ready-made interpretations, but are gradually relying on their own ideas of what Islam entails.[5] Although this development cannot be said to represent a new phenomenon as such, there has been a noticeable growth during the last decade in the number of ordinary Muslims who participate in producing knowledge on their own religion[6] More and more Muslims ask themselves what it means to be a believer, and consult and interpret religious sources for themselves in order to figure out how to guide their behaviour. The task of deciding what Islam is and says is no longer seen as the preserve of *ulama*, but questions that an increasing number of ordinary Muslims can ask and provide answers for themselves.

As part of this trend, a range of new voices has been heard in regard to Shari'a. What constitutes 'authentic' interpretations of

Shari'a is a core issue of debate among Muslims nowadays and also a noticeable feature of contemporary family law debates in several Muslim countries. There are numerous voices and interpretations to be found expressing what should be seen as 'correct' and 'authentic' models and norms for gender, in particular in regard to women's rights in Islam. Such demands are not limited to questions of how to pray or what to eat. In addition, issues of Islamic jurisprudence are up for debate. A plethora of women's rights organisations and activists engage in Muslim family law debates locally, for instance in Morocco, Tunisia, Egypt, Iran and Malaysia (Tucker 2008 and Moghadam 2013b), or take part in global movements and networks like Women Living Under Muslim Laws, Women's Learning Partnership for Rights, Musawah, or Sisters in Islam (Moghadam 2013a). How to codify a Muslim family law that is in line with Shari'a and at the same time safeguards women's rights represents a continual struggle in most Muslim societies.

Such endeavours are thus not particular to Iran, nor can they be seen specifically as 'new' trends. Rather, the upsurge of Muslim women's rights activism goes back at least to the early nineteenth century, and attempts to define 'authentic' models of gender in Islam have taken place in different historical periods in most Muslim societies. [7] What is new, however, is the breadth that these debates on Islam have assumed in recent decades. Whereas previously reserved as the domain of religious authorities alone, a number of 'ordinary' people today take part in defining what constitutes 'correct' and 'authentic' Islam. Consequently, issues of Muslim family law and Shari'a are no longer the privileged area of *ulama*, but are also up for debate by a range of Muslims and subject to profound processes of change.

Nevertheless, the concept of authority still lies at the heart of these developments. Religious authority takes many forms and is contingent on both formal and informal power structures, and is also linked to the concept of legitimacy. According to Max Weber, authority involves accepting power as something legitimate by those subjected to it (1964: 382). In this view, the changes taking place with regard to religious authority in Islam are thus inextricably connected to the believers who start to question and seek alternative solutions to the authorities that they no longer see as legitimate. Thus, the study of changes in religious authority should start from the believers' point of view. Krämer and Schmidkte, however, rightly point out that this does not so much involve a fragmentation of religious authority, but rather a proliferation of religious knowledge, actors and normative statements (2006: 12). Thus, the developments signify a shift in religious knowledge in Islam. This is the case for Sunni and Shi'a Islam alike. The ongoing family law debate in Iran and the women's rights activists presented in this book can be seen as part of this trend of disseminating Shi'a religious knowledge in contemporary Iran.

The contribution of this book

In recent years a growing strand of research has been dealing with contemporary Muslim family law debates.[8] However, the ways in which family law debates and women's rights activism intersect have not been adequately covered. This book seeks to address this gap in research in both areas. The overall research questions are: How do Iranian women's rights activists conceive of family law as expressed through the concepts of Shari'a and women's rights, and what kinds of intersections exist between women's rights activism and family law debates in contemporary Iran? Moreover, what do the intersections convey in terms of dissemination of Shi'a religious knowledge?

The methodological approach, as well as the choice of methods and sources, relate to the overall hypothesis. My own point of departure as a researcher is that when people engage in debates about religion and gender, they do so in relation to broader issues of concern in their lives and societies. On this basis, I have decided to inquire into the ways in which women's rights activists in this research conceive of family law. The study thus elaborates on how their views depend on and are conditioned by their various situations and how they relate differently to aspects of religious legitimacy and authority. The situatedness of women's rights activists is reflected in the dual conditions of subjective perceptions and context.

Although as a researcher I have by and large been inspired by Talal Asad's call to approach Islam as a discursive tradition (1986), one of my main concerns is not to ascribe to Islam a too unique or prominent role when studying Muslims. In most current research, Islam is considered a discursive tradition on the premise that it represents 'simply a tradition of Muslim discourse that addresses itself to conceptions of the Islamic past and future, with reference to a particular Islamic practice in the present' (op. cit.: 14). The Asadian approach reveals a vast amount of studies on Islam at the present time. Recently, though, such studies have received criticism. Mainly, the critique relates to how Asad's approach to Islam builds on a static division between a 'western' and a 'non-western' world that takes no account of the different notions that Muslims hold of the secular (Bangstad 2009) and fails to address aspects of change and breaks with the religious tradition (Schielke 2010). Moreover, it is argued that the role of Islam is favoured in the construction of Muslim identity over that of other factors (Ismail 2004: 617).

This critique has proven highly relevant for this study. The women's rights activists presented here conceive of Shari'a and women's rights in highly diverse ways. However, the complexities of Muslim women's rights activism are often incompletely studied or even ignored. In this book, I therefore seek to understand how perceptions of family law are shaped and conditioned by larger frames of references pertaining not only to religion, but also to other frameworks, and how they are related to aspects of legitimacy and authority both historically and today. Instead of analysing the conceptions of family law presented here as either mere outcomes of changes or continuations of Islam, aspects of both processes will be addressed.

As part of this approach, a processual and actor-oriented methodological approach towards Shari'a is deployed. Shari'a is not understood normatively or from an insider's perspective, but as consisting of various fields of knowledge. Rather than seeking only text-based, formal and authoritative sources and definitions of Shari'a, the book elaborates on everyday, informal and subjective conceptions of what is referred to and perceived as Shari'a. Consequently, the ways in which specific topics of family law are debated serve to illustrate various fields of knowledge in Shari'a – the ideal, the practice and the conceptions of the topics in question. This triangular division of Shari'a is based on the findings of this study and will figure throughout the book. The three fields of knowledge pertain to what is considered to be 'Islamic', or 'in accordance with Shari'a', or 'in line with women's rights'. Such considerations are again contingent on the larger context in which the issue is practised and on who is speaking. The ongoing debate of the Family Protection Bill will therefore be mainly addressed from the perspective of various women's rights activists in Iran, which is the conceptual level of Shari'a. This represents an important perspective in studies of what is referred to as Shari'a, as well as in relation to the research on gender and Islam, because of its focus on the process and actors behind such constructions.

This book also offers a new approach to the issues of representativity and difference among Muslim women's rights activists. It moves away from identitarian-based categories, and strives instead towards incorporating the various conceptions of women's rights activists on a common basis. Most studies of contemporary women's rights activism connect a religious identity to the kind of categories employed, by characterising the activists as 'Muslim', 'secular', and 'Islamic'. This study, however, follows Iris Marion Young's alternative way of thinking of gender as a social collective (1997),[9] and strives to include aspects of difference that are often ignored in identitarian-based group conceptualisations. Instead of 'Islamic' and 'secular', the categories 'rejectionist', 'revisionist', and 'loyalist' are applied. [10] They are built on Carolyn Osiek's typology of hermeneutical perspectives on the Bible (1985). These categories draw attention to the centrality of religious texts that is common among the activists, but also reflect different ways of approaching religious sources – which can be found in other religions such as Christianity and Judaism. Also, the categories of rejectionist and loyalist serve to denote positions that often have been excluded from studies of gender and Islam.

Consequently, the results of this study contradict the notion that women's rights activism in Iran takes the form of a uniform 'Islamic feminism', but rather show that there is a plurality of ideas about the combination of Shari'a and women's rights. In this way, the categorisation applied does not necessarily presume that the conceptions put forward take secular-liberal, feminist, or merely religious outlooks on women's rights as an ultimate aspiration, but rather denotes how secular and religious-based sources intersect in approaches to family law.

Methods and sources

In order to address the above-mentioned topics, the research presented here is based on a variety of sources. The major ones are elite interviews and unstructured interviews and conversations with women's rights activists collected mainly in Tehran, but also in some European cities in 2002,[11] and between 2008 and 2011. In addition to the interview material, a number of different textual source have been used. First, some legal codes. The 1928 Iranian Civil Code (*Qanun-e Irani-ye Madani*) was drafted between 1928 and 1936 and represents Iran's first civil code. Its sources are Shi'a law,[12] the Napoleonic Code and European codes of law. I also make use of Fakhreddin Badrian's translation of the Iranian Civil Code from 2002. In addition, the study is based on several textual sources published online. Some references are also made to the 1967/75 Family Protection Law and to the 1979 Constitution of the Islamic Republic of Iran. The full texts of these legal codes are available online.[13] The 2007 and the 2010 versions of the Family Protection Bill are referred to and are also published online.[14] Although the final fate of the bill remains to be seen, I have limited the debate on it to August 2011, when the overall discussion on the 2010 version of the bill was diminishing. Moreover, a vast amount of the information about the debate of the Family Protection Bill has been derived from the internet. Some of the main sources of this study are articles and statements published by women's rights activists on the 2007, 2010 and 2011 Family Protection Bills, as well as alternative drafts of family law bills such as that of Mehrangiz Manoochehrian from 1963/64 and the proposition of 'women from different Iranian cities', both of which are available online (Fair Family Law website, henceforth FFL, 8.5.10 and Manoochehrian 1963/64).[15] Among the most cited websites are Fair Family Law (*Qanun-e Barabari*),[16] the websites of the One Million Signatures Campaign (*Yek Milyun Emza-ye Baraye Taghir-e Qavanin-e Tab'iz Amiz*),[17] the Feminist School (*Madrese-ye Feministi*)[18] and Meydan (Women's Field).[19]

Obviously, these online publications have made the field more accessible to me as a researcher. Following the presidential election in 2009, I was not able to return to Iran as intended in 2010 and 2011. Considering these difficulties, the online publications have been invaluable in order to follow the debate. Had it not been for the publications on the websites of Fair Family Law for instance, a great deal of information about the Family Protection Bill would never have been available to me. Collecting data and conducting research online does, however, provide a set of challenges. Daniel Varisco has described internet-based research as 'being there online', or 'conducting ethnography in cyberspace' (Varisco 2000 and 2002). He claims that many researchers today engage in 'participant webservation'. Although there are some new challenges that emerge as part of these technological developments, the same methodological and epistemological issues are relevant in cyberspace research as in other kinds of research, as pointed out by Hakken (1999). For instance, the importance of situating the problem of the study and having the necessary academic training and language knowledge remains the same.

By means of the internet, though, the field that previously was 'out there' and far away, is now brought closer and demands new questions on the researcher's own impact on the topic in study. We are online as users, but also as researchers. The technology enables a greater flow in terms of intersections of local and global contexts. By means of the increased globalisation and flow of information across borders via the internet, the researcher's and the interviewee's fields are connected in new ways. Thus, new ethical challenges have developed as a result of internet-based research and webservation.

The interviewees

A total of 28 women's rights activists were interviewed for this study.[20] They can all be defined as women's rights activists, meaning that in one way or another they are preoccupied with issues of women's rights. They include activists engaged in women's and family NGOs and state organisations, or working on an individual basis. By profession, they are professors, lawyers, journalists, researchers, students or government employees. Twenty-six of the interviewees are female, and two are male women's rights activists. One had previously worked for a women's rights NGO and the other for the One Million Signatures Campaign (OMSC). Also, four of the interviewees were interviewed in different European cities. Two of them I met only outside Iran, and the other two were interviewed both in Tehran and after moving into exile in Europe. In terms of background, most of the older interviewees such as Afsaneh, Bahareh, Parisa, Maryam and Arezoo belong to the upper strata of society. Many of them also obtained PhD degrees after studying abroad (Europe or the United States) and returned to Iran either just before or shortly after the 1979 Revolution. The social backgrounds of the younger interviewees, however, varied. Some belong to the upper middle classes (such as Ziba), whereas others (such as Leyli, Shahla and 'Ali) come from rural areas and the lower classes. In general, there seem to be larger social and class differentiations among the younger activists included in this book than among the older ones.

The selection of interviewees was primarily made by the so-called snowball method (Repstad 2007). I started the investigation in 2008 with four key interviewees (Afsaneh, Parisa, Bahareh and Arezoo) who introduced me to others. Later, some others became key persons advising me whom to talk to next. The snowballing method has certain implications. A limitation of selecting interviewees in this way is whether a representative number from different groups have been recruited. Most of the interviewees in this study can be categorised as elite women's rights activists belonging to the upper strata of society. Such a social background can hardly be said to signify women's rights activism in general. Moreover, most of the interviewees represent revisionist views on family law. Without being too categorical, it is possible to say that about 20 of the interviewees represented revisionist outlooks, whereas the remaining eight were rejectionists and loyalists. This uneven representation can be seen as a consequence both of the methodological basis of the study and the method of selecting interviewees. Both the processual and actor-oriented approach and the snowballing method impose limitations on the representativeness of the research. There is thus no claim that this study is representative beyond the interviewees included here, or that the broader population of Iran shares these points of view. Instead, the study illustrates the different opinions and perceptions of family law legislation of some women's rights activists in contemporary Iran.

Outline of the book

The Family Protection Bill is linked to quite specific ideas of women's rights and Islam in present-day Iranian society. These ideas are, however, also connected to some of the recurrent definitions of genderhood and sexuality to be found throughout Iran's modern history. The eight chapters of this book seek to capture aspects of change and continuity encapsulated by the contemporary family law debate. Chapter One looks into concepts related to Shari'a and Muslim family law debates with a special emphasis on the importance of authority. In Chapter Two, the significant role of marriage in Islam is discussed. In particular, the ways in which the issues of dower, polygyny and temporary marriage have been regulated and organised in various Muslim family law codifications will be explored comparatively. The chapter also examines the fields of knowledge that inform issues of Muslim family law. Marriage-related issues are conditioned and established not only by religious prescriptions as defined in the Qur'an and *ahadith*, or as interpreted by Islamic scholars. They are shaped by everyday experiences and conceptions. The ideal, the practice and the conceptions that inform the issues of dower, polygyny and temporary marriage are brought out in Chapter Two. In Chapter Three, the content, breaks and continuities of the Family Protection Bill are explored, in particular the three issues of dower, polygyny and temporary marriage. The two subsequent chapters address the question of how family law is debated and conceived by the women's rights activists in this study. The general elaborations by various women's rights activists on the issues of Shari'a and family law are presented in Chapter Four, and Chapter Five examines the particular ways in which they relate to issues of dower, polygynous and temporary marriage.

Both family law reforms and women's rights activism have, however, been important for definitions of genderhood in Iran for decades. Such definitions are not fixed once and for all, but have been constantly changing over time. Chapter Six therefore explores different periods of women's rights activism in the country, and Chapter Seven correspondingly inquires into the shifting paradigms on gender and sexuality that have existed in Iran from the early 1900s until the present. Thus, Chapters Six and Seven discuss the ways in which models of genderhood have been constructed, negotiated and transformed throughout Iran's modern history. Finally, Chapter Eight investigates the means by which women's rights activists' conceptions of family law are legitimised and authorised in contemporary Iran. In doing so, it reports on how women's rights activists included in this study engage in present-day quests for authentication of their views on family law. Lastly, some final remarks sum up the main contributions of this book.

CHAPTER 1

SHARI'A AND FAMILY LAW

Shari'a is a multifaceted term and may refer to several levels of meaning. On the one hand it is said to express the idea of a divine law, and on the other hand a legal system that regulates economic, political, religious aspects of society and relations between people. The term Shari'a is also complicated, as it refers to a range of ideas, practices and perceptions. It builds on Islam's sacred sources of Qur'an and Sunna, entails a set of different codifications enforced in various contexts over centuries, and refers to numerous interpretations made either from scholarly or everyday points of view. The call to lead a life according to Shari'a is seen as an important guideline in the lives of many Muslims, and thus represents different meanings. Literally, Shari'a means 'the path to the waterhole', which is often interpreted as a metaphor for the way to God's will. Shari'a is believed to be both an expression of divine will to guide the conduct of Muslims in this life and the hereafter, and the basis for social and human relations. Moreover, Shari'a involves a legal evaluation of actions ranging from the obligatory (*wajib*) to the prohibited (*haram*).[1] The tension between Shari'a as a guide for social, religious and human conduct and as divine will has been recurrent throughout the history of Islam.

Shari'a, *fiqh*, or Islamic law?

A set of conceptual problems arises with the study of Shari'a, which falls into the category of religious law. Similar to Jewish law,

Halakha, Shari'a refers to the notion that the word of God is law as expressed in the religious sources. The sources do not, however, represent conventional material for a legal code; nor do they deal with legal topics comprehensively. Rather, they contain universal principles, doctrines and injunctions that can be used in the making of law. Thus, it becomes important to make a distinction between various concepts used.

In most research literature the concept of Shari'a is translated as 'Islamic law', but this has been criticised on several grounds. First, the very term 'law' is said to relate to cultural and conceptual ambiguities, in which Eurocentric approaches tend to form the basis for understanding other legal systems (Hallaq 2009: 1). Shari'a does not have a counterpart, for instance, in European codes of law, and remains distinct from systems of common law or codified law, for example the Napoleonic Code. Due to the central position of the mufti in elaborating on Shari'a,[2] it has rather been referred to as juristic law (Vikør 2003: 18–19).[3] The term 'Islamic law' is often used as a parallel both to Shari'a and *qanun*, but without distinguishing between these two levels of meaning. The concept *qanun* is most closely referred to as legislation, but may also imply regulations, codifications, acts or statutes (Khan 2010: 112). Consequently, some are of the opinion that Islamic law is an inaccurate term. According to the renowned scholar Wael Hallaq, the straightforward academic approach towards Shari'a remains particularly problematic because of the Orientalist failure to distinguish between law and morality in Shari'a, and – according to Hallaq – it is a topic that has not been adequately problematised by scholars of Shari'a (2009: 2). On this basis, the very term 'law' remains difficult and problematic when used as replacement for the concept of Shari'a.[4]

Second, a general distinction is often made between Shari'a and *fiqh*. Whereas the former refers to the idea of divine revelation, the latter corresponds to human interpretation or understanding of Shari'a (Mir-Hosseini 2000a: 5). *Fiqh* is thus the methodological basis of Shari'a, and researchers of Shari'a often translate *fiqh* into Islamic jurisprudence and as representing a science of law or systematised knowledge used in developing law (Khan 2010: 112).

According to Noel J. Coulson, the science of *fiqh* refers to understanding and ascertaining Shari'a by means of classical legal theory (1964: 75–6).[5] Among believing Muslims, there is not usually a tendency to distinguish between these two levels of understanding, but such a division is often made by researchers of Shari'a for analytical purposes. The distinction, however, is difficult to grasp because the concepts Shari'a, *fiqh* and *furu'* may be applied interchangeably.[6] What is more, Muslims themselves often blur these levels of understanding. Codified laws may be seen as representing Shari'a, although several variations of codification on one and the same issue may exist. The meaning of the different concepts used is therefore highly dependent on their context (Vikør 2003: 308). Some researchers, however, maintain this difference as a basis for analysis. Ziba Mir-Hosseini claims that Shari'a can never be understood or applied completely as it represents a divine ideal. She thus distinguishes between ideal and reality, or theory and practice. Accordingly, she states that the only aspect available for humans is the level of *fiqh* – Shari'a in reality or in practice (2000a: 8).

Third, there is some debate over the analytical conception of Shari'a, and most recently over the use of 'Islamic law' *vs.* 'Muslim law'. This distinction also contributes to underline both the ideal and applied levels that the concept of Shari'a represents. Whereas the use of 'Islamic law' implies a fixed and determined version of law, the concept of 'Muslim law' is said to refer to a notion in which the agency of Muslims is accounted for. Moreover, 'Muslim law' can be seen as encapsulating Shari'a as a product of social, political and historical developments, whereas 'Islamic law' is said to project a more static and ahistorical approach. In this regard, it could be added that the term 'Islamic law' entails emic and somewhat normative evaluations of what can be seen as representing the 'Islamic' or not. For instance, can one codification of Shari'a be more 'Islamic' than another, and who is to decide the 'Islamicness' of a legal code? The labelling 'Islamic law' can thus be said to have normative implications, which is also a reason for why some researchers prefer the term 'Muslim law', as it opens up a higher degree of flexibility and inclusion of different interpretations of Shari'a. The term

'Muslim law' was previously frequently used in research literature from the 1960s and 1970s, but with the wave of Islamisation that hit many predominantly Muslim countries in the late 1970s and 1980s[7] the term 'Islamic law' gained ground. There are now signs that 'Muslim law' is reappearing in studies of family law in particular. The approach towards Shari'a as 'Muslim law' has emerged as a result of contemporary transformations in research of Shari'a as a topic of everyday negotiations and public debate, which are discussed further below.

First, however, it is necessary to clarify the main differences between Shi'a and Sunni conceptions of Shari'a. In legal practice, there are more similarities than differences between these two directions of law. The divergences are mostly found in inheritance law and with regard to temporary marriage (*mut'a* or *sighe*). Shi'a inheritance law is more complex than the Sunni version, and whereas Shi'a law accepts temporary marriage, Sunni schools of law have prohibited the practice. The Ja'fari school of law is sometimes referred to as the fifth school of law, in addition to the four Sunni schools of law.[8] The formative period of the major Sunni schools of law took place between 700 and 1000 CE, whereas the Ja'fari school of law developed in a formative period from approximately the year 1000 until the fourteenth century.

The Shi'a branch of Islam has three main schools of law.[9] The Ja'fari school of law is that of the Imamis (*Ithna 'ashari* or Twelvers), named after the sixth Shi'a Imam Ja'far as-Sadiq (d. 765). The Ja'fari school is dominant in Iran, and mainly relies on hadith transmitted by the Prophet or his family via the heirs of 'Ali and Fatemeh. The Zaydi school of law has its name from the fifth Shi'a Imam Zayd ibn 'Ali (d. 740). The school belongs to Zaydis (or Fivers) and is mostly found in Yemen. They are seen as inspired by the Sunni view on legal issues (Vikør 2003: 123). The Isma'ili school of law is the school of Isma'ilis (or Seveners), named after the seventh Shi'a Imam Isma'il ibn Ja'far (d. 755). It was the dominant school of law during the Fatimid Empire (909–1171) and is based on principles derived by Qadi al-Numan (d. 974). The Shi'a schools of law were developed under living Imams for a certain period of time, and thus relate quite differently to the principles of shari'a from the Sunni schools of law. In particular, Shi'a concepts of *qiyas* and *ijma'*, as well as of authority, differ from those of Sunni schools of law (Momen 1985: 185–8). The concept of *ijma'* for Shi'a jurisprudence points to the consensus of the imams as expressed mainly in the Sunna. In addition, the Shi'a school of law has formally rejected the concept of *qiyas* and rather relies on *'aql* (reasoning) as a source of Shari'a, which has laid the ground for a more widespread use of the principle of *ijtihad* (independent reasoning) in Shi'a jurisprudence. Among the traditional sources of jurisprudence for the Ja'fari school of law are the works of Muhaqiq al-Hilli (d. 1277) and Shahid Awwal (d. 1384). More contemporary sources of importance are publications by Ayatollah Ruhollah Khomeini (1902–89) and Ayatollah Morteza Motahhari (1920–79).

Authority and legitimacy

Shari'a has never been devised by one book or compilation. There is no one Shari'a, nor is there a single textbook that summarises what Shari'a entails. Rather, there are a number of *ulama* from different schools of law (*madhahib*) who elaborate in written or oral form on their opinions of what Shari'a represents in various cases. Shari'a is the result of ongoing efforts and inquiries relating to the Qur'an and ahadith (pl. of hadith) made by *ulama* on the basis of certain principles and methods. Thus, there is no consensus as to what Shari'a involves, despite the belief that it should be based on and express a divine will in Islam.

Authority is therefore a key concept, and writing on the topic of Shari'a is impossible without making reference to authority and legitimacy. As Wael Hallaq put it: 'To say that authority is the centrepiece of Islamic law is merely to state the obvious' (Hallaq 2001: xi). Authority, according to Hallaq, has evolved around 'the *power* to set in motion the inherent processes of change and continuity' in Shari'a throughout history (ibid.). Said Amir Arjomand further suggests that we take 'the right or legitimate claim to obedience as the essential component of the notion of authority' (1988: 1). An interpretation of Shari'a is dependent on the legitimacy it holds in the Muslim community (*umma*). In the case of a fatwa for instance,[10] the idea is that a Muslim can choose which fatwa he or she wishes to follow in a particular case. The decision often rests on what kind of *madhhab* the person belongs to, as well as which religious authority (*'alim*) he or she has confidence in.

The question of the authority and legitimacy of an interpretation of Shari'a thus results from a combination of religious affiliation and geographical position. For instance, whereas in Sunni Islam the appointed caliphs are considered the successors of the Prophet and should receive obedience on this basis, Shi'a conceptions of authority developed differently.[11] In Shi'a Islam, the legitimacy of the caliphs is rejected, and it is rather the leadership of 'Ali ibn Abi Talib and his descendants that is seen as representing the legitimate successors of the Prophet. On this basis, the supreme guidance of the imams is not only established, but also linked to the notion of their possession of *'ilm* (science/knowledge) (Arjomand 1988: 3). The importance of *'ilm* is further underlined by the transfer of authority from the imams to contemporary Shi'a *ulama* through the occultation of the twelfth Imam. The concept of the *'ilm* of the Shi'a imams has no counterpart in Sunnism, and represents a distinctive feature of Shi'a authority. Arjomand thus asserts that the two most distinctive features of the Shi'a concept of authority are linked to the imamate and to *'ilm* (op. cit.: 3).

Shi'a religious authority, however, is constantly being challenged. The first schism between state and religious authority in Iran was introduced during the Safavid dynasty in 1501. Following a doctrinal split in Shi'a theology,[12] a hierocracy that later became independent of the state was established during the Qajar era. However, yet another chapter in the relationship between the state and religious authority was initiated with the establishment of the Islamic Republic of Iran in 1979. Ayatollah Khomeini presented a novel principle of state religious authority under the idea of the guardianship of the jurist (*velayat-e faqih*). Since its introduction, Khomeini's theory has been a source of tension and debate for Shi'a religious authorities.

However, with the controversial presidential election in 2009, the ongoing struggle between state and religious authority reached a new high. According to Arjomand, a new phase of hierocracy–state relations was inaugurated after 2009 (2010). Moreover, the demonstrations that followed the election contributed to accentuate the debate over the principles of the Islamic Revolution and the basis of the Islamic Republic. Arjomand further adds that:

> The eruption of the Green Movement in Iran has occurred in conjunction with birth of a new oppositional Shi'ite jurisprudence whose roots may be traced to the reform movement that emerged during the first year of Khatami's presidency. (2010)

Shi'ite jurisprudence and Shari'a are thus being challenged in contemporary Iran on more than one level. The degree of legitimacy that an interpretation of Shari'a may represent is not only dependent on formal aspects of authority, but also to a high degree on the level of religious authority held by the person behind the interpretation. In fact, it may go beyond the titles of *faqih*, mufti and *mujtahid*. In order to reveal the level of access a person or a group has to religious authority and legitimacy, there is thus a need to move beyond the formal levels of authority in Shari'a. The concept of religious proximity can be helpful in this regard. Erica Appelros has introduced the analytical concept of 'religious proximity', and claims that religion as a power structure operates within higher and lower degrees of religious proximity (2007).[13] A formalised or institutionalised religious position, such as the one held by the Pope in Catholicism or by the Shi'i *ulama*, represents the highest degrees of formal religious proximity. There are, however, also informal degrees of religious proximity that relate to people who lack the institutionalised forms of authority, but who make up for it by other means, for instance their level of religious knowledge, piety, or religious affiliation. Because of their knowledge of religious sources, exemplary behaviour, or role in the religious community, some may be able to acquire a higher degree of religious proximity than their position would imply. Religious proximity thus highlights the fact that authority and legitimacy may vary according to where you are standing, i.e. the situatedness of the person or group.

In order to grasp this dimension of religious authority, understanding it in terms of a formalised or institutionalised positioning or a person's religion can prove to be inadequate. Religious authority is not only restricted to titles or positions of leadership, but may also appear in unexpected circles and places. Moreover, religious authority endorses a kind of power relation that is not only limited to gender and class, but may also intersect and be dependent on other power structures. These may result in various configurations of religious proximity. For instance, a Muslim woman does not traditionally hold the authority to become an *'alim* mainly because of her gender.[14] Due to her level of religious knowledge and piety, however, she may prove to be acknowledged as one, despite lacking formal qualifications. This was the case with Banu Amin Esfahani, for instance, who was recognised as a female *mujtahid* in Qom in the 1960s.[15] In addition, other power structures may have influence on the notion of religious proximity. One example can be found among some contemporary women's rights activists and female politicians in Iran who because of their political and/or family relations in the Islamic Republic obtain a higher level of religious legitimacy than other women. Both A'zam Taleqani and Faezeh Hashemi are examples of women who have gained both political and some religious influence based on their family affiliations.[16] Thus, religious proximity reveals not only power structures within formal religious hierarchies, but also within informal hierarchies such as those that go beyond categories of class and gender and rely instead on the importance of religious knowledge, devoutness, and religious and political affiliation.

To approach the issue of authority and legitimacy in Shari'a in terms of religious proximity is a way of drawing attention towards informal and formal power structures that are at play. As discussed in the introduction, Shari'a may represent various fields of knowledge depending on which approach is applied. Some of the women's rights activists in this study tend to present controversial views on Shari'a.

For instance, they do not rely on formal sources or structures of authority, but rather build on subjective understandings of what the principle of *ijtihad* or the practice of dower involves. For this reason, it is helpful to examine some informal and subjective sources and structures of authority, as well as contextual and processual aspects of their understandings. The topic of family law is a prominent example in which not only the gendered aspects of Shari'a may be approached, but also how alternative versions of Shari'a are constituted, constructed and perceived.

Family law as the last bastion of Shari'a

Family law is often described as the last bastion of Shari'a, because it regulates issues in the so-called private realm of society. Family law affects practices between individuals in familial relationships, such as marriage, divorce, inheritance and custody of children, etc. Ziba Mir-Hosseini claims there are mainly two reasons for the privileged position of family law in Shari'a. First, Qur'anic provisions dealing with family law issues are the most explicit in terms of personal relationships, and are thus perceived as pertaining to a core area representing the 'sacred' in Shari'a (2000a: 12). Whereas most predominantly Muslim countries have sought to replace Shari'a-based legislation with laws founded on European codes of law in areas such as economy and administration, family law has remained governed by Shari'a. Second, Mir-Hosseini claims that the reform of other areas of Shari'a has thus left the field of family law as a highly sensitive and disputed issue (2000a: 12). Consequently, family law has remained the privileged area of law guided by Shari'a in many countries. It is also a highly gendered issue, dealing with rules and regulations related to gender relations and sexuality. For this reason, family law has emerged as the preferential symbol of Islamic identity in many countries experiencing processes of Islamisation (Hélie-Lucas 1994: 391). What is more, family law signifies a divisive topic in debates over conflicting prospects for the role of Islam for society both in national and global contexts. It has therefore been connected to politics of imperialism and projects of modernisations

(Ahmed 1992: Chapter 8). As a key area of Shari'a, family law issues reveal struggles over fundamental aspects of national politics and religious issues, as well as identity politics.

Over the last two decades, family law reform has emerged as a conflict-ridden area in many Muslim countries, such as Mali, Yemen, Morocco, Palestine, Syria, Egypt, Sudan and Iran.[17] Debates in these countries illustrate that family law signifies an ongoing struggle between different notions of the kind of role Shari'a should play in contemporary societies. The struggle involves tugs of war between concepts of tradition and modernisation, as well as processes of Islamisation and secularisation. Léon Buskens, for instance, argues that the debate of the reform of the Mudawwana (the Moroccan Family Law Code) entailed conflicting visions of society, family and Islam in Morocco (2003). Because family law has become a symbol of the place of Islam in society and of the right to participate in politics, it reveals confrontations between different world-views and identities (op. cit.: 121–2). A similar struggle can be found in the recent debate over the so-called *khul'* law reform in Egypt, which increased women's right to divorce (*khul'*) (Sonneveld 2009).[18] This debate signifies conflicts over wider issues of concern in Egyptian society, and Sonneveld argues that it is linked not only to the role of Islam and Shari'a, but also to everyday life (op. cit.: 247). Similarly, there is an ongoing debate over the direction of the Islamic Republic in contemporary Iran.

CHAPTER 2

MARRIAGE IN MUSLIM FAMILY LAW

Marriage has a prominent role in Islam and a central position in Shari'a. It comes into the category of *mandub* actions – recommended for all Muslims. Marriage is seen as an ideal living arrangement for Muslims, which is both religiously rewarded and recommended, and also performs a significant function for society as a whole. Several rules are set out to regulate the act of marriage. For one, the Islamic marriage contract (*'aqd al-nekah*) is considered to be a civil contractual agreement between the two parties. The contract is an essential part of the marriage and without a valid contract a marriage is not considered legitimate. Moreover, most schools of law require the woman to have a male guardian (*wali*) when contracting the marriage (Tucker 2008: 31). In addition, there are substantial elaborations on the question of the minimum age of marriage (op. cit.: 72), the rights and duties of the spouses (op. cit.: 50–9), and regulations in case of divorce (op. cit.: 84–101).

Furthermore, marriage is highly relevant to debates on women's position and rights in Islam. Consequently, it has constituted a central topic of Muslim family law debates not only in Iran, but also in the debate over divorce reform in Egypt in 2000, the discussion on polygyny in Malaysia in 2003 and the family law reform in Morocco in 2004.

Marriage regulations reveal significant aspects of Shari'a, as the many perceptions of the practice relate to fields of knowledge –

ideals, conceptions and practices – that may involve Shari'a. First, marriage is connected to the normative field of ideals in Islam. There are several verses in the Qur'an and numerous hadith stories dealing with marriage. Some Qur'anic verses refer to those who are considered to be suitable spouses (2: 221, 4: 22–5, 5: 5), while others deal with different kinds of marriage arrangements (4: 3, 4: 24 and 4: 25) and the rights and obligations, as well as the relationship, between the spouses in marriage (4: 34, 9: 71, 51: 49). The many Qur'anic references underscore the ideals of marriage in Islam.

Second, marriage is a preferential topic of Shari'a and has been dealt with in detail by a number of *ulama* who have elaborated on the specific rules and regulations pertaining to marriage. On this basis, marriage relates to *fiqh*, on a practical level that involves principles of jurisprudence as well as actual codifications. Numerous *ulama* have dedicated much effort into clarifying directions for marriage, serving both as guidelines for married couples and as a basis for state laws that regulate the society as a whole. As a result of the many Qur'anic prescriptions and jurisprudential inquiries, there is a vast array of regulations dealing with marriage.

A third field pertains to conceptions of marriage. Representing an issue of everyday life for the great majority of Muslims, marriage and married life is something on which many people hold an opinion. Marriage is thus also shaped by subjective experiences and opinions, and is often described and discussed according to the various perceptions and actual experiences of it.

In regard to the Family Protection Bill, marriage is a significant topic of debate. In particular, polygyny, temporary marriage and dower have become contested issues. The debates serve to illustrate various fields of knowledge in Shari'a. The three fields of the ideal, the conceptions and the practice pertain to what is considered to be 'Islamic' or 'in accordance with Shari'a', or 'in line with women's rights' based on the different sources and perspectives of the knowledge applied. Whereas the sources and legal theory behind the practices of dower, polygyny and temporary marriage reveal one kind of knowledge of Shari'a, the functions, debates, reforms, procedures and contemporary situation of such practices tell a different story.

Hence, the following analysis of the contemporary debate in Iran is based on not only how the issues of polygyny, temporary marriage and dower are presented in the Family Protection Bill, but how they are regulated in other contexts and represent various fields of knowledge.

Dower

Dower (*mahr* in Arabic and *mehrieh* in Persian) is a mandatory part of the marriage contract and represents important functions for women both in marriage and in the event of divorce.[1] The practice of dower is mentioned in several places in the Qur'an and it is thus held to be an obligatory part of the marriage (2: 236, 2: 237, 4: 4, 4: 24 and 4: 25). A marriage is not even considered lawful without dower. The Qur'an states: 'And give the women [upon marriage] their [bridal] gifts graciously. But if they give up willingly to you anything of it, then take it in satisfaction and ease' (Qur'an 4: 4). The mandatory character of dower is also made clear in a hadith story about a man who says to the Prophet that he has nothing, not even an iron ring, to offer his new wife as dower. The Prophet is then said to propose that the man offers his Qur'an as dower. The story is seen as underlining the binding character of dower in the Islamic marriage, regardless of its value and form (Khan 2010: 3–4).

In classical legal theory dower is divided into different categories:

1. The specified dower (*al mahr al-musamma*), which is determined when entering marriage and registered in the marriage contract by the *qadi* in charge of the ceremony.
2. The unspecified or stipulated dower (*mahr al-mithl*), which is used when the dower is not fixed upon marriage. In such cases, due to the mandatory character of dower, the amount is decided on the basis of the qualities of the bride (age, beauty, fortune, understanding, virtue, if she has previously been married, and so on), as well as the social status of her family (DeLong-Bas and Esposito 2001: 24).

Furthermore, the dower is divided into two portions. The first is the prompt dower (*muqaddam*), which can be claimed in its entirety upon consummation of marriage. The second portion is the deferred dower (*muakhkhar*), which refers to an amount paid out to the wife only in the case of dissolution of marriage. The prompt dower is the gift the wife receives at the time of marriage and the deferred dower is what is promised to her if she is divorced or widowed (Moors 1995: 77).

Dower and Nafaqa

Although dower is the property given to the wife at marriage, the practice is also significant for defining the relationship between the husband and wife and the position of the woman in the marriage. In addition to dower, *nafaqa* – maintenance during marriage – is among the husband's main obligations towards his wife, as stated in the Qur'an (2: 233) and in several ahadith (Tucker 2008: 50–1).[2] In Iran, a wife is expected and required to perform obedience or be submissive (*tamkin*) to her husband, signifying compliance and sexual services during the marriage. On the basis of performing *tamkin* she is entitled to *nafaqa*.[3] In the event of a wife's disobedience or not fulfilling her responsibilities towards her husband (*nushuz*),[4] however, she could lose her right to *nafaqa*. Consequently, the doctrines of *nafaqa* and *nushuz* are highly interconnected, as the latter decides the wife's obligations towards her husband in order to receive maintenance and mostly concerns making her body available to her husband. There is thus a clear distinction between *mahr* and *nafaqa*, in that the former is paid partly or in its entirety at marriage to the bride and is recognised as her own property, whereas the latter represents the husband's financial obligation to provide for his wife and children in marriage (food, clothes, housing, etc.), in return for her obedience and availability.

Dower and divorce

Another topic that underlines the relevance of dower is divorce. In fact, the various aspects of dower are hard to grasp without relating it to rules of termination of marriage. There is an inextricable connection between deferred dower and divorce, conveyed in a

Persian proverb that says: 'I give up my dower to make free my life' (*Mehram halal janam azad*) (Mir-Hosseini 2000a: 82). The saying refers to the importance of dower as a bargaining factor in case of divorce and the fact that many women are willing to give it up in return for divorce.

The two issues of dower and divorce are highly interrelated and mutually relevant. In contrast to Christianity, but similar to Judaism, Islam contains the right to divorce in marriage. The married couple, however, has different access to the dissolution of the marriage. In short, the husband has the unrestricted right to dissolve the marriage, whereas the wife is only allowed to do so on a few specific grounds. There are four main types of dissolution of marriage.

The first form is divorce (*talaq*). The procedure is based on a Qur'anic verse (65: 1–2), and is referred to simply as *talaq* (repudiation). *Talaq* is made on the initiative of the husband and is his unilateral right to divorce, as mentioned. It is the most common form of divorce in Shari'a. The procedure is quite simple. A husband expresses a divorce formula, usually 'I divorce myself from you', three times in the presence of two male witnesses. A formula of divorce unconfirmed by witnesses is seen as invalid, but the wife does not need to be present, nor is her consent needed in order for the divorce to be effected. *Talaq* comes in two forms, however. *Talaq al-sunna* is the regular kind of divorce, in which the different modes depend on the number of times the divorce formula is pronounced and the revocability of the divorce. *Ahsan* is considered the best type of *talaq al-sunna* and requires the husband to articulate *talaq* when the wife is not menstruating. She then enters the waiting period of *'idda*; which lasts for three menstrual cycles and involves sexual abstinence (mentioned in the Qur'an 65: 4).[5] The divorce is completed after these three months, but during this time it is still revocable.

Hasan is the second best type of *talaq al-sunna*. It is effected if the husband utters the divorce formula three times during the wife's *'idda*. Afterwards, *hasan* is irrevocable, unless the wife marries another man who divorces her or dies in the meantime (Mir-Hosseini 2000a: 37). *Talaq al-bid'a*, the second main kind of *talaq*, is considered an irregular form of divorce, meaning that the Qur'anic prescriptions for divorce have not been followed. Nevertheless, it has become common practice (Mir-Hosseini 2000a: 37). It requires the husband's pronunciation of *talaq* three times in a row, and the wife then immediately enters *'idda*. In case of *talaq*, in either of the two kinds, the wife is entitled to the deferred amount of dower.

Khul' is the second main form of marriage dissolution. It is made on the wife's initiative and depends on the husband's consent, which is normally based on some sort of financial compensation, often in the form of dower. Mir-Hosseini notes that *khul'* means 'to take off' and signifies the wife's reluctance towards her husband (2000a: 38–9). In practice, though, all divorces of mutual consent are of the *khul'* kind, as they are dependent on the approval of the husband (op. cit.: 39). In the end, it is the husband who decides if he wants to divorce or not in exchange for a financial transaction. And as a result, the husband can benefit financially from the wife asking for a divorce instead of initiating *talaq* himself.

Still, divorces by mutual consent are most commonly referred to as *mubarat* (Tucker 2008: 98). According to Articles 1146 and 1147 in the 1928 Civil Code of Iran, there is a distinction between *khul'* and *mubarat,* and both are irrevocable kinds of divorce. *Khul'* divorce is initiated by the wife and the consent of the husband is given after he receives payment of compensation. *Mubarat* divorce depends on mutual agreement and the payment of compensation to the husband should not exceed the amount of dower (Articles 1146 and 1147 in the Civil Code). Whether the *khul'* or *mubarat* form of divorce is instigated, a consequence of a woman-initiated divorce is that she loses any form of economic maintenance, in addition to dower.[6]

Tatliq (judicial dissolution) is a third form of marriage dissolution, meaning that the marriage is terminated in court. *Tatliq* refers to conditional divorce (Tucker 2008: 79). Most commonly, *tatliq* is resorted to if the husband refuses to agree to divorce. Then, the court must either induce him to agree or pronounce divorce on his behalf. In cases of *tatliq*, the wife is given the right to deferred dower. The *tatliq* divorce procedure, in which the marriage is annulled on the basis of an error in the marriage contract or a shortcoming of either the husband or wife, has often been presented as the wife's divorce (op. cit.: 95). In Sunni schools of law there are usually several preconditions before a woman can file for divorce, and here the Maliki School represents the most broadminded. For instance, the impotency, sickness, or absence of the husband were considered valid grounds for a woman to obtain divorce (op. cit.: 92–5). In the Ja'fari Shi'a School of Law, though, there has traditionally been only one condition under which a wife can demand divorce, namely impotence (ibid.).

Tafriq or *faskh* is a fourth form of dissolution of marriage. It involves an annulment of the marriage based either on an error in the marriage contract or a shortcoming of either the husband or wife (infertility). Most commonly, a marriage is declared annulled on the basis of impotence or infertility of the husband (Vikør 2003: 282), but has also been held to be available to the husband by some Shafi'i jurists (Tucker 2008: 93). *Tafriq* is, however, seen as a preferential procedure of divorce for a wife, as she keeps her rights both to dower and maintenance during *'idda*. Although described as separate forms of divorce, the conditional and judicial divorce (*tatliq*) and the divorce by annulment (*tafriq*) are used interchangeably, as the one tends to precede the other and because of their mutual dependency in the process of divorce (Welchman 2000b: 320).

Historically, though, the most common forms of divorce have been *talaq, tafriq* and *khul'* (Tucker 2008: 86). Nonetheless, the question of maintenance and dower after divorce has been prominent, and in particular the wife's right to the deferred dower. In the case of divorce, the deferred dower serves very different functions for women from the prompt dower. Although deferred dower is said to pertain to both divorced and widowed women, the number of widowed women demanding deferred dower has decreased with time (Moors 1995: 147). According to Moors, there has also been a remarkable increase in the position of the deferred dower (ibid.). Both the use of and the amounts of deferred dowers have increased. In spite of the importance of deferred dower in recent years, only a few women actually obtain it after termination of marriage. Women are given the right to the deferred amount of dower if they are widowed, divorced by repudiation (*talaq*), or have a recognised reason to file for divorce (*tafriq*). If the wife should file for divorce on her own initiative (*khul'*), however, she will not be entitled to the deferred dower (op. cit.: 147–8).

Different functions of dower

Dower serves several functions that go beyond its most basic intention and ideals as presented in legal sources and theory. First, dower has become significant for the position and rights of women. Its most obvious function is with regard to finance, as it can leave the wife in a better financial position in case of divorce. This has proved to be important, especially for those women who have not earned their own income during marriage. Second, dower can serve as a means for women to delay or prevent an unwanted divorce. If a husband threatens to perform *talaq*, he might think twice when reminded about his obligation to pay the dower. Also, and maybe more importantly, dower can function as a bargaining tool for women in order to obtain a divorce (Mir-Hosseini 2000a: 71–82). As mentioned, the husband is expected to receive some kind of compensation for granting his wife divorce (*khul'*). By employing the dower as a means of negotiation and agreeing to give up part or the whole amount of dower, the woman can achieve divorce from her husband even though he did not give his consent to begin with.

In the documentary *Divorce Iranian Style* (Mir-Hosseini and Longinotto 1998), we follow a young woman who ultimately and after some discussion hands back half of her dower in order to obtain a *khul'* divorce. Many women choose this negotiating strategy. If they are willing to give up part of or their entire dower, they might have a stronger case with regard to obtaining divorce, or even custody of the children after divorce. Thus, dower may enable greater access to divorce for a woman, and make her financially secure in the event of divorce.

Debates and reforms relating to divorce

The correlation between divorce and dower also serves to illustrate the connections between Shari'a on an ideal level and a conceived level, and in particular the problems when the two fields of law meet.

The unequal rights of men and women regarding access to divorce have been a recurrent topic of family law debates since the early 1900s. Rather than outlawing men's unilateral right to divorce as such, regulations have been put in place to restrict and regulate its use. In recent years, most Muslim family law codifications demand that *talaq* be registered in court, and this is now the case in contemporary Iran, Algeria, Lebanon, Pakistan, Jordan, Egypt and Singapore (Tucker 2008: 116). Moreover, the Iranian Civil Courts Act from 1979 demands either the consent of the wife or permission from the court in order for a husband to perform *talaq* (Mir-Hosseini 2000a: 55). In 1992, Amendments to Divorce regulations were ratified in Iran, which further restricted the husband's access to *talaq* and granted the wife increased financial rights after divorce on the basis of an estimated price for her housework during marriage (*ujrat al-mithl*) (Mir-Hosseini 1996: 144). The regulations enacted in different contexts bring to mind the importance not only of applying family law codes that are in accordance with Shari'a, but also those that support notions of women's rights to various degrees.

Talaq al-bid'a has, however, represented the most troublesome procedure of divorce. In fact, it is seen as an irregular form of divorce and is regarded as morally reprehensible by most *ulama*. The Ja'fari school of law does not recognise forms of *talaq* apart from the regular ones (*talaq al-sunna*) and completely rejects *talaq al-bid'a*, as it requires strict adherence to the procedure of pronouncing divorce in the presence of two witnesses (Ferdows 1985: 28). Nevertheless, there are instances of *talaq al-bid'a* being practised in Iran, where it is referred to as *seh-talaq* (third or triple divorce) (Kamalkhani 1996: 191). In general, though, the Shi'a school of law represents a stricter view on *talaq* than most other schools of Islamic law (Vikør 2003: 135 and Tucker 2008: 88–9). The procedure is, however, still known to happen especially in Sunni Muslim majority countries. In recent years there have been stories about men pronouncing divorce by text messages sent to the wife's mobile phone (*ABC Science*, 30 July 2003), and *Talaq al-bid'a* by text message has been approved by Malaysian *ulama* in 2003 (Knickmeyer 2008, and Kinninmont 2011: 59–60).

There are also stories of *talaq al-bid'a* being performed through the software application Skype. A young Indian man living in Qatar wrote the word *talaq* three times during a Skype chat with his wife. Later, he said he did not intend to divorce his wife. Although the husband insisted that *talaq* was not done intentionally, the fatwa section at the Islamic University of Darul Uloom Deoband in India nevertheless said that the pronouncing of *talaq* is binding (Siddiqui, 27 October 2010). Such a ruling is in accordance with Hanafi rules, which generally emphasise the wording and not the intention of the action. In 2004, a debate on the practice of triple *talaq* emerged in India. A campaign addressed the need to ban triple divorce on the grounds that it caused harm to Muslim women, was considered 'un-Islamic' and should be outlawed in countries like Algeria, Iran, Iraq and Indonesia (Tucker 2008: 125). The All India Muslim Personal Law Board, however, argued in favour of maintaining the procedure as a means of protecting India's Muslim minority rights in 2004, and went against a ban (op. cit.: 125–6). Instead, the Board made the decision to discourage the practice (op. cit.: 127).

Rather than abolishing *talaq*, the legal grounds on which women may seek divorce have been extended. In Egypt, for instance, women's rights activists focused on the issue of *khul'* as a means of addressing women's restricted access to divorce. The campaigns advocated *khul'* by the use of arguments in favour of securing women's rights in Shari'a (op. cit.: 129). Finally, in January 2000 the *khul'* law was ratified in the Egyptian Parliament. The amendment remained a contested issue, however. It was disputed whether the law contravened Shari'a by not demanding the husband's consent. In 2002 the Supreme Constitutional Court in Egypt ruled that it did support Qur'anic prescriptions, but the success of the *khul'* law remains in women's actual use of it law (ibid. and Sonneveld 2009). So far, the law has not proved an immediate success, as both the law and the women filing for *khul'* divorces have been discouraged as being immoral and 'un-Islamic' (Tucker 2008: 130).

The correlation between the practice of divorce and the deferred dower, and the efforts to restrict and regulate men's unilateral access to divorce, are reminders of the dependency of one area of Shari'a on another, as well as of the importance and relevance of socioeconomic and cultural contexts for legal practices. On this basis, it is worth looking into the various functions and aspects pertaining to dower and also how it tends to be perceived.

Changes in the use of dower

Historical studies have examined the link between changes in the practice of dower and aspects of gender, economy, class and education. Judith Tucker's study on family law in the seventeenth- and eighteenth-century Ottoman Empire shows that dower was a marker of difference between middle- and upper-class women, and that lower-class women would register a significantly smaller dower in their marriage contracts (1998). Tucker asserts that dower played a more important role for the lower classes than for middle- and upper-class women, because they had other means of securing their property and wealth (op. cit.: 177). Kamalkhani's research from Iran also reports on a tendency towards class-based demands for dower; the more educated the bride, the less dower is requested (Kamalkhani 1996: 190). After this research was conducted, however, significant changes both in the use of and rules on dower have been enacted in Iran. Similarly, Moors has elaborated on the ways in which payments and amounts of dower have generally followed larger economic trends in Palestine from the early 1900s and have continued to vary throughout different historical periods (1995: 5). Moors points out an interesting shift. Throughout the twentieth century, dower as defined in the marriage contract was not as easily linked to social or class background as it had been previously (op. cit.: 94).

Nevertheless, these studies illustrate the ways in which dower reflects broader trends in society. The actual dower practice has been shown to go beyond the dower as an important religious prescription in marriage. As a result of shifts in gender relations and class affiliation, dower has come to exist on two levels. On the one hand, Ron Shaham notes in his study of Shari'a courts in Egypt in the first half of the twentieth century (1997) that there is a twofold development in the practice of registering dowers. Whereas many couples registered a high amount of dower in the actual marriage contract, namely a 'public dower' (*mahr al-'alaniya*), the real dower being paid to the wife proved to be a substantially lower amount, a 'secret dower' (*mahr al-sirr*) (op. cit.: 29). For this reason, Shaham asserts that high amounts of dower were 'a source of prestige in society', and that in cases of divorce the husband would thus claim that the 'public dower' was not to be considered binding (op. cit.: 30).

On the other hand, though, transformations in relation to dower can be seen as the result of shifts in gender relations and signal a move away from 'traditional' forms of marriage. Annelies Moors' study reveals how token dowers have been increasingly registered in marriage contracts in Nablus from the 1960s until today (1995). In the marriage contract, one amount of dower is registered. However, the stories of the women Moors interviewed reveal that the token dower does not necessarily match the dower actually received. For some, dower represents an old-fashioned element in marriage. They therefore refrain from registering anything but a token amount in their marriage contracts. The significance of not demanding a dower, but rather gifts, became increasingly common during the 1970s (1995: 108–9). This tendency was seen not only among the urban and wealthier sector of the population, but also among the rural and poorer classes. On this basis, Moors claims that the registration of a token dower is a step towards 'modernity' for many women in this region (2008: 88). The trend seems to rely on shifts in ideas of marriage and gender relations, rather than being merely an issue related to social and class background.

Similar tendencies can be traced in Iran, where the most absurd items and quantities of dowers have been inserted in the marriage contract. Ziba Mir-Hosseini tells the story of a woman who was furious to discover that her once so 'romantic' dower in the form of a ton of jasmine flowers, turned out to be completely useless when her divorce was enacted many years later (2000a: 75). Similar stories have come to light more recently. In 2008, the story of an Iranian couple who had registered 124,000 roses as dower in the marriage contract was broadcast worldwide (BBC, 3 March 2008). Shortly after the marriage, the wife discovered that her husband was very stingy and would not even buy her a cup of coffee. Thus, she decided to teach him a lesson. She went to court and demanded that he pay her what he had promised in the marriage contract. The court then ordered the husband to give his wife 124,000 roses, because it was her right to demand and receive the promised dower. Whether the husband was able to pay the promised dower remains unknown, but the story characterises a trend among young couples getting married. For some Iranian couples, dower represents the sale of a woman in marriage that contradicts their idea of a love marriage. They therefore choose to insert a symbolic amount of dower in the marriage contract, as seen in the examples from Egypt and Palestine. The educational level of the married couple is also seen as relevant to the amount and kind of dower registered in contemporary marriages in Iran. Despite higher dower claims from many young couple's families, many students refuse to register higher dowers in their marriage contracts because it is seen as contradicting their idea of marriage (Rezai-Rashti 2011: 58).

Against these studies, though, are statistics pointing towards a general increase in the cost of marriage, and an overall trend in recent years has been the demand of excessive dowers (Singerman 2010: 10). This is not limited to Iran, but is a more widespread trend (Moors 2008, Layish 2006, Tucker 2008). Consequently, some *ulama* have criticised it as 'a social evil' (Amin 1996: 59) and as 'contrary to honour and religion' (Layish 2006: 62). Still, there are instances of *ulama* who have opposed rules limiting the practice (op. cit.: 56–7). Thus, the article on dower in the Family Protection Bill in Iran is quite remarkable in its attempt to introduce legal boundaries and restrictions on the practice. The high cost of marriage is a result not only of high amounts of dower, but also of expensive housing and costly marriage ceremonies. Despite this trend, marriage is still a universal norm in Muslim countries and many have policies to encourage the marriage of young couples. Iran and Egypt, for instance, are two states that have experienced a demographic transition, with reduced fertility, delayed marriage, increased public education, reductions in the literacy gap between men and women and improvements in public health and access to contraception

(Singerman 2010). It is expected that countries like Egypt, Iran, Iraq, Jordan, Libya, Oman, Pakistan, Saudi Arabia, Sudan, Syria and Yemen will experience a further explosion of youth over the next twenty years (ibid.).

There is a general tendency to register increasing amounts of dower in Muslim marriage contracts. In turn, the escalating dower claims prevent young couples from getting married due to financial shortfalls. Such shifts in the practice of dower correspond to trends in society pertaining to transformations of gender relations, religiosity, economy, class and status. In this way, dower represents a gateway into perceptions not only of dower, but also of the various aspects relevant to Shari'a and women's rights more generally.

Debates and reforms relating to dower

The issue of dower has not been a topic in family law debates to the same extent, for example, as polygyny. Dower has represented neither a major issue of legal reform nor a preferential topic of religious elaboration. Still, the practice has been subject to some regulations relevant to conceptions of the role of Shari'a in contemporary state legislation and of women's rights in society. For instance, some countries have fixed a limit for dower in order to prevent excessive demands for it. The value of dower can be used to signify the status of the bride or of her family. In the family law of South Yemen in 1974, it was decided that dower (both prompt and deferred) could not exceed 100 dinars (Khan 2010: 8). Similarly, the Somali Family Code from 1975 permitted a maximum dower of 1,000 local shillings. The Moroccan Code of Personal Statutes from 1958 restricted the marriage guardian (*wali*) from opposing marriage because of inadequate dower, if the bride herself was willing to accept it (ibid.).[7] The determination of the amount of dower in legal disputes has been made in Egypt, Lebanon, Jordan, Sudan and Morocco (ibid.).

More recently, though, the issue of dower has been indirectly relevant in family law reforms. In the 2004 reform of the Moroccan Mudawwana, dower is stated to be only symbolic (Labidi 2005: 276), but is maintained in the actual law code (Buskens 2010: 115).

Dower has also emerged as a divisive issue in regard to the ratification of international conventions for women's rights. Egypt expressed reservations to Articles 15 and 16 in CEDAW (Convention on the Elimination of All Forms of Discrimination Against Women), because of their incompatibility with Shari'a and its provisions for dower (Tucker 2008: 80).[8] CEDAW allows for such reservations 'on the ground that national law, tradition, religion or culture are not congruent with Convention principles' (United Nations website). A quite different use of dower served to legitimate a new Shi'i family law in Afghanistan in 2009. Representing a religious minority in Afghanistan, the Shi'i Muslim population has a separate code of personal status law, which was drafted in 2009 (based on Articles 2 and 113 in the 2004 Constitution of Afghanistan). The law gives a husband nearly unconditional rights to sexual intercourse with his wife on the basis of paying her dower, and thus invokes the previously mentioned aspects of *tamkin* – that a wife is expected to remain obedient to her husband in return for maintenance (*mahr* and *nafaqa*). This law has been labelled 'the rape law' in international media due to the restricted role it offers women and the privileged position it assigns to men (Yassari and Saboory 2010: 299–301).

Debates and reforms relevant to dower in Iran

Dower has also been a relevant topic in family law debates and reforms in Iran. In the Iranian Civil Code from 1928, Articles 1078 to 1101 in Chapter Seven are dedicated to dower and are called 'About Dower' (*Dar Mahr*). According to Article 1078, anything that can be called property and can be owned and possessed, can be designated as *mehrieh*. Dower is considered as payment for a woman's sexual favours, and this is underlined in Article 1085 in the Civil Code:

> So long as the marriage portion is not delivered to her, the wife can refuse to fulfil the duties which she has to her husband provided, however, that the marriage portion is payable at once. This refusal does not debar her from right of maintenance expenses.

In addition to dower, a wife is entitled to maintenance (*nafaqa*), as stated in Articles 1106 and 1107. *Nafaqa* entails costs for 'dwelling, clothing, food, [and] furniture' (Article 1107). However, the Civil Code clearly states that 'If the wife refuses to fulfil the duties of a wife without legitimate excuse, she will not be entitled to the cost of maintenance' (Article 1108).

The topic of dower did not emerge as an issue of family law debate in Iran until the late 1980s. In July 1989, a bill was presented in the Majles (Parliament) proposing the transfer of the power of divorce from the husband to civil courts. The debate among the bill's supporters and opponents dealt mainly with two concerns. Opponents of the bill argued for the preservation of the Qur'anic-prescribed right of the husband to repudiate his wife at any time. Supporters of the bill, however, urged the state to make sure that the number of divorces decreased as part of the state's responsibility to protect the family by limiting these. The Divorce Reform Bill (*Layehe-ye Eslah Talaq*) received major support in the Majles, and was then approved by the Guardian Council (*Shura-ye Negahban*). In December 1992 the Majles ratified a law called 'Amendments to Divorce Regulations'. It consisted of a single article with seven notes and introduced changes in four main areas (Mir-Hosseini 1996: 144). First, no divorce without a court certificate could be registered. Second, female judges could be appointed to assist male judges in court. Third, the court calculated a price on women's housework during marriage (*ujrat al-mithl*). This section was highly controversial and is still perceived as remarkable in terms of women's right to maintenance in Muslim family law codes. Women's rights activists in Iran, however, sustained their argument that Islam does not require women to do housework in their husband's house, and even that the husband is obliged to pay for the wife to breastfeed her child (Hoodfar 1999: 16). A fourth aspect of the law demanded that all couples asking for a divorce go through a mandatory process of arbitration, in the presence of one mediator representing each party. If reconciliation failed, the court could declare a *talaq-e raji'*[9] that was final only after the wife had fulfilled *'idda*, and the husband had paid the wife both her *mehrieh* and *ujrat al-mithl*, unless he could convince the court that he was unable to pay (Mir-Hosseini 2000a: x). On this basis, the 1992 amendment restricted the husband's right to *talaq* and increased the wife's financial rights after divorce.

Again, with the 1992 Divorce Reform Bill, the close connection between divorce and dower was established. In fact, Mir-Hosseini claims that 'What is clear at this stage is that, at least in theory, the 1992 amendments do offer a better deal than the Family Protection Law did to women who enjoy little economic independence' (Mir-Hosseini 1996: 152). One reason for her claim is that the reform extended the divorced wife's financial rights by granting her the right to sue for payment for household services during marriage. Women were therefore put in a better bargaining position as a result of an increase in financial rights after 1992. For example, dower could be used as a bargaining card to achieve custody immediately after divorce (op. cit.: 152).

Only a few years later, the issue of dower once again became the focus of law reform debate. In 1997, a law that introduced the re-evaluation of dower with inflation was passed in the Majles. The main reason was that the amount of dower in many marriage contracts resulted in substantially lower sums at the time of payment because of inflation. After divorce, many women were therefore put in a difficult financial situation. Marziyeh Sediqi, a female Majles representative, said that for some women the dower 'won't even cover her taxi fare to court' (Halper 2007: 1180). The new law was therefore implemented to ensure that the marriage gift retained its original value regardless of what was stated in the marriage contract, by valuing it according to inflation.[10] The law caused debate in the Majles. Its opponents claimed that it would 'disable the traditionally recognized warm sphere of family life' and 'destroy the economic basis of the country' (op. cit.: 1184).[11] Supporters of the law, however, argued that it was in line with Shari'a, by granting women the marriage gift they were entitled to according to the Qur'an. Eventually the bill was ratified in the Majles. As usual when a bill is acknowledged by the Majles, it is passed on to the Guardian Council for approval. The Guardian Council did not, however, ratify the 1997 law because of what they claimed were inconsistencies with

Shari'a. In fact, it had to be sent on to the Expediency Council (*Majma'-ye Tashkhis Maslahat-e Nezam*) for approval, which passed the law as legitimate despite protests from members of the Guardian Council.

Polygyny

Polygyny is often referred to as *ta'adod al-zojat* in Arabic and as *chandzani* in Persian.[12] In Islam, polygyny has a clear Qur'anic legitimation and the rules regarding the practice are clearly stated:

> If you fear that you shall not be able to deal justly with the orphans, marry women of your choice, two or three or four; but if you fear that you shall not be able to deal justly (with them), then only one, or (a captive) that your right hands possess, that will be more suitable, to prevent you from doing injustice. (4: 3)

On this basis, all four Sunni schools of law recognise polygynous marriages in legal theory. Polygyny is a typical *mubah* Shari'a action, which means that it is permitted. In most cases, however, *mubah* actions like polygyny do come with restrictions of some kind. In polygyny, for instance, it is generally believed that unless a man is capable of taking care of a plurality of wives, he should abstain from polygyny. Still, a plurality of marriage is allowed for men. In the main, the Shi'a view on permanent marriage corresponds to the Sunni view. With regard to views on temporary marriage, however, the Shi'a Ja'fari School of Law differs substantially from the Sunni schools of law. In the Ja'fari school, marriage takes at least two forms: permanent marriage (*nekah*) and temporary marriage (*nekah mut'a* or *sighe*). Similar to Sunnism, a man is allowed to marry up to four wives at the same time. In addition – and this is unique to Shi'ism – he can also contract an indefinite number of temporary marriages, either simultaneously or serially. The practice of temporary marriage marks a remarkable difference between Sunni and Shi'a schools of law.

Contemporary situation of polygyny

Polygyny lies at the heart of debates on women's rights in Islam and is also highly relevant for the role of Shari'a in a society. Statistics, however, are difficult to find. They are either difficult to produce or simply unreliable. There are various reasons for this. In countries where polygyny is restricted, for example, people may want to hide the fact that they are in a polygynous marriage in order to avoid financial penalties or imprisonment, or simply because it is sometimes seen as stigmatising. Another challenge is that statistics in this area are produced either by opponents or proponents of polygyny, and thus often unreliable because of their purpose.[13]

What is relevant for this book, however, is to point to the current situation of polygyny in Muslim majority countries. On the basis of accounts from women's rights groups in Malaysia, polygyny seems to be increasing because of a relaxation in governmental sanctions (Sisters in Islam, 28 December 2006). There are also reports indicating a rise in promotion of polygyny in Iraq (Ayoubi, 26 January 2011), as well as in Malaysia (Gooch, 5 January 2010) and Indonesia (Vaswani, 17 December 2009). Moreover, in Saudi Arabia the practice of polygyny has increased, in particular since the recent boost in oil revenues (Yamani 2008: 215). Yamani claims that the Saudi state has promoted polygyny as part of pro-Islamic values in society and in response to pro-polygyny policies by the Iranian government (ibid.). On the other hand, though, the practice of polygyny has decreased in Morocco, both as a result of the French protectorate in the country from 1912 until 1956 (Zeitzen 2008: 177), and after the 2004 Mudawwana reform in which polygyny was restricted (Buskens 2010: 114).

Other statistics point towards high rates of polygynous marriages in the Gulf region (Fakhro 1996), and report that less than 4 per cent of the population practice polygyny in Egypt, 9 per cent in Mauritania and 17 per cent in Sudan (Souaiaia 2008). Among the motivating factors for polygyny in rural Egypt, Laila Shahd's fieldwork shows that economic, cultural, social and sexual motives are important (2003). Also, the infertility of a wife, a wife giving birth to daughters but no sons, problems with in-laws, and making political alliances to enable advancement in political structures may serve as motivations for entering polygynous marriages (Welchman 2007: 77). Among middle-class Muslims in South Africa, however, studies indicate that such reasons for polygyny do not work (Bangstad 2007). Instead, most of them refer to notions of marriage based on 'western' ideas of 'romantic love' (op. cit.: 128), although the situation might prove to be different for the poorer classes. However, there seem to be few studies examining religious motivations for engaging in polygynous marriages.

Debates and reforms relating to polygyny

Polygyny has represented one of the most troublesome areas of Muslim family law debates. The legal approach towards the practice varies from prohibition on the one hand to encouragement on the other. According to Tucker, the issue was treated with complete tolerance in the Ottoman Law of Family Rights from 1917, and continued to be so in later codifications in Egypt and Jordan (2008: 75). At the other end of the scale, Turkey prohibited the practice of polygyny in 1926 and Tunisia followed suit in 1956. Tunisia's President Bourguiba asserted that polygyny did not contravene Islam, but that it 'had become inadmissible in the twentieth century and inconceivable to any right-minded person' (Welchman 2007: 78). In Iraq, Syria and Morocco, however, the issue has been dealt with in-between these two edges of the debate, treating polygyny as legally restricted based on the permission of the court, in order for the marriage to be lawful (Tucker 2008: 75).

Few countries have sought to abolish polygyny on the basis of refuting its Islamic character. Rather, a general trend towards limiting the legal grounds for polygyny has been to introduce stricter procedural conditions. According to Lynn Welchman, four conditions are most often used to obtain the consent of the court for polygynous marriages in contemporary Muslim family law codes. First, a husband needs to prove his financial ability to provide for more than his current wife and family. In most cases, the requirement for financial ability is combined with other conditions. In the 1977 Civil Code of Afghanistan, for instance, it is combined with the demand for the consent of first wife as a basis for permission

(Yassari and Saboori 2010: 305). If a husband should break any of these conditions, the first or second wife is allowed to apply for divorce based on *darar* (harm), but in the event of an additional marriage of the husband, the second marriage will still be valid (ibid.).

A second criterion relates to the existence of a 'lawful benefit' for the polygynous marriage dealing with the circumstances (and in most cases deficiencies) of the first marriage (infertility, absence or illness of the wife). The 1974 Indonesian Marriage Act states that monogamy is the basis for marriage, but that a man can apply to the court for permission to marry additional wives if various conditions are met (Otto 2010: 467).[14] If these conditions are fulfilled, the court may grant permission for polygyny. But if it turns out that a polygynous marriage is contracted without permission, the husband will be given a fine, and the registrant of the polygynous marriage will face sanctions and possibly imprisonment (Otto 2010: 469). The second criterion therefore results in what Welchman refers to as a 'lawful benefit', namely that the wife is unable to fulfil her 'duties' as a wife, or is unable to give birth to children. Such circumstances are seen as legitimising additional marriages and are made with reference to the first marriage. Similar cases can be found in the 1984 Algerian Family Law Code, the 2001 Jordanian Code and the 1992 Yemeni Code (Welchman 2007: 80). Another variation of the demand for 'lawful benefit' can be found in provisions added to the Iraqi Family Law Code in the 1980s, which allowed polygynous marriage where the bride's status as a widow was inserted into the contract. Welchman notes, however, that this amendment was done with reference to the situation of a 'surplus of women' as a result of many men losing their lives in the Iran–Iraq war (op. cit.: 80).

A third kind of condition requires the fair and just treatment of all co-wives. This basis for polygynous marriage was inserted both in the United Arab Emirate's 2005 law and the Sudanese Family Code of 1991. The condition is intended to ensure that all wives are treated equally and are not forced to share households against their will. Welchman points out that this requirement has resonance in classical jurisprudence, in interpretations of the Qur'anic verse 4: 3 in which the principle of 'fair treatment' is mentioned (op. cit.: 81). Thus, in polygynous marriages the co-wives are by no means expected to live in the same house, but can expect to have their own households and separate living arrangements.

A fourth criterion for polygyny has been based on notification requirements related to asking the consent either of the court or the first wife as a means of restricting polygyny (op. cit.: 81–2). The issue of notification is based on consent, and can be entered as a stipulation in the marriage contract in Morocco, for instance. According to Léon Buskens, the process of restricting polygyny has taken place gradually in Morocco. In the 1958 Mudawwana, polygyny was considered lawful, but was seen as a source of possible *darar* (harm for the wife) and thus provided legitimate grounds for divorce (Buskens 2003: 74). In the 1993 revision of the Mudawwana, however, polygyny was made further dependent on the permission of the court (op. cit.: 80), and the 1998 proposal for Mudawwana reform introduced clear restrictions on polygyny, as a man could marry another wife only if the first wife consented and with the permission of a judge (op. cit.: 86). In the 2004 Mudawwana these provisions were conjoined, as women now are allowed to insert a condition for monogamy in their marriage contract, and a subsequent marriage is made dependent on the permission of both the first and second wives as well as a judge (Buskens 2010: 115). If the husband still marries a second wife and breaks these conditions, the first wife is entitled to apply for divorce. Moreover, the number of wives allowed in a polygynous marriage is limited to two in the 2004 Mudawwana (Labidi 2005: 276).

Polygyny has proved to be a subject that goes beyond debates on codification of family law. In countries like Malaysia, Indonesia, Morocco and Egypt, polygyny represents an area of debate relevant to larger social and political issues. Buskens writes that the issue of polygyny has been an important symbol in the struggle for reform of family law, both for progressives who claim it is a sign of inequality and for conservatives and Islamists who claim it is a God-given right of the husband (Buskens 2010: 115). Similarly, John R. Bowen maintains that despite being a practice restricted by law, the issue represents a symbolic position in debates about the role of Islam in Indonesian society (2003). Moreover, a number of so-called pro-polygyny voices have emerged in public in recent years (op. cit.: 224–7).

The review of rulings on polygyny in Malaysia in recent years shows a similar situation. The 1984 Family Law Code stated that a man should fulfil five conditions in order to be able to contract additional marriages (Harding 2010: 516).[15] Then, in 1994, the requirement for having a judge's consent to a polygynous marriage was removed, and in 2004 the condition for proving that a polygynous marriage was 'just *and* necessary' was altered into 'just *or* necessary' (Hamza and Othman 2010). On this basis, the women's rights group Sisters in Islam (SIS) has claimed that that the Malaysian state is currently promoting polygyny, or at least ignoring what they maintain is an increasing use of it (ibid.). For this reason, SIS launched the Campaign for Monogamy in 2003.

In Egypt, there is an ongoing debate that resembles the one in Malaysia, in which different positions towards the practice are revealed. In 2004, the National Council for Women suggested the introduction of fines and sanctions on men contracting polygynous marriages. The influential Al-Azhar University in Cairo, however, refused to approve the proposal (Welchman 2007: 86). In Morocco, claims of absolute prohibition of polygyny were launched by groups of women's rights activists in relation to the 2004 Mudawwana reform, and in Palestine there are women's rights groups arguing for prohibition, as well as some who seek only to restrict the practice (op. cit.: 87). In Algeria, demands for reform of the 1984 Family Code towards prohibition have also been initiated (ibid.).

To sum up, there are three general approaches to codifications of polygyny. One relates to prohibition of the practice and is to be found in countries where polygyny is made illegal, such as in Tunisia, Turkey and Fiji.[16] Another is to make polygyny conditional, as in Indonesia, Malaysia and Morocco, as well as Bangladesh, Pakistan, Singapore and the Philippines. A third approach can be found in the Gulf countries, like Kuwait, Oman, United Arab Emirates and Qatar, where polygyny remains more or less unrestricted (op. cit.: 86).[17]

Debates and reforms relating to polygyny in Iran

Similar to other Muslim countries, polygyny has been a contested subject in family law debates in Iran and has gone through changes. In the 1928 Iranian Civil Code, a section called 'About Marriage' (*Dar Nekah*) is dedicated to marriage and divorce-related issues. Here, permanent marriage is elaborated on with regard to rules for contracting a marriage, regulations on who is considered a legitimate spouse, and the rights and duties of both husbands and wives. There is, however, no single article that explicitly deals with polygyny. Article 942 states that: 'if there be more than one wife, the fourth or eight part [of inheritance], which belongs to the wife, will be divided equally among them' (Article 942). Moreover, Article 119 states that:

> The parties to the marriage can stipulate any condition to the marriage which is not compatible with the nature of the contract of marriage, either as part of the marriage contract or in another binding contract: for example, it can be stipulated that *if the husband marries another wife* [author's italics] or absents himself during a certain period, or discontinues the payment of cost of maintenance ... or treats her so harshly that their life together becomes unbearable, the wife has the power, which she can also transfer to a third party, to obtain divorce after establishing in the court the fact that one of the foregoing alternatives has occurred and after the issue of a final judgement to that effect. (Article 119 in the Iranian Civil Code)

Thus, polygyny is dealt with indirectly in the Iranian Civil Code. In the 1967 Family Protection Law, however, amendments were introduced that did not outlaw polygyny as such, but introduced clear restrictions.[18] First, the husband was required to have the consent of his first wife in order to marry additional wives. Second, a court confirmation of the capability of the husband to provide financial and psychological support for several wives at the same time was required. Third, if a polygynous marriage was contracted without the court's approval, the husband was sentenced to up to two years of imprisonment. The marriage was, however, still considered valid (Hinchcliffe 1968: 521). The exceptions to these restrictions were if the first wife could not bear children or was unable to have sexual relations with her husband. On the basis of these incapacities of the wife, the court could approve a polygynous marriage without her consent. Otherwise, both the consent of the first wife and permission from the court were demanded. Thus, polygyny was not made illegal after 1967, but was restricted by law. With the establishment of the Islamic Republic in 1979, the Family Protection Law was formally abolished. In September 1979, under the Special Civil Courts Act, religious courts replaced the family courts introduced in 1967. As a result, polygyny was again left unrestricted. It has, however, continued to be a recurrent focus of family law debates in the Islamic Republic of Iran, as it has in other Muslim countries.

After 1979, the first significant amendment to family law came in 1982, when new marriage contracts were introduced. The 1982 amendments allowed both parties the right to insert conditions into the marriage contract. This can be seen as a contradiction to the husband's unilateral right to divorce (*talaq*) at any time he wished, as defined in Article 1133 in the Iranian Civil Code. The wife's right to enter stipulations into the marriage contract was underlined by Ayatollah Khomeini in a speech on 6 March 1979:

> There is one particular question to which attention should be paid. When women wish to marry, there are certain prerogatives they can stipulate for themselves that are contrary neither to the Shari'a nor to their own self-respect. For example, a woman can stipulate that if her future husband turns out to be of corrupt moral character or if he mistreats her, she would possess the right to execute a divorce. This is a right Islam has granted to women. If Islam has imposed certain restrictions on both women and men, it is for the benefit of both. Similarly, just as Islam has granted man the right to divorce, it has also granted it to woman, on the condition that the parties have stipulated at the time of marriage that if the husband behaves in a certain manner, the wife will have the

> right to execute divorce. Once the man has accepted such a stipulation, he can never repudiate it. Apart from making it possible to include such a stipulation in the marriage contract, Islam forbids the husband to mistreat his wife; if he habitually mistreats her, he is to be punished and the *mujtahid* will grant the wife a divorce. (Algar 1981: 264)

The speech was given legal significance. In 1982, Article 1130 of the Iranian Civil Code was altered and new marriage contracts were issued:

> In the following circumstances, the wife can refer to the Islamic judge and request for a divorce. When it is proved to the Court that the continuation of the marriage causes difficult and undesirable conditions, the judge can for the sake of avoiding *harm* (*'asr*) and *difficulty* (*haraj*) [author's italics] compel the husband to divorce his wife. If this cannot be done, then the divorce will be made on the permission of the Islamic judge. (Article 1130 in the Civil Code)

Thus, there are corresponding links in the post-1979 reform to stipulations allowed for in the 1967 Family Protection Law. Although family law after 1979 sought to distance itself from the laws during the Pahlavi era, there seems to be some continuity in practice. For instance, Mir-Hosseini claims that there are striking similarities between the 1967 and 1982 amendments, as both were made on the basis of procedural rules. Instead of addressing the theory of Shari'a, the reforms simply changed the procedural rules for contracting and dissolving marriages (Mir-Hosseini 1996: 145). The reforms were therefore easier to apply because they did not deal with the theological and legal basis of Shari'a. Also, Mir-Hosseini notes divergences with regard to theory and practice. Although the Family Protection Law was abolished in 1979, it was never formally repealed and some procedural rules continued (ibid.). This law had introduced restrictions on contracting polygynous marriages. Not only was the consent of the first wife still demanded, but court approval recognising the marriage contract and confirming the husband's ability to support more than one wife was also requested. Otherwise the husband would have to serve up to two years in prison.

In theory, it was an offence to register a polygynous marriage without court approval also after 1979, but in practice it entailed no punishment, as the courts did not uphold it. It was not, however, until August 1984 that the Assembly of Experts (*Majles Khobregan*) removed the penalty for contracting polygynous marriages without court approval. Thus, the actual practice depended on the outlook of the judge registering the marriage, as the theoretical basis of the law did not require it (op. cit.: 146). This is only one example of a case where Mir-Hosseini traces a continuity between the Family Protection Law and the reforms enforced after 1979.[19]

In general, the amendment of Article 1130 is based on the Shari'a concept of *'asr va haraj* (harm and difficulty) (Mir-Hosseini 2000a: 65).[20] If a marriage involves harm to the wife, the judge can make the husband dissolve the marriage or do it on his behalf. On the basis of Article 1130, the judge could thus dissolve the marriage on behalf of the wife if one or more conditions in the contract had been broken.[21] For instance, a woman could demand divorce if the husband contracted a second marriage without her consent or because of his failure to treat his wives equally, if this had been inserted in her marriage contract as a valid ground for divorce (op. cit.: 57). Like the issue of dower, polygyny is therefore intrinsically connected to divorce, and references to the principle of *'asr va haraj* or *darar* have become quite common in divorce cases since 1982 (Mir-Hosseini 2003: 25).

Temporary marriage

The practice of temporary marriage represents a major area that divides the Sunni and Shi'a branch of Islam. Temporary marriage is a pre-Islamic tradition of Arabia that is still legitimised among Twelver Shi'ites (Haeri 1989: 49). Shi'as find justification for the practice in the Qur'an and also claim that the Prophet Muhammad allowed it. Sunnis, however, rely on the opinion of the second Caliph

'Umar, who denounced the custom in the seventh century. For Shi'as, though, the judgement of 'Umar is not considered binding.

Verse 4: 25 in the Qur'an classifies three types of marriage: permanent marriage (*nekah*),[22] slave marriage (*nekah ima'*) and temporary marriage (*nekah mut'a*) according to Shi'ism (op. cit.: 30). According to Sunni schools of law, only the two former kinds of marriage are allowed, and temporary marriage is considered an illegitimate form of Islamic marriage. The Shi'a religious legitimacy of temporary marriage derives from verse 4: 24 in the Qur'an: 'Such wives as you enjoy (*istamta'tum*) thereby, given their wages apportionate; it is no fault in you agreeing together, after the due apportionate' (4: 24). The Arabic word *istamta'tum* forms the basis for Shi'ism to legitimise temporary marriage (Haeri 1989: 61). According to Shi'i scholars, there were four main reasons for the Prophet's approval of temporary marriage in the early Islamic period: (1) it provided a legal framework for individuals to engage in sexual relations in times of war when men were separated from their families; (2) it satisfied an individual's needs; (3) it represented a way for war widows to be provided for; (4) it provided legitimacy and inheritance rights to children born to individuals engaging in extramarital relations (Ghori 2008: 35).

In Shi'i legal tradition, temporary marriage is legal and has at times even been encouraged. The founder of the Shi'i Ja'fari school of law, the sixth Imam and *'alim*, Imam Ja'far al-Sadiq, is reported to have said: 'I do not like a Muslim man who passes out from this world without having practised one of the Prophet's traditions. One of these traditions is *mut'a* of women' (Haeri 1989: 49). For these reasons, temporary marriage is seen as a legitimate form of marriage in Shi'ism.

Temporary marriage in Iran

The institution of temporary marriage is known as *mut'a*, *sighe*, *ezdevaj-e movaqat* or *nekah movaqat*. The term *mut'a* means 'marriage of pleasure'.[23] *Sighe* is the colloquial phrase describing the practice. *Sighe* literally means 'concubine' and refers to the type of marriage contract (op. cit.: 50). *Sighe*, however, is never used for a man.

As Haeri writes: 'A man does *sighe*, whereas a woman, ambiguously enough, either becomes a *sighe* or is a *sighe*' (op. cit.: 51).[24]

The temporary marriage takes the form of a contract (*'aqd*), where a man and an unmarried, divorced or widowed woman agree on the duration of their marriage (from one hour to 99 years), and after the period has ended there is no need for divorce. The duration of the marriage and the amount of dower (*ajr*)[25] must be specified in the marriage contract in order to be considered valid (op. cit.: 53). Whereas some consider permanent marriage as a sale of a woman's sexuality, temporary marriage corresponds to a contract of lease (op. cit.: 59). Witnesses are not required, the marriage does not need to be registered and there is no prerequisite for the consent of a guardian (*wali*), although these practices have changed according to local requirements (op. cit.: 56). Prior to 1979, an adult virgin Shi'i Muslim woman (over 18 years) could contract her own marriage without the authorisation of a male guardian in certain cases. After 1979, however, Khomeini issued a fatwa stating that the permission of a male guardian was required regardless of whether the marriage was permanent or temporary (op. cit.: 40). The degree of autonomy given to the woman, however, is highly dependent on socioeconomic factors and local variations. The spouses in temporary marriage have no inheritance rights,[26] nor is the wife entitled to financial support during marriage (*nafaqa*), and the waiting period after divorce (*'idda*) lasts two menstrual cycles (45 days), in contrast to the *'idda* in permanent marriage which is three menstrual cycles.

A man can contract as many temporary marriages simultaneously as he wants, while a woman can marry only one man temporarily at a time.[27] According to Haeri, this is required in order to identify the father of a child born in the temporary marriage. The child has equal status (at least in theory) to that of children stemming from permanent marriages. According to Haeri: 'Here lies the legal uniqueness of *mut'a*, that which distinguishes it ideologically from prostitution, despite their striking resemblance.' (op. cit.: 2) Haeri therefore claims that it would be a mistake to view temporary marriage as just another form of prostitution, or to discuss it primarily from that perspective. Still, these aspects have made temporary marriage a dilemma to research, since it on the one hand constitutes a legal provision of Shi'a Islamic jurisprudence, and on the other hand has several parallels with the act of prostitution (op. cit.: 59).[28]

Contemporary situation of temporary marriage

The issue of temporary marriage does not have the same history in terms of regulations and reforms as polygyny and dower. The simple explanation is that temporary marriage has only been accepted and legitimised by the Ja'fari Shi'a school of law,[29] and is plainly outlawed in Sunni schools of law. Temporary marriage is also practised outside Iran, however. In Lebanon, there are young, unmarried, male members of Hezbollah who contract temporary marriages in order to engage in religiously accepted sexual relations with women (Worth, 20 November 2008). There are also cases to be found beyond predominantly Shi'a communities. In Tanzania, for instance, the arrangement has been controversial since the early 1990s (Nagar 2000). In Dar es Salam, temporary marriage is promoted by Shi'a *ulama*, who underline the practice as an Islamic alternative to the '"decadent" western style of "free" [heterosexual] relations' taking place in Tanzania today (op. cit.: 663). Sunni Muslim women from lower classes tend to engage secretly in temporary marriage with wealthy Shi'a Muslim men in return for payment. Thus, the practice of temporary marriage in Tanzania reflects hierarchies in Tanzanian society based on gender, religion, ethnicity and class (ibid.).

In Syria, there are cases of temporary marriage being performed as so-called *nekah 'urfi*, or customary marriages.[30] Although the Syrian state actively tries to control and regulate this kind of marriage arrangement by state-codified law, *'urfi* marriage is widespread and a commonly debated topic in Syria (Rabo 2011: 35). Young people get married in unconventional ways in order to engage in 'lawful' sexual relations. Such marriages are often conducted illegally, without formal registration, and frequently lack a proper marriage contract (*'aqd nekah*). Besides, the occurrence of so-called 'tourist marriages', in which wealthy men from the Gulf region marry young Syrian women for a short period of time, and already married men secretly enter into *'urfi* marriages, is widespread in Syria (ibid.).[31] Also in

Norway there are reports of young Muslims, both Sunni and Shi'a, who engage in what they refer to as temporary marriage as a sort of trial marriage, in order to have a religiously accepted love relationship outside of marriage (Bøe 2012). Thus, marriage practices that share similarities with those of temporary marriage are not limited to predominantly Shi'i areas or to Shi'i Muslims.

Nonetheless, the difficulties in obtaining information about the practice of polygyny also relate to temporary marriage, as a type of marriage often performed with discretion. As a religious practice, temporary marriage has been little researched. The anthropologist Shahla Haeri is one of the few who have studied this phenomenon in Iran in recent years (Haeri 1989). Such research is fraught with challenges. First, it is a practice that is often conducted in secret, and a shameful subject because of its association with extramarital sexual relations (*zina*), which are outlawed in Shari'a.[32] Thus, many people are reluctant to talk about the subject for fear of social stigma, and the stories told about temporary marriage may have a strong element of rumour or gossip.

The problem with secrecy and lack of registration of temporary marriage is illustrated in the Iranian film *Hemlock* (*Showkaran*) by Behrouz Afkhami from 2000. The film shows the fairly open debate on Islam in today's Iran and the ideological boundaries surrounding it (Mir-Hosseini 2007). It describes the ways in which temporary marriage is practised today and its possible consequences. The main characters, Mahmoud and Sima, engage in a temporary marriage. It must be kept secret from Mahmoud's first wife and is thus not registered, which is not uncommon in Iran. Mahmoud and Sima start to talk about temporary marriage after knowing each other for a relatively short period of time. Mahmoud says: 'I have certain convictions, like temporary marriage, if a relationship is about to lead to sin.' Sima laughs: 'You don't appear like the kind of guy to believe in such things!' Mahmoud is still serious and says: 'What's wrong with doing things in a legal and moral way?' Sima continues to laugh, and replies: 'I don't know. I think people should get married when they like each other.' Mahmoud nods and says: 'Yes, exactly. And that is exactly what temporary marriage is. It has certain conditions and it can lead to a permanent marriage at a later stage.' Sima continues to laugh, and Mahmoud asks her in an irritated manner why she cannot have a serious conversation about this topic. Sima looks at him again and replies: 'Maybe because I have already taken this relationship more seriously than this?'

Sima and Mahmoud thus have quite different expectations of where their relationship is going. While Sima wants to marry Mahmoud on a permanent basis, Mahmoud seeks a short-term relationship and a diversion from his daily family life. Mahmoud soon finds out that it is difficult to keep his relationship with Sima a secret from his wife. After a while, he wants to end it. He leaves a message on Sima's answering machine and delivers seven gold coins to her as dower. At this point, Sima has just found out that she is pregnant and the situation becomes more tense. Sima has decided to keep the baby and does not want to end the relationship. At least, she wants Mahmoud to agree to register the marriage so that her unborn child can have the necessary identification papers. When Mahmoud tries to persuade her to have an abortion and wants her out of his life, Sima becomes frustrated and threatens revenge. The film ends tragically when Sima dies in an accident, and the film shows Mahmoud driving past the scene of the accident together with his wife.

The film caused a huge debate in Iran, as it dealt with problems in Iranian society connected with drug abuse, prostitution, corruption, and misuse of religious prescriptions such as temporary marriage (Mir-Hosseini 2007). The debate revolved around those who saw the film as presenting a legitimate critique of family policies in Iran, and those who claimed it merely made fun of religious laws and regulations (op. cit.: 618). Moreover, the film illustrates the procedure under which temporary marriages are conducted in contemporary Iran, and also points to the possible consequences of an unresolved legal issue both for children and for the women who engage in unregistered temporary marriages.

Debates and reforms relating to temporary marriage

Historically, temporary marriage has been primarily an urban phenomenon in Iran, associated with pilgrimage and long-distance travelling and especially common among salesmen (Haeri 1989: 1). More recently, the practice has figured in the state's family policy plans. After the Revolution in 1979 (and particularly during the Iran–Iraq war), the promotion of temporary marriage was part of a policy called the 'universalisation of marriage' (Paidar 1995). Temporary marriage and polygyny were justified as a means of protecting the family from single women, adultery, divorce and prostitution.[33] During the 1990s the discourse on 'universalisation of marriage' decreased, but again in 2007 Iran's Interior Minister, Mostafa Pour-Mohammadi, started to promote temporary marriage as a solution to the country's social problems (Harrison, 2 June 2007). Pour-Mohammadi claimed that temporary marriage should not be used just for sexual pleasure, but to solve what he saw as problematic areas for society such as increasing numbers of divorced and single women, and a rise in marriage age (ibid.).[34] Still, many Iranians see temporary marriage as just a form of permitted prostitution, legitimised within a Shi'a Islamic framework by putting 'a religious hat on it', so to speak (Haeri 1989: x).

Recent family law codifications have for the most part taken up the issue of temporary marriage indirectly. In the 1928 Civil Code, however, there is a section in Book 7 on marriage and divorce, called temporary marriage. It contains three articles: One deals with a short definition of temporary marriage (Article 1075); the second states that the duration of the temporary marriage must be defined (Article 1076); and the third article makes it clear that the same regulations concerning dower in general are valid also for marriages of a temporary kind (Article 1077). On the issue of dower, temporary marriage is equated with permanent marriage according to several articles of the Iranian Civil Code (Articles 1095,[35] 1096,[36] 1097,[37] 1098[38] and 942).[39] Article 940, however, states, 'A married pair, married permanently, and not restrained from inheriting, take inheritance one from the other.' Thus, there are no inheritance rights in a temporary marriage. Temporary marriage, however, is nowhere mentioned in the 1931 Marriage Law or in the 1967 Family Protection Law (Mir-Hosseini 2000a: 166).[40] According to

Mir-Hosseini, leaving temporary marriage out of these reforms may be seen as a way of limiting its legal legitimacy:

> Thus, prior to 1979, although the Shari'a validity of *mut'a* marriage was not directly challenged, its legal validity was seriously curtailed. The aim was to discourage and even ban this type of marriage without offending the clergy and challenging the Shari'a directly. The end-result was that *mut'a* became a mutilated form of marriage with no legal consequences. (ibid.)

The description of temporary marriage as a 'mutilated form of marriage' is still applicable, though. Despite the legal provisions connected to this form of marriage, the practice is often maintained in secret and outside the court system. A relevant issue for temporary marriage therefore deals with the demand for registration. Whether this is required or not for temporary marriage has remained an unresolved issue for years. In the 1931 Marriage Law, registration of all marriages became a legal requirement. In practice, however, this law had little effect on the registration of temporary marriages, due both to the lack of legal representatives outside urban centres and lack of knowledge of the law (Haeri 1989: 215, note 17). Thus, the legal provisions for registration have not been as strictly enforced for temporary marriages as for permanent marriages, and the act of offering and acceptance may therefore be performed privately by either the man or the woman, or by a mulla (op. cit.: 51). In most cases, though, it is probable that couples tend to contract their own marriages without any kind of official registration. Consequently, as a practice most often performed outside the court system, temporary marriage has entailed limited rights both for the wife and child in the marriage and has therefore been subject to debate. Temporary marriage also highlights the contentious nature of areas of family law, as they tend to involve disputes about what is seen to be in accordance not only with notions of Shari'a, but also of women's rights.

CHAPTER 3

THE FAMILY PROTECTION BILL

The Family Protection Bill was initially introduced by the cabinet (*Dolat*) of President Ahmadinejad in 2007, but has clear links to previous amendments and debates that have characterised the area of family law for decades. Since its first introduction, the bill has been subject to revisions and debates in the Majles, as well as in public, involving both religious and academic scholars and women's rights activists. In order to fully understand the content of the Family Protection Bill and not least the debate that has followed, the background, breaks and continuities that the bill offers to the topic of family law in Iran will be given. Also its 2007, 2010 and 2011 versions will be reviewed, particularly in light of changes offered to previous family law reforms in Iran. The development of the bill has, however, been quite difficult to follow because of its contentious nature and the limited information available on Iran's internal politics. It is therefore important to stress that the following presentation is not intended to give a complete overview of the process of debate on the bill. Rather, it offers an insight into some of the significant topics of debate and changes from 2007 until 2011. The legal–historical context of the bill is given particular emphasis, and although the debate and revision of the bill has not ended, this presentation draws a line in August 2011.

Background of the Family Protection Bill

Although the Family Protection Bill was first presented in 2007, initial preparations go further back and can be summarised in three main efforts. The first attempt to define a new family law was initiated after the Constitutional Revolution in Iran (1905–11) and drafted in the Iranian Civil Code between 1928 and 1935. In 1928, the Iranian Civil Code represented a shift from preceding family law rulings. The 1931 Marriage Law, which was the most important reform at the time, introduced registration of all marriages in courts and enabled women to initiate divorce proceedings in civil courts. Whereas family law was previously governed by *ulama* alone, reforms enacted in relation to the draft of the Iranian Civil Code between 1928 and 1935, and not least the 1931 Marriage Law, brought the definition and administration of family law under state control. The Iranian Civil Code was the only European-based law code enacted in Iran at the time that contained references to Shari'a,[1] and most of its articles can be seen as simplifications and codifications of the majority opinion within Shi'a jurisprudence (Mir-Hosseini 2010: 327). *Ulama* had previously been in charge of family law issues. Now civil courts under the rules of the Ministry of Justice were established to register and manage all marriages and divorces (ibid.).

The second initiative of codification came during the Pahlavi era and resulted in the Family Protection Law in 1967 and 1975. Mainly, the 1967 Family Protection Law introduced equal access to divorce, while in 1975 further amendments allocated child custody to both men and women and Family Protection Courts were set up. With the establishment of the Islamic Republic of Iran, though, the Family Protection Law was formally abolished in 1979. Shortly afterwards, the call for a return to Shari'a was announced and the Special Civil Courts Act was introduced to secure this goal. Although the 1979 Act allocated the authority of civil courts to a *mujtahid*,[2] pre-revolutionary reforms continued to have procedural influence over family law issues in practice (Mir-Hosseini 2000a: 25). Following the establishment of the Islamic Republic, family law rulings have continued to be made mainly according to the Iranian Civil Code. Parts of the Family Protection Law were, however, maintained in practice after 1979 as the basis for judgements in family law courts (Halper 2005: 97 and Mir-Hosseini 2000a: 25). What is more, the 1967 Family Protection Law has gradually been reimplemented since 1979 through singular reforms of the Civil Code, and the 1998 Family Court Law represents the final fulfilment of the amendments abolished in 1979 (Halper 2007, Mir-Hosseini 1996 and 2000a).

Since the 1979 Special Civil Court Act, only isolated reforms have been passed in the area of family law. They signify attempts to develop legislation appropriate for the Islamic Republic, and were eventually defined in the Family Protection Bill of 2007. This bill was originally prepared by the Legal and Judicial Committee in the Majles (*Komisiun-e Qazi-ye va Hoqoqi-ye Majles*) in 2007, and was the third initiative for codification of Iranian family law, intended to replace preceding codifications. Later the same year President Ahmadinejad's government took up the judiciary's draft, and additional changes were made. The 2007 Family Protection Bill was not, however, a final version that received unanimous consent or approval. Rather, the quest for family law legislation has continued in the debates over the content of the bill since its introduction.

Content of the Family Protection Bill

On 24 June 2007, the cabinet of Ahmadinejad introduced an amended version of the 2007 Family Protection Bill. During that summer, it was presented to the seventh Majles. As the bill was being clarified for ratification in the Majles in the early autumn of 2008, a widespread public debate about its content developed. As a result of the extensive protests and debates mainly in the Majles, but also among religious and academic scholars and women's rights activists, the 2007 Bill was sent back to the Legal and Judicial Committee in the Majles for review. Primarily, the disputes arose over three articles:

(1) Article 22 on registration of temporary marriage (*sabt-e ezdevaj-e movaqat*);[3]

(2) Article 23 on conditions for authorisation of plurality of marriage (*ta'adod-e ezdevaj*);[4]
(3) Article 25 on provisions for deciding standardised dowers (*mehrieha-ye balatar az hod mo'taraf*).[5]

The overall content of the 2007 Family Protection Bill represents both a break from, and continuity with, previous family law reforms in Iran. Its introductory text states:

> Considering that certain parts of the laws concerning rights of the family have been found incompatible with the Shari'a and the legal vacuum arising therefrom, in view of the confusion in the rules in this sphere, lack of clarity as to which of those rules are outdated and which are not, leading to harmful effects and numerous problems. (Introduction to the 2007 Family Protection Bill)

The need for clarification of the present legislation is based mostly on two grounds: first, to fulfil Article 21 of the 1979 Constitution of the Islamic Republic, which is to 'ensure the rights of women in all respects, in conformity with Islamic criteria';[6] and second, to carry out the requirements of Article 158 of the Constitution by 'drafting judiciary bills appropriate for the Islamic Republic'.[7] The declared aim of the Family Protection Bill, in its introduction, is 'to reduce or resolve the problems existing in the rules of family rights, to settle the ambiguities, contradictions and vacuum within the currently applicable family laws'. The need to adopt a comprehensive family law codification that corresponds both to concepts of women's rights and Shari'a is thus officially stated in the draft.

There seems to be a general consensus among politicians, religious and academic scholars and women's rights activists on the need to revise current family law legislation. Which laws require amendments and what the reforms should contain, however, remain divisive topics. The particular laws defined as problematic by the 2005 cabinet are specified in Article 53, the last clause of the bill. If ratified, the Family Protection Bill is said to replace family law rulings identified as ten previously enacted laws, among them the Family Protection Law from 1967/75 and the amendments made with regard to dower and divorce in the late 1990s.[8]

The Family Protection Bill consists of six chapters. Chapter One deals with family courts and Chapter Two with family counselling centres. Both are related to the constitutional aim of establishing 'courts to protect and preserve the family' (Article 21 in the 1979 Constitution of the Islamic Republic). Chapter Three is on marriage, mostly a revision of the Law of Marriage ratified in 1931. Chapter Four takes up the Amendments to Divorce Regulations from 1992 and clarifies judgements on divorce. Chapter Five involves custody rights and maintenance of children and is meant to replace the Law on Right of Custody from 1986. Chapter Six deals with penal provisions and will replace amendments made to Articles 645 and 646 in the 1996 Islamic Penal Code.

The amendments proposed in Chapters One and Two of the 2007 bill mostly represent continuities of previously enacted policies. The section on family courts can be seen as an extension of the 1997 Family Courts Law. Article 1 states:

> In exercise of Paragraph 3 of Article 21 of the Constitution of the Islamic Republic of Iran and for the purpose of investigating family affairs and disputes and offences subject to the present law, the Judiciary is required to establish an adequate number of family court branches in all judicial districts of cities. (Article 1 of the 2007 Family Protection Bill)

The endeavour to bring family disputes into the judicial sphere has become a continuing objective in the history of family law in Iran. The 1935 Iranian Civil Code initiated a process of judicialisation of family matters;[9] in particular the 1931 Marriage Law, which transferred marriage and divorce from the preferential domain of *ulama* in Shari'a courts to official state-defined courts (Mir-Hosseini 2000a: 23–4). This was reinforced in the 1967 Family Protection Law, with the establishment of designated family courts. After the 1979 Revolution there were attempts to reverse the judicialisation process, in particular by the closing down of family courts and their replacement by special civil courts. These lasted until 1994, when the Law of Formation of General Courts was ratified. The special civil courts now disappeared and family disputes moved into general courts that dealt with all kinds of legal cases. Mir-Hosseini writes that having all sorts of cases in one court soon led to chaotic conditions, as only two courts dedicated to family matters were opened within each general court (Mir-Hosseini 2000a: ix). Gradually, the process of bringing family matters into courts was re-enacted and finalised in the 1997 Family Courts Law. By removing family matters from the exclusive domain of the *ulama*, the judicialisation of family law involved a move away from Shari'a courts and towards increased secularisation of the legal system. In the light of this development, however, Chapters One and Two of the 2007 Family Protection Bill represent continuities with previous efforts towards judicialisation of family matters. In addition, the establishment of family counselling centres is advocated in Article 17 of the 2007 Bill.

Controversies about the Family Protection Bill

The 2007 Family Protection Bill also caused contention over efforts to develop a codified family law. To begin with, three articles in Chapters One, Four and Six of this bill were considered controversial, mostly by various women's rights activists. First, Article 2 of the bill, dealing with requirements for judges in court, has been a subject of debate.[10] In a statement from women's rights activists criticising the Family Protection Bill,[11] Article 2 is opposed because the removal of the obligatory presence of one female judge is seen as a step backward for women's rights (FFL, 9 September 2007). The discussion on having female judges in family courts derives from an old debate, pushed forward especially by female members of the Majles during the 1990s on the basis of Article 21 in the Constitution, which reads that 'The government must ensure the rights of women in all respects' and 'establish competent courts to protect and preserve the family'.

In the 1992 Law of Amendment to Divorce Regulations, it was stated in note 5 that the appointment of female advisory judges to work in cooperation with the senior judge was allowed (Mir-Hosseini 2000a: x). The argument for the 1992 Bill had been made in favour of the protection of the family and to guarantee women the lawful rights granted to them by Islam. The ratification of the Family Courts Law in 1998 established designated family courts to replace the general courts. The law included the stipulation that judgements should, as far as possible, be made in consultation with female legal advisers, and it was specified that each court should have at least one female adviser whose view on the case should be presented before a sentence was determined (Mir-Hosseini 2000a: ix). The law re-established pre-revolutionary family courts, which were given the exclusive right to treat cases dealing with family matters. Thus, Article 2 of the Family Protection Bill represents breaks with the 1997 Family Courts Law. A coalition of women's rights activists therefore opposed Article 2 on the basis that it did not promote the need for female judges, but instead reversed the legal status of women to the situation before the 1967 Family Protection Law: 'the bill proposes to move back women's status 42 years' (FFL, 9 September 2007).

Second, Article 28 of the Family Protection Bill, which introduces new routines for women applying for divorce, has received attention.[12] Divorce regulations were subject to reform in the Family Protection Law of 1967 and in the 1992 Law of Amendment to Divorce Regulations. Both reforms restricted men's unilateral right to divorce (*talaq*), as discussed in the previous chapter. Divorce, however, is considered one of the most problematic areas of family law because of men's unrestricted and women's limited access to the marriage dissolution process. Therefore, many anticipated a change in divorce rights for women in the new family law proposal. According to 'The 2008 Statement of the Coalition of Women's Rights Activists and Groups opposing the "Family Protection Bill"' this was not achieved in the 2007 Bill, which rather contributed to the deterioration in women's access to divorce (We Change website, 18 August 2008).

Third, Article 46, which deals with penalties for a marriage between a non-Iranian man and an Iranian woman without proper authorisation, has been questioned.[13] In such a case, the foreign man will risk between 90 days and one year of imprisonment, and the woman (if married at her own free will), her father (if he gave permission) and the marriage officiant will be sentenced as accomplices. Article 46 also relates to the issue of women's citizenship, which has been at the heart of the debate on Iranian women's rights and is also relevant to the rights of children. In Iran, women are defined as citizens mainly on the basis of their role in the family (Article 21 in the Constitution). Article 1060 of the Iranian Civil Code states that 'Marriage of an Iranian woman with a foreign national is dependent . . . upon special permission of the Government' (Article 1060). Based on these directives, the status of women in Iran is often considered a second-class citizenship. Article 46 of the 2007 Bill is thus seen as reinforcing this status further by imposiing penalties for marrying a non-Iranian man without permission, as the government then demands to act as the guardian (*wali*) of the woman.

Women's rights activists, mainly outside Iran, have contested Article 46, which they consider a major step back in terms of women's rights. The article is seen as particularly discriminatory to Iranian women living outside Iran. Elahe Amani, an exiled Iranian activist living in the United States, writes that the impact of the bill on Iranian women living abroad is that: 'Iranian women married to foreign men will not be able to obtain citizenship for their children, even if these children are born and raised in Iran' (Amani 2008).

Fourth, there have been widespread protests against amendments proposed in Article 53 of the Family Protection Bill, which states that with its ratification a number of previous laws and amendments will be replaced. This article has aroused general concern among those promoting reform of Iran's legal system on the basis of what are seen as gender discriminatory laws. Among previous laws that will be overruled are the 1931 Marriage Act, which required the registration of marriages of all kinds in court, and the 1992 Law of Amendment to Divorce Regulations, which demanded that a husband pay compensation to his wife in the event of a divorce that is not initiated by or cannot be the fault of the wife. Thus, issues of marriage registration procedures and divorce in the Family Protection Bill have been controversial.

Continuities and breaks in the Family Protection Bill

In particular, three articles in Chapter Three have stood out as the most contentious parts of the 2007 Bill. Articles 22, 23 and 24/25 have been the reason for the initial review and the prolongation of the Family Protection Bill. These articles are said to represent breaks with the 1931 Marriage Law, the 1967/75 Family Protection Law, the 1982 Amendments on Marriage Contracts, the 1992 Amendments to Divorce Regulations and the 1997 Amendments on Dower. In the 2007 Bill, Article 22 on registration of temporary marriage states:

> Registration of permanent marriage [*sabt-e 'aqd-e nekah-ye dayem*], its voluntary or compulsory revocation, divorce, reunion [in the marital state] and pronouncement of annulment of marriage and divorce are mandatory [*elzami*]. Note: Registration of temporary marriage [*sabt nekah movaqat*] shall be subject to Rules of Procedure [*ayin-e tabe'*] to be approved by the minister of justice. (Article 22 of the 2007 Family Protection Bill)

The 2007 version of the article thus asserts that the question of registration of temporary marriages is to be subject to 'rules of procedure', and therefore signifies that temporary marriage will continue to be an unresolved issue in family law. Formally, temporary marriage came under the 1931 Marriage Law, which required the registration of all kinds of marriages. In practice, though, provisional types of marriage have been contracted in private outside the formal legal system. With temporary marriage continuing to be an unsettled legal issue, controversies emerged around the proposed Article 22 of the 2007 Bill and remained a divisive topic of debate in the 2010 version.

Another controversial proposal is Article 23 on the conditions for a husband receiving legal permission to contract a plurality of permanent marriages:

> Marriage to a subsequent permanent wife [*hamsar-e badi*] shall depend on court authorisation upon ascertainment of the man's

> financial capability and undertaking to uphold justice [*'edalat-e ejrae'*] among his wives. Note: In the event of plurality of marriages [*ta'adod-e ezdevaj*] and should the marriage portion [*mehrieh*] mature and the wife demands it, the authorisation to register the new marriage [*ezdevaj-e mujadad*] shall depend on payment of the marriage portion to the first wife. (Article 23 of the 2007 Family Protection Bill)

Article 23 changed the 1982 Marriage Contract Amendments by replacing the consent of the first wife with the authorisation of the court as the sole ground for contracting a polygynous marriage, and simultaneously made a clean break with the 1967 Family Protection Law, which had also established restrictions on polygyny. Moreover, the article states that registration of a subsequent marriage presupposes the payment of dower to the first wife, if she asks for it. In short, there have been adverse reactions to Article 23 on the basis that it removed the demand for the consent of the first wife, and was seen as introducing easier access to polygyny and in effect promoted the practice.

In addition, there were protests about Article 25 on deferred dower:

> At the time of registration of marriage, the Ministry of Economic Affairs and Finance [*Vezarat-e Umur-e Eqtesadi-ye va Darai-ye*] is required to collect tax [*maliyat*] on unreasonable and higher-than-conventional marriage portions [*mehrieha-ye balatar az had mota'araf va qeyr manteqi*], in view of the condition of the couple and the national economic issues, progressively in ratio to the increase in the amount of marriage portion. The amount of conventional marriage portion and the amount of tax shall be determined with a view to the general economic conditions of the country by rules of procedure to be proposed by the Ministry of Economic Affairs and Finance and to be approved by the Council of Ministers. (Article 25 of the 2007 Family Protection Bill)

The proposal for a financial tax on dowers that exceed the official amount is seen as breaking with the practice of dower in three main areas.[14] First, the idea that the Ministry of Finance was to decide on a conventional amount of dower and then collect tax on amounts above this was seen as breaking with dower as a religious prescription. Second, the latter was further seen as divergent from dower as a private agreement between the parties in marriage and an amount to be decided in the marriage contract. Third, the provisions of Article 25 were considered to undermine dower as a woman's financial property, and also to limit women's ability to make use of dower as a means of negotiation in obtaining divorce (*khul'*). The debate about the three articles mentioned is further discussed in Chapter Five.

The Family Protection Bill review process: 2007–10

In August 2007, the first draft of the 2007 Family Protection Bill was presented to the Legal and Judicial Commission in the Majles. In July 2008, the Legal and Judicial Committee passed the bill and the following month it was presented to the Majles for ratification. The bill provoked disputes both in the Majles and among the general public. A group of women's rights activists led by Shirin 'Ebadi, Mahboobeh Abbasgholizadeh and Simin Behbahani arranged a sit-in at the Majles on 31 August 2008, where they discussed the contents of the bill with some members of the Majles (FFL, 31 August 2008). Because of the controversies over the content of the bill, and in particular over Article 23 on polygynous marriage, it was sent back to the Legal and Judicial Commission for review in September 2008. In autumn 2009, the review process ended and the Legal and Judicial Commission approved a new version. In 2010, this was introduced to the Majles. The Proposed Amendments to the 2010 Family Protection Bill included revisions of the legal procedures of temporary marriages (Article 22), polygyny (Article 23) and dower (Article 24).

The 2010 version of Article 22 specifies a legal procedure under which temporary marriage should proceed. It includes mandatory registration if the wife is pregnant and if both parties agree on registration. Thus, it represents a break with previous rulings on temporary marriage. The 1931 Marriage Law established a dual validity with regard to temporary marriage. On the one hand, registration of all kinds of marriages was required. On the other hand, such marriages were practised outside the court system and left as an unresolved issue. There is also a clear difference between the 2010 Family Protection Bill and the 1967 Family Protection Law in that the latter has no reference at all to temporary marriage, let alone not requiring it to be registered. The article in the 2010 Bill, however, states:

> Registration of temporary marriage [*sabt-e ezdevaj-e movaqat*] or expiration time [*enqeza-ye modat*] or to terminate temporary marriage before the agreed expiration date [*bazl*] if the wife is pregnant is mandatory, and expiration time or date does not prevent registration in the event of marriage. In other cases, registration of a temporary marriage is done when there is mutual consent from both parties. In the event of mutual consent of both parties for registration of temporary marriage, it is not required for it [the marriage] to be written in [the] identity card [*shenasname*], but if both parties agree on this form of registration it can be done. Note: Registration of the details of this article and previous articles in the official marriage and divorce office is according to the resolution that is reached within one year proposed by the Minister of Justice and dependent on the approval of the head of the judiciary. Until this resolution is ratified, regulations in the mentioned Article (1) authority still remains as the amendment of the law regarding marriage approved in 1316 [1937]. (Article 22 of the Family Protection Bill 2010)

Thus, the 2010 version of Article 22 introduced a clear break with previous enactments on temporary marriage, as it proposes to demand registration in the event of pregnancy and if the two parties allow the temporary marriage to be registered in their identity cards. On this basis, the amendment demands a similar registration of both temporary and permanent marriages.

In the 2010 edition of Article 23, the provisions for a man to contract more than one permanent marriage were extended from the 2007 version of Article 23 that demanded court authorisation, husband's financial ability and his capacity to 'uphold justice among his wives' (Article 23 of the 2007 Family Protection Bill). The 2010 version added ten conditions under which a husband is permitted to contract additional permanent marriage(s):

> The court allows the husband to apply for permission for permanent renewed marriage [*ezdevaj-e mujadad-e dayem*] on the basis of the following circumstances: (1) The consent of the first wife; (2) Inability of first wife to perform marital duties; (3) Lack of obedience of wife after court verdict; (4) Wife infected by madness or incurable disease; (5) Confirmed conviction of wife for deliberate crime to one year of imprisonment or incapacity to pay a fine resulting in a year of custody; (6) If the wife has had any harmful addiction that, according to the court, is affecting family life; (7) Unacceptable behaviour of wife so that life is made unbearable for the husband; (8) A wife leaves marital life for six months; (9) Sterility of wife; (10) The absence of the wife for a year. Note: The applicant must prepare and present his petition with causes and reasons as above and submit it to the court. (Article 23 of the Family Protection Bill 2010)

The contractual stipulations detailed in Article 23 of the 2010 Bill refer to different aspects of the marriage contract. The concept of a contract is significant not only for interpersonal obligations and financial transactions, but also as a model for gendered relationships in Iranian culture and it can thus be considered the backbone of marriage institutions (Haeri 1989: 65). The concept of a contract has also been used as a paradigm for introducing reform to family law, for instance by allowing for the possibility of including conditions in the marriage contract to limit a man's right to a plurality of marriages and his unilateral right to divorce. On the basis of introducing stipulations in the contract, the 1967 Family Protection Law was abolished in 1979 (Hinchcliffe 1968: 521). It is thus interesting to note that similar conditions are now being proposed in the 2010 Bill. The use of contractual stipulations in both the 1967 Family Protection Law and the 2010 Family Protection Bill represents a continuity in family law reform. In comparison, though, the 1967/75 Family Protection Law introduced three conditions for contracting a polygynous marriage: the consent of the first wife, court confirmation of the husband's capability to provide financially and psychologically for several wives, and up to two years of imprisonment if a polygynous marriage was contracted without the approval of the court (Hinchcliffe 1968: 521).

The main difference between the 2010 Family Protection Bill and the 1967/75 Family Protection Law lies in the nine conditions to prove deficiencies of the first wife in the performance of her 'marital duties'. Thus, the conditions of the 2010 Bill for polygyny are clearly situated within conditional restrictions introduced to polygyny as seen in countries like Egypt, Indonesia and Morocco (Welchman 2007: 87). Still, the 2010 version of Article 23 signifies a shift from the 1967/75 Family Protection Law's requirement for the husband to prove and adjust to provision for the marriage, towards a focus on proving shortcomings on the part of the wife.

In the 2010 version of Article 24 (which replaced the former Article 25), the demand for taxation of dower is removed. Instead, the article states that the judiciary should decide a standard rate for dower every three years, and if the husband should fail to pay the dower upon request (within the conventional limits) he will be sentenced to prison. The amended article states:

> Government agencies must promote marriage culture through cultural and public media and be sure to take necessary action to produce and establish ordinary and common dowers [*mehriehha-ye mota'araf*]. Note 1: A normal rate of dower based on the country's general economic situation is announced once every three years by the head of the Judiciary. Note 2: If the *mehrieh* at the time of marriage contract is at a normal [*mota'araf*] and lawful [*halal*] rate and if the husband should

> refuse to pay *mehrieh*, he is subject to the provisions of Article (2) of the law of financial convictions. Note 3: If the amount of dower is more than conventional at the time of the marriage contract, the excess *mehrieh* (*mazad*) is dependent on the financial status of the husband. Note 4: It is necessary to consider the current price level when calculating *mehrieh*. (Article 24 of the Family Protection Bill 2010)

Although the demand for tax on dower was removed, the 2010 version of the article continues to diverge from the ways in which previous family law codifications have dealt with the issue. Nevertheless, the effort of the judiciary to establish a standardised rate for dower remains a stipulation never seen before in Iran.

The Family Protection Bill review process: 2010–11

Up until 2011, the Family Protection Bill continued to be a contentious issue in the Majles, and revolved particularly around Articles 22, 23, and 24. In August 2010, 'Ali Ardashir Larijani, Speaker of the eighth Majles, announced that Articles 22, 23 and 24 would be sent to the Majles's Legal and Judicial Commission for further investigations (FFL, 12 November 2010). Various statements and proposals for replacing the three articles were then raised by the end of September 2010. Farhad Tajri, vice-president of the Majles's Legal and Judicial Commission, said that because of the vast amount of proposals and statements presented to the Commission, Articles 22, 23 and 24 were passed on to the Committee of Private Rights (Komite-ye Hoqoq-e Khososi) for further examination. Tajri also stressed that there was no reason to remove the three articles from the proposed bill, but if comprehensive and useful proposals for reform were presented, then the Committee of Private Rights would make use of them when reviewing the articles (FFL, 12 November 2010).

Mosa Qurbani, a member of the Legal and Judicial Commission, stressed that the review process of the Commission of Private Rights could continue indefinitely as no time limitations had been decided. On behalf of the Judicial and Legal Commission, Qurbani said that the Commission had come up with a proposal for removing Articles 22 and 24 from the bill, and instead of Article 23 the Commission suggested that three additional articles should be inserted. According to Qurbani, one of these should discuss women's right to divorce, and the second article would deal with the right of men to contract a polygynous marriage. A third article was recommended by the Legal and Judicial Commission in order to address the rights of children. Later, Amir Hossein Rahimi, spokesman for the Commission, proposed that the first of these articles dealing with women's rights to divorce should be added to Article 23 (FFL, 12 November 2010).

None of these suggestions was, however, ratified by the end of 2010. Instead, provisional resolutions were made with regard to the future of these articles. Muhammad Dehghan, a Majles representative, said in an interview with Mehr News Agency: 'The process of reviewing the remaining articles of the bill has yet to be completed and only Article 22 has been approved with modifications' (Campaign for Equality website, 7 November 2010). Dehghan referred to the last modifications of Article 22 and said:

> The content of Article 22 has not changed significantly, but a provision has been added to it. In addition to requiring that temporary marriages [*sighe*] be registered in the event of pregnancy, or the agreement of the parties, conditions specified in the marriage contract make registration of temporary marriage obligatory. (Campaign for Equality website, 7 November 2010)

Thus, the registration of temporary marriage in the event of pregnancy and if both parties in the marriage agreed, had been made mandatory. The issues of polygyny and dower, however, still presented complex legal challenges. According to Dehghan, the ratification of Articles 23 and 24 was not a pressing issue and could easily be postponed. Instead, he highlighted the need to seek expert opinions on these two articles, so that members of the Majles would have grounds for accepting the proposed amendments:

> We are not in a hurry to review and approve the two remaining articles and we are trying to invite expert opinion on these two articles and after utilizing expert opinions we will address this issue. In this way, our fellow parliamentarians will also be better convinced to accept the recommendations of the Commission. (Campaign for Equality website, 7 November 2010)

Article 24 in the 2010 Family Protection Bill encountered problems based on deciding what was a 'standard [*mota'araf*] and lawful [*halal*] rate' for dower (Article 24 of the Family Protection Bill 2010). As a result, the Legal and Judiciary Commission of the Majles announced in November 2010 that Article 24 might be deleted due to problems in setting a standard and a limitation of dower (FFL, 12 November 2010 and Campaign for Equality Website, 7 November 2010). Shortly after, it was announced that the article had been removed altogether (FFL, 12 November 2010).

The process of review of Article 23, the most controversial part of the Family Protection Bill, was more time-consuming. Muhammad-Reza Rahimi, spokesperson of the Legal and Judicial Commission and the first vice-president of Iran, referred to female Majles deputies who had been present to discuss the issue: 'The proposals of these representatives of different periods were important and useful in reforming Article 23' (FFL, 12 November 2010). Rahimi added that because of the length of the debate, the Legal and Judicial Commission had not been able to take a vote on Article 23. Moreover, some female members of the Majles and several women's rights activists have protested against paragraph seven of the 2010 edition of Article 23, which referred to 'unacceptable behaviour of the wife such that life is made unbearable for the husband' (FFL, 12 November 2010). Consequently, grounds were laid for new rounds of debate on the content of Article 23.

Then in late July 2011, it was announced that Article 23 had been omitted from the 2011 version of the bill, and that the 2011 version of it would be reintroduced in the Majles shortly (Mardomak News, 26 July 2011, BBC Persian, 30 July 2011, Karmand News, 13 August 2011). Moreover, it was reported that divorce rights were allocated to women in cases where a man had contracted a polygynous marriage without her consent (Icana News, 13 August 2011 and Farda News, 13 August 2011). Thus, for the first time since the introduction of the Family Protection Bill in 2007, Article 23 and the issue of polygyny had been removed from it. The reason for the omission was said to be the amount of protest and fierce debates that the article had caused in the Majles, as well as among *ulama* and women's rights activists (FFL, 29 July 2011). For instance, Ayatollah Sane'i protested against the article and said that if a man marries without the consent of the first wife, this is 'unlawful, forbidden and a sin', and he believed that 'even on the basis of the principle of *tamkin* [obedience and docility of the wife], the man is forbidden to remarry' (Mardomak News, 26 July 2011).

Although the article on polygyny was removed from the Family Protection Bill, this was not seen only as beneficial for the position of women. In an op-ed published on the Feminist School website, it is noted that although Article 23 had been removed this does not mean that polygyny has ended as a practice in Iranian family law (Feminist School website, 31 July 2011). The op-ed also stated that 'What we really want is divorce rights and generally equal rights for women' (ibid.). A similar point is made in a piece published on the Fair Family Law website a few days after the news about Article 23 was known: 'Article 23 has been removed and there is now silence on the subject of polygyny' (FFL, 4 August 2011). Thus, the deletion of Article 23 may signify that polygyny is left as an unresolved issue in the 2011 version of the bill. To the question of introducing divorce rights for women in the event of the husband contracting a polygynous marriage without her consent, women's rights activists responded negatively. In an article published on the Fair Family Law website, the provisions on divorce were said to be uncertain because the full text of the 2011 Family Protection Bill had not yet been published (FFL, 4 August 2011). Moreover, in an article a few days later it was argued that divorce rights were not enough, and that polygynous marriages (permanent and temporary ones) should be outlawed entirely (FFL, 16 August 2011).

Main positions on the Family Protection Bill

Positions vis-à-vis the Family Protection Bill have mostly been divided between those who support and those who oppose it. They are also closely connected to attitudes towards Islam and Shari'a, views of women's rights and stances in Iranian national politics. They result in various interpretations of how family law is defined, its use, and what kind of sources a codified family law can draw upon. For example, Zohreh Elaheyian, who supports the Family Protection Bill, is a neoconservative member of the Majles and represents the current government. Her outlook on family law is confined to the Islamic framework and builds on a notion that Islam and complementary gender roles benefit women's rights and the nation. Elaheyian underlines parts of the bill that she deems favourable for women's rights. 'Regarding the custody of children and ... family courts, new modifications in the law are in favour of women', she said in an interview (Iranian Labour News Agency, ILNA, 25 August 2010). Mostly she emphasises the establishment of designated family courts in every Iranian city to deal with family disputes and that these courts will also have female judges, something Elaheyian sees as positive features of the bill (FFL 19 October 2010).

In addition, she maintains that 'Those who are not in favour of the law are against the system and anti-women's rights' (ILNA, 25 August 2010). She has stressed that it is not the legislation itself that is discriminatory towards women, but rather the altering of its contents by the western media. Elaheyian mentioned Shirin 'Ebadi in particular as someone who has spread negative information about the bill in the international media by her comment that it primarily calls for polygyny (FFL, 19 October 2010). Elaheyian considers the bill to be favourable for the protection of family and women's rights, and sees ratification as the best option for avoiding international pressure on Iran to sign CEDAW (FFL, 19 October 2010). Also, she says that those who oppose the bill want Iran to join CEDAW, which according to Elaheyian is equivalent to taking action against women's rights and the system of the Islamic Republic (ILNA, 25 August 2010). On this basis, Elaheyian's view of the family law can be labelled as loyalist, and her opinions on to the Family Protection Bill also project a neoconservative political view.

On the other hand, Zahra Rahnavard is a representative of those who oppose the bill. Rahnavard is associated with the reformist wing of politics in Iran. She was a political adviser to President Khatami and is also known as the wife of the reformist politician Mir-Hossein Mousavi.[15] Like Elaheyian, Rahnavard views Islam as potentially beneficial for women's rights. They do, however, differ in how they view the current implementation of family law. Although they both support the Islamic Republic and look primarily to Islamic sources for defining women's rights, Rahnavard criticises the current government and the enforcement of family law. She has on several occasions spoken out against the bill, both in its 2010 and 2007 forms. Mainly she argues that the Family Protection Bill will have adverse effects on women's rights on the basis of Article 23 dealing with polygyny, because it 'Gives more power to men to have polygamy without the wife's consent and harshly discriminates against the women even further than the circumstances women are suffering today in Iranian society according to the current laws.' (Rahnavard 21 August 2010)

Rahnavard's objection to the bill, however, does go beyond the issue of women's rights as she connects its implementation to the foundation of the Iranian nation. She writes that 'Removing the so-called "Family Protection" bill from the Majles's agenda is not a feminine demand but is rather a symbol of the national demand for the prosperity of the Iranian nation and the stability of the Iranian families' (ibid.). Although Rahnavard rejects the overall content of the bill, she projects revisionist perspectives of family law.

Between these two positions are those who support the Family Protection Bill in general, but oppose some of the articles. Elahe Rastgoo, for example, a former reformist Majles representative, has criticised Articles 22, 23 and 24/25 of the bill and tried to prevent its implementation (ILNA, 24 August 2010). Thus, Rastgoo can be said to reflect revisionist views on family law. Interestingly, such a view appears to have the support not only of members of the Majles, but also of some *ulama*. The debate in the Majles on the content of

Articles 22, 23 and 24/25 reveals that many of the same arguments are in use by revisionist women's rights activists. For instance, the way in which the amount of dower is limited in the Family Protection Bill – although supported by many loyalists – has been opposed by revisionist women's rights activists and a majority of politicians and *ulama* alike in the Majles. Because of the revisions that the Family Protection Bill has been subject to in recent years, there is reason to believe that revisionists like Rastgoo actually represent broader views prevailing in the Majles about what legal regulations of dower, temporary and polygynous marriages should involve than those of the loyalist approach. As mentioned above, the conservative branch of politics is currently split in Iran. Consequently, loyalists do not necessarily represent the overall conservative political view in the Majles, but are challenged by conservatives who represent views more in line with revisionist perspectives. In addition to the loyalist and revisionist positions on the bill, there are groups of women's rights activists who not only oppose the three articles in question, but also reject the Family Protection Bill in its entirety. They may be referred to as having a rejectionist view of family law, but they are not found in the current Majles. A coalition of women's rights and human rights groups has together drafted statements opposing the Family Protection Bill. Their 2008 statement said that 'Women's lack of legal rights has been reinforced through this bill' (We Change website, 18 August 2008). The various conceptions of the so-called rejectionists, revisionists and loyalists on the Family Protection Bill and issues of Shari'a and women's rights more generally are discussed in detail in Chapter Four.

CHAPTER 4

CONCEPTIONS OF SHARI'A AND FAMILY LAW

The two subsequent chapters deal with how the women's rights activists in this study approach family law. Chapter Five addresses the particular ways in which they relate to issues of dower, polygynous and temporary marriage. In this chapter, however, more general views about Shari'a and family law are examined. Even though Shari'a is considered an integral part of the legal system in Iran, there is no consensus on what it represents as a legal source or on its content. Thus, Shari'a is a highly controversial issue. Women's rights activists, too, elaborate on the historical and contextual meaning of concepts relevant for family law legislation, such as law (Shari'a *vs. qanun*), reform (*eslah*), independent reasoning (*ijtihad*), consensus (*ijma'*), common good (*maslaha*) and justice (*'edalat*). The following is an overview of the main controversies among women's rights activists holding so-called rejectionist, revisionist and loyalist perspectives on family law.

Rejectionists, revisionists and loyalists

An overall distinction is made in this book between the three general understandings of family law in contemporary Iran: rejectionist, revisionist and loyalist. This distinction is made in order to explain various approaches that the women's rights activists take towards

Shari'a. It mostly refers to the kind of sources they take into account when advocating their views. However, there seem to be certain recurrent references that are relevant to all three positions and to the family law debate in the Islamic Republic more generally. At the same time, it is possible to draw out some basic lines of difference between these three positions.

The rejectionist view

First, the typical rejectionist position claims that Islamic sources of law have been so influenced by patriarchy that they need to be rejected as a whole. Consequently, this approach rejects the practices of dower, polygyny and temporary marriage and sometimes the entire tradition of Islam. Most of them claim that the Family Protection Bill must be rejected in its totality, and argue in favour of an abolition or overall reform of current legislation. The rejectionist approach relies on sources of law such as CEDAW, or an amended version of the 1928 Iranian Civil Code, that have little or no validity in the official family law debate in Iran. In order to make some impact on the debate, those who hold a rejectionist view sometimes adopt a revisionist approach towards family law for practical reasons. A clear-cut rejectionist position is therefore not commonly utilised in the official public debate, although there are examples of it being presented online and among a few of the interviewees. Important sources of reference for the rejectionists tend to relate to women's rights as inherent aspects of Iranian history (*Iraniyat*). Thus, they often referred to Mehrangiz Manoochehrian's draft of an alternative family law bill from 1963/64. Among the interviewees, Afsaneh and Touran represent outspoken rejectionist views.

The revisionist view

The revisionist approach accepts that the practices of family law have a divine origin and are based on Islamic sources, but seek to adapt them to the current Iranian society and context. Most often this involves some kind of legal regulation of the practices of dower, polygyny and temporary marriage. Revisionists argue for the amendment of the existing family law legislation, which they consider should be based on different sources. Both Shari'a and principles of women's rights are recognised as sources of law. The revisionist approach is thus more in line than the rejectionist one with the accepted conditions for the official public debate, because they establish their arguments more or less within the framework of Islam and the Islamic Republic. However, those who hold revisionist views tend to combine a range of sources, such as the Qur'an, ahadith, *usul al-fiqh*, CEDAW, Mehrangiz Manoochehrian's draft of an alternative family law bill from 1963/64 and references to the teachings of Ayatollah Sane'i. In addition, the revisionist position makes use of other sources of legitimacy based, for instance, on notions of Islamic-ness (*Islamiyat*) and Iranian-ness (*Iraniyat*). The majority of the interviewees represent revisionist conceptions of family law: Elham, Zahra, Leyli, 'Ali, Assieh, Arezoo, Minoo, Bahareh, Parisa, Rokhana and Zohreh.

The loyalist view

Relating ideas of family law to Islam and the Islamic Republic of Iran are also significant for the loyalist approach. However, the pace, extent and reasons for adjusting contemporary family laws are framed in a different manner. Among recognised sources for family law legislation are the Qur'an, *ahadith*, *usul al-fiqh,* the 1928 Iranian Civil Code and Iran's 1979 Constitution. Strong arguments are also often made against the CEDAW. The loyalist approach tends to address the religious texts literally, accept the practices of dower, polygynous and temporary marriages as founded on divine revelation, and be reluctant to endorse wide-ranging reforms that discard authoritative and established interpretations of these practices. The starting point of the loyalist position is not primarily to safeguard women's rights, but rather to preserve the protection of the family as a founding principle of the Islamic Republic. Loyalists who take part in the contemporary debate on family law do, however, tend to adopt arguments in favour of maintaining women's rights to some degree. They also make reference to Islamic-ness (*Islamiyat*) and Iranian-ness (*Iraniyat*) in order to gain legitimacy. Maryam and Leyla were among the few loyalists found among the interviewees, but this position is held by many contemporary members of the Majles who are active in the Family Protection Bill debate.

'Shari'a, it's different from law'

A basis for the rejectionist approach to family law legislation is that there should be a clear distinction between the concepts of Shari'a and law (*qanun*). Whereas Shari'a is seen as representing a divine legislation that is inaccessible to humans, law refers to a codification with clear sources and principles. The concepts of Shari'a and *qanun* are often used interchangeably without any distinction between their different levels of meaning, and this is one of the inherent conceptual problems with Shari'a. Rejectionists assert that such a division is fundamental to codifications of family law, and they argue that Iran's family law should be based on codified legislation and non-Islamic sources. Ideally, many rejectionists seek a complete secularisation of the Civil Code of Iran, in which Islamic sources would have no influence.

A clear rejectionist position was expressed by Touran. She explained why she did not believe in a mere revision of existing family law legislation. When we met in August 2011, only days after the removal of Article 23 of the Family Protection Bill was publicly known, she said:

> I cannot be happy about this [the removal of Article 23] ... This law is from Shari'a, it's different from law [*qanun*]. And if [Article 23 is] deleted from law, it [polygyny] is still in Shari'a, and many people will do it outside the law. And it is very dangerous, I think more dangerous. (Interview with Touran, August 2011)

As Shari'a still constitutes a basis for current family law legislation in Iran, Touran expected more substantial changes to the legal system. She continued:

> As a secular activist, I believe that all law should be outside Shari'a. It is not one reason for us that one article of this law is

> deleted, because we believe that when Shari'a can influence the law, it can come back to law. Because you know that if deleted now, a new election for the Parliament, and a new play with opinion [will follow] ... Because when an article is issued in Parliament, the Guardian Council [*Shura-ye Negahban*] should confirm it. And they will not confirm it, I think ... And that's a game, a play. (Interview with Touran, August 2011)

As long as Shari'a is said to influence the legislation, Touran believes that it does not matter how practices such as polygyny are legally defined. She thinks that people will continue to practice it and the Guardian Council will permit it as long as the legislation is founded on Islamic sources and Shari'a. Touran's view of the legal system is characteristic of the rejectionist approach. Many rejectionists advocate a complete secularisation of the legislation.

'Family law is not sacred'

There are several similarities between the rejectionist and the revisionist approach to family law. A similar point of view to Touran's can be found among the revisionists, and one of their recurrent arguments is that there is a difference between Shari'a and law (*qanun*). Zohreh, a lawyer, explained to me first, that there is a difference between Shari'a and '*urf* (custom), and second, that there are two kinds of law in Iran:

> Part of the law is from Shari'a and the other side is law [*qanun*]. As in other countries, rulings regarding warfare are law [*qanun*], but a very big part of laws in Iran comes from Shari'a, for example inheritance [*ers*] and stoning. These are different from ordinary law [*qanun*]. (Interview with Zohreh, August 2011)

The difference between Shari'a and *qanun* referred to here relates to a distinction often made between Shari'a and *fiqh*. The different conceptions of Shari'a and *fiqh*, discussed in Chapter One, showed that the distinction is relevant for a scholarly perspective (*etic*) as well as for believers (*emic*). Whereas Shari'a represents 'divine law', *fiqh* is considered to be the human understanding of it. Thus, Shari'a may refer to a level of ideas and *fiqh* to actual codifications derived from human interpretations. On the emic level, such a contextual reading of Shari'a can be found, for instance, in Muhammad Mojtahed Shabestari's writings. Shabestari is a Shi'a *'alim* who has defended the possible combination of Shari'a and human rights. As a result, he is referred to as representing 'post-Islamist thinking' (Selvik and Shahibzadeh 2003). He claims that there is no such thing as 'eternal' or 'uncontested' Shari'a, and that Shari'a must be perceived as a continuing process of elaborations of *fiqh*. Furthermore, he argues that the religion of Islam should not be confused with a legal system, because religion is a spiritual and inner experience for humans (ibid.).

A similar distinction forms the basis of the revisionist (and to some degree the rejectionist) approach towards Shari'a and family law. An overall starting point of revisionists is that family law legislation is a subject that can be debated and changed. In the outline of alternative family law drafts published online it is stated: 'Family law is not sacred, therefore it is possible to discuss and talk about it and challenge it' (FFL, 8 May 2010). Similarly, the lawyer Gity Porfazel argues that any legislation should be subject to public debate and conform with the demands of the people. She states: 'The laws must be in accordance with the societal and cultural demands of the people. If not, the society will experience tension and turmoil ... Therefore the laws must be consistent with the development of the community' (FFL, 26 July 2008).

Although there are overlapping opinions on family law between the revisionists and rejectionists, an important dividing line can still be found in the sources that they take into account. Whereas the rejectionist approach generally discards Islam and argues in favour of secularised laws, the revisionists tend to engage with Islamic sources and legal principles. This difference between the two approaches is evident in the revisionists' references to concepts in *fiqh* such as *'edalat* (justice) and *ijtihad* (the process of independent reasoning).

'If there is justice, there is no polygamy'

Article 23 of the 2007 Family Protection Bill underlines the need to 'uphold justice' (*'edalat-e ejrae'*) between the wives in a polygynous marriage. Accordingly, the concept of justice (*'edalat*) is a significant term in the approach to polygyny among the revisionist women's rights activists. Revisionists do, however, tend to elaborate on what justice involves in a broader contextual sense, rather than as merely as a principle of *fiqh*.

Gity Porfazel claims that 'If there is justice [*'edalat*] there is no polygamy.' (FFL, 26 July 2008) She goes on to question how there can be justice in a marriage if, for instance, the age difference between a husband and a wife is 30 years. On a more general basis, she argues that the kind of justice that lawmakers are promoting in the Family Protection Bill is based on finance alone. Porfazel writes: 'We cannot define it this way . . . *Tamkin* [obedience of the wife] allows for financial support for housing, clothing and shopping; but this is not justice [*'edalat*]' (ibid.). Instead, she defines the concept of 'edalat in a wider sense, in which the wife's psychological and emotional well-being is emphasised and not merely the financial needs. Porfazel's attitude to the concept of justice signifies the revisionist approach, because it maintains the need to 'uphold justice' as defined in the Family Protection Bill, but revises the meaning of justice and relates it not only to the financial rights granted to the wife as a result of performing *tamkin* towards her husband, but also to her broader well-being.

Theologically, the concept of justice (*'edalat* or *'adl*) plays a significant role in Shi'i *fiqh*. It is also a noteworthy doctrinal difference between Shi'ism and Sunnism.[1] Although more widely referred to in Shi'ism, the Shi'a concept of justice has been called on by *qadi*s in Sunni courts as well, in order to maintain a notion of justice (*'adl*) within the limits of Shari'a (Shehada 2005: 13). Typically, not so much attention has been given to textual sources in such court rulings, but rather to the context of family law disputes (ibid.). Sometimes the concept of *'adl*, as derived from Shi'i *fiqh*, has been referred to by Sunni *qadis* as a means of showing sensitivity towards the 'weak party' in cases when family law has not proved suitable for a *qadi*'s ruling. On this basis, the concept of *'adl* has allowed for a more 'progressive' attitude than the application of customary laws (op. cit.: 13–14). In a similar manner, revisionists raise aspects of justice (*'edalat*) as a means of limiting the grounds for polygyny in the Family Protection Bill. References to*'edalat* thus give support to their contextual reading of polygyny and justify their understanding of the concept of justice as going beyond its definition in the Family Protection Bill.

'Everybody can do it, it's Islamic'

Another recurrent revisionist reference is to *ijtihad*. *Ijtihad* refers to a process of independent reasoning and is a principle of *usul al-fiqh* that has been important in the development of Shi'i Shari'a in particular.

Elham legitimises her idea of Shari'a primarily on the basis of the Qur'an, which she sees as the most authoritative source of Islam. When I first met her in 2002, she asserted that there is no basis for discrimination against women to be found in the Qur'an, and emphasised that she has discussed this with a number of *ulama*. She said:

> I had many interviews with Islamic scientists and I have read all of the Qur'an, and there is nothing that says that man is superior to woman. Even when it comes to children, the Qur'an says that both the mother and the father should have council with them. And these disqualifications [that men are in charge of women, and that the custody right belongs to the father] in our culture are not from the Qur'an. Almost all of it is from the non-documented talking that has come over the years, but there is no [supporting] document . . . And in Islam, the Qur'an is the most important document you can refer to. (Interview with Elham, November 2002)

Similarly, Parisa made a distinction between primary and secondary laws. She claimed that if a primary law that has a Qur'anic reference cannot be implemented, it can be subject to change:

> The Islamic laws are of two kinds. One kind comes from the Qur'an . . . Islam said that if a law in the Qur'an cannot be done, you could change it . . . And all of the clergymen accept this. And these are called secondary laws. Not primary laws like the one in the Qur'an. (Interview with Parisa, November 2002)

Thus, in Parisa's view, any secondary law can be changed at any given time:

> And when we change the law it is secondary law. As a secondary law you can change it just like that. Just like music or chess. You know that chess was forbidden in Islam? But now it is OK. Music was *haram* in the last century, but now it is OK. Because as secondary laws you can change these laws. In the beginning of Islam maybe men could divorce their wives at any time. But these days, no . . . It was Arab culture and not Islamic. Islam does not belong to the Arabs. These laws belong to the cultural Arabs of the past. (Interview with Parisa, November 2002)

To distinguish between so-called primary and secondary laws is seen by the revisionists as foundational for law reform. In addition, revisionist interviewees made reference to principles of *usul al-fiqh*. Previously, Elham mentioned the importance of having the support of the *ulama* consensus (*ijma*), which is seen as an important concept of *usul al-fiqh*. *Ijma'* has a different significance in Shi'ism than in Sunnism. Based on the perception of the occultation (*ghayba*) of the Twelfth Imam, Shi'a Muslims generally hold that the consensus of Shi'i *ulama* also represents the opinion and consent of the Twelfth Imam. The idea is that the Twelfth Imam is still in contact with contemporary *ulama*, as explained in the doctrine of *ghayba*. Therefore, if contemporary Shi'i *ulama* have arrived at a common agreement, one can assume that the Twelfth Imam also agrees and that the decision is sound and religiously legitimate.

References to the principle of *ijma'* are thus considered an important and valid source of legitimation in Shi'i *fiqh* and are recurrently used by revisionist interviewees. For instance, they consistently make reference to quotes from Ayatollah Yousef Sane'i (1937–) on the position and rights of women in Islam. Unlike many other contemporary Shi'i *ulama*, Ayatollah Sane'i is known to be outspoken on women's rights. For instance, he has declared that women can qualify to become a *mujtahid* (Kian-Thiébaut 2002: 70); he has issued a fatwa in support of women's inheritance rights (We Change website, 16 February 2008) and has challenged the practice of polygyny and the Family Protection Bill (We Change website, 28 July 2011). For this reason, Ayatollah Sane'i has often been mentioned as a source of legitimation by revisionist interviewees.

Another recurrent reference in the revisionists' understanding of *usul al-fiqh* was related to the principle of *'asr va haraj* or *darar* (hardship and harm). The 1982 legal amendment made it possible for couples who were about to get married to insert certain stipulations into their marriage contracts. Bahareh explained to me how the principle of *'asr va haraj* could serve to change the legislation even further and allow women greater access to divorce:

> So as you know the right of divorce is with men in Islam. It cannot be changed. But it has been changed in Iran; it is sometimes the judge who decides. *'Asr va haraj* is a bad situation which you can't tolerate anymore. When somebody is in this situation she can bypass the laws and go further. For example, imagine someone in a desert who has no food, but there is a pig there and pigs are forbidden [as food] in Islam. But in this situation you can eat it. Or if somebody points a gun towards him and makes him eat, then he should eat. This is the way: that when you are in a bad situation you should bypass. It is the same with divorce. If a woman can show that she is in a bad situation which she can't tolerate, then she can go and request this type of divorce. (Interview with Bahareh, November 2002)

The concept of *'asr va haraj* is a principle of *usul al-fiqh*, which allows a rule to be lifted if it creates hardship. A woman can thus obtain a divorce if she can prove that her marriage imposes harm (*darar*) on her. Robert Gleave describes the concept of harm in this context:

> The avoidance of harm is said to be the underlying intention (*maqsad*) of the Shari'a. When implementing a legal rule which causes an immediately recognizable harm (considered to frustrate the general intentions of the Shari'a), the legal rule should be suspended and a more benevolent rule set in its place. Such a procedure, which appeals to a jurist's (personal) understanding of God's aims and intentions in instituting the Shari'a, was highly controversial in the classical period; for some jurists it gave fallible human judgement a decisive and regulatory role over God's law. (Gleave 2007: 80)

Although it has been a controversial principle of Shari'a, *'asr va haraj* or *darar* has provided a rationale for women's access to divorce in Iran since 1979 (Mir-Hosseini 2000a: 65). The principle is thus used to a high degree according to subjective understandings of the intention of Shari'a (*maqsad*).

Many of the interviewees went even further and advocated the increased use of *ijtihad*. Arezoo explained:

> This [*ijtihad*] is a way that the Shi'a believes in and not the Sunni. The situation in Saudi Arabia or in Afghanistan under the Taliban, was and is worse. Because the main reason is that they don't believe in *ijtihad* and think according to today's needs. So in Saudi Arabia women can't drive cars or have ID cards. They are part of men's property. And also the situation in Afghanistan under the Taliban, women can't even come out of their houses. (Interview with Arezoo, November 2002)

References to *ijtihad* were recurrent among the revisionists. Their reading of it does not, however, necessarily correspond to conventional understandings of the concept. Some of the interviewees held quite radical views. Parisa, for instance, believed that any Muslim with sufficient knowledge about Islam, even women, could perform *ijtihad*. She said:

> *Ijtihad* means that a person, who can know Islam well, not only clergymen, it means everybody who knows Islam can say: 'I am

> a Muslim and I tell you that the real Islam is this'. They can change it {the law} . . . It is not my opinion. Everybody can do it, it's Islamic. Every Muslim can do it. In Iran we have some women *mujtahid*. And I myself know Islam well. Not only me, but also many of the law students and lawyers. (Interview with Parisa, November 2002)

The call for conducting *ijtihad* in order to improve women's rights has been made by other women's rights activists as well, such as Mehrangiz Kar in the journal *Zanan* in 1993. The conventional idea of *ijtihad*, however, is that only those who qualify to be appointed as *mujtahid* may perform *ijtihad*. The formal preconditions for qualifying are based on the criteria of maturity, being male, of legitimate birth, of Shi'a faith, and having a high level of intellect and justice (integrity) (Momen 1985: 202). The condition of being male, however, is controversial. Although there are Shi'i sources supporting the assertion that women cannot quality to be a *mujtahid* due to biological differences (Fischer 2003: 162), there are women who have been recognised as *mujtahid*. For instance, Banu Amin Esfahani authored a number of Qur'an commentaries (*tafsir*). Informally, she was referred to as a *mujtahid* and was also declared to have the required licence (*ejaze*) from a respected *mujtahid* (op. cit.: 163). Women are allowed to study both *usul al-fiqh* and *tafsir* in contemporary Iran, but are generally not seen as qualified to exercise *ijtihad*. Still, after 1979 quite a few women were engaged in these studies, and the debate continues over the appropriate qualifications of a *mujtahid* (Kian-Thiébaut 2000 and Tajali 2011). For Parisa, however, the case is clear. The criteria do not rely on gender, but rather on a person's level of knowledge of Islam.

'All of the changes should be in accordance with Shari'a'

The loyalist approach favours maintaining the existing legal structure. Although there is also a demand among loyalists for changing some laws, the changes advocated were generally believed to come with time, so that no drastic measures should be taken.

Maryam represents the loyalist position. She underlined the need for reform (*eslah*) or adjustment of the current family law legislation, but in a more restrictive manner than some of the rejectionist and revisionist interviewees:

> I think that this law has been codified according to Islamic Shari'a and ... our civil law [the Civil Code] also has some combinations from French law, and is according to Iranian culture and the current situation. This law is for protection of women and family, and we have exercised it and used it for many years. Now the situation has been changed, for example, from 50 years ago and ... it is a trend to have some other changes in family law. But one thing I should say is that all of the changes should be in accordance with the Shari'a. Of course, many great religious leaders are considering new interpretations, and it is more appropriate for women, as for example I myself appreciate, but I really should say that maybe in some aspects we have law, but sometimes people are more advanced than law. If we could not change some of the things, with interpretation of Islam and with people who are well-educated, [but] all of them look at Islam as a source of family relationship and they believe in it. I think you know that Iran is more than a religion, it is a mode of thought, it is a mode of living, it is a way of life, and I think that we could have better and [more] friendly interpretations of family law, but all of them should be in accordance with the Shari'a law in Iran. (Interview with Maryam, March 2009)

Maryam's perspective on reform (*eslah*) is characteristic of the loyalist position. Primarily, the loyalists seek solutions that are 'in accordance with the Shari'a in Iran', as expressed by Maryam. It is possible to detect certain parallels between the loyalist and the revisionist approaches to Shari'a, because both rely on concepts of *usul al-fiqh*. A major difference, however, concerns the loyalists' attitude to the Islamic Republic, as they tend to support and be loyal to state-defined versions of family law. As Maryam points out, she does not consider it enough simply to initiate family law reforms. The amendments should also be in agreement with the 'mode of thought' and 'way of life' in Iran. This is a recurrent concern of the loyalists and also emerges in their views on the debated articles in the Family Protection Bill.

The main differences between the three approaches to Shari'a and family law refer to which sources are considered the basis for legislation. For the rejectionist position, secular-based sources of law are considered most appropriate, while the revisionists advocate a combination of sources that are both secular-based and Islamic. The loyalist approach mainly relies on Islamic sources as most appropriate for the Islamic Republic. Another striking aspect is the several overlapping arguments. First, both the rejectionists and the revisionists differentiate between concepts of Shari'a and *qanun*. Second, revisionists and loyalists express the need for adjustments of contemporary family law legislation, although they differ with regard to the degree of reform. Nevertheless, both revisionist and loyalist stances relate to concepts of *usul al-fiqh* as a means of reform. In spite of their different approaches and opinions on Shari'a and family law, the women's rights activists draw on similar sources and concepts.

CHAPTER 5

CONCEPTIONS OF DOWER, POLYGYNY AND TEMPORARY MARRIAGE

Dower

Despite the central position of dower in marriage arrangements, it has not been among the most significant topic of family law debates in Muslim majority countries. Nevertheless, dower often figures indirectly in public debates because of its relevance for economic and marriage policies and thus for society at large. In the 1928 Iranian Civil Code, dower is described in Articles 1078 and 1085. These provisions were left unaltered in the 1967 Family Protection Law, in which divorce, custody of children and polygyny were all reformed. The issue of dower was not dealt with directly in Mehrangiz Manoochehrian's alternative family law bill draft of 1963/1964, which treated issues of divorce and marriage in detail. Not until the 1997 Amendments on Dower was dower subject to state reform, when its revaluation in line with inflation was introduced. The new law thus ensured that the marriage gift retained its original value regardless of its nominal value in the marriage contract.

Dower was again a topic of public debate with the introduction of the Family Protection Bill in August 2007. Article 25 of the bill dealt with dower, and in particular, the statement 'required to collect tax on unreasonable and higher-than-conventional marriage portions' evoked reactions and public debate. After the sit-down demonstration in the Majles on 31 August 2008 organised by a group of women's rights activists, the bill was sent back to the Judicial Commission in the Majles for review. In January 2010, the Family Protection Bill was reintroduced by the Judicial Commission with minor alterations. In the article on dower, now labelled Article 24, the tax obligation on dower was removed. Instead, the article suggested that dower should be limited to a standard sum to be decided by the head of the judiciary.

The controversies over dower in Iran in recent years have been substantial. The debate over the implementation of Article 25/24 of the 2007 Family Protection Bill reveals how the issue is being perceived and practised in contemporary Iran. As mentioned, dower is also subject to larger socioeconomic and cultural changes. On the one hand excessive demands, and on the other hand the trend towards amounts of dower that are only symbolic, continue to be parallel but still paradoxical tendencies. The various functions of dower point to broader concerns in Iranian society, and the rejectionist, revisionist and loyalist approaches all illustrate how dower correlates with aspects of gender, class, lifestyle and piety.

Prohibition of dower

As we have seen, rejectionist conceptions of family law tend to reject religiously defined sources and practices as a basis for state legislation. Consequently, rejectionists call for the elimination of dower because of its adverse effects on women's rights and position in society.

Touran was frank in her opinion of dower regulations and saw the provisions in the Family Protection Bill as connected to women's limited legal rights in Iran:

> Touran: Of course, it {*mehrieh*} is a joke. Because you were in Iran, and many people laugh at this law and I am ashamed to have this law in my country! But it exists . . . {but} I believe this is a new situation in law for *mehrieh*, it depends on the other laws and rights of women. When you limit the rights of women, you have to make a new situation for them. *Mehrieh* for

> them [the lawmakers] is a deal for this. You take many rights from them [women], and you pay *mehrieh*. It is not bad laws; it is bad culture in all traditions in Iran.
>
> Marianne: Is the whole tradition of *mehrieh* bad?
>
> Touran: Yes. For example I said to my youngest sister when she wanted to marry, I told her you can ask him for rights to divorce, and you say I don't want *mehrieh*. But she told me: 'what would his family think about me when I tell him I want divorce rights?' You know? It's a bad culture! But I think we should talk about this before marriage. Because after marriage it is finished. Women have *mehrieh*, but don't have rights to continue their life. (Interview with Touran, August 2011)

According to Touran, if women were given improved divorce rights, there would be no need for dower.

The sociologist Shahla E'zazi has also elaborated on the function of dower in society, saying: 'Our legislators don't understand that our society has changed' (Feminist School website, 12 February 2010). She explains that the conditions for what she labels the 'pre-modern family' have changed, and with it the need for dower. 'Therefore, *mehrieh* [used to have] different forms, but these concepts in the contemporary world have lost their functions.' She continues, 'I think marriage should be based on love, not based on women's fear over dower' (ibid.). Moreover, E'zazi sees a connection between the interpretation of dower and violence against women, because dower is sometimes considered payment for a woman's sexual favours. She says that 'Sex between the two partners should be based on desire. If the woman is not always ready to provide sexual services, a form of violence against women is conducted and it may result in rape' (ibid.). Thus, E'zazi does not focus on the socioeconomic aspects of dower addressed in the Family Protection Bill. Her reasons for rejecting the practice are that it represents an old-fashioned arrangement, enables violence against women and is therefore contrary to her perception of women's rights.

Maryam Ghanbari, a lawyer, follows E'zazi's line of argument. On the Meydan website she writes: 'But I do not know why with this article, one simply protests to have tax put on dower, and not to remove it' (Meydan, 10 August 2008). Ghanbari points to the fact that many women's rights activists tolerate the practice of dower on the basis that it can function as a tool for negotiation in cases of divorce and child custody. She, however, regards a search for those who question the practice of dower as 'an insult to human dignity' and wants to remove the practice altogether (ibid.). These rejectionist approaches point to gendered aspects of dower, and in particular what are seen as its discriminatory consequences.

Against taxation of dower

The revisionist approach relates dower to a larger context. Both its religious premises and the broader legal and societal aspects are emphasised. In particular, the revisionists oppose demands for taxation and standardisation as proposed by the Family Protection Bill.

Afsaneh, one of the women's rights activists with a revisionist view on family law, explained why she saw the tax demand on dower as an amendment with financial consequences for women:

> Before a man had to pay *mehrieh* when a wife asked for it. It was his duty. Lately we have seen that many women ask for bigger and bigger *mehrieh* and therefore they [the government] want to change it. In Article 25 it says that it should be the judge that decides when, and how much a woman should get in *mehrieh*. How is this possible? If a man says he doesn't have any money and hides it somewhere else, then women will lose their money! (Interview with Afsaneh, February 2009)

Afsaneh's attitude to Article 25 represents one of two approaches to the issue of taxation on dowers. She supports those who oppose the idea of taxation for the reason that dower often remains only a promise granted in the marriage contract – it is deferred dower. In cases where the marriage does not end in divorce or is otherwise terminated, dower is left unpaid. On this basis, some women's rights activists have questioned how it is possible to demand taxes on something that is often unpaid. Their 2007 statement opposing the Family Protection Bill states that Article 25 would have deteriorating effects on women's rights vis-à-vis other areas of law such as divorce:

> While women still have no rights to divorce and can no longer even object to their husband taking on a second wife, you are asking new wives to pay a tax to the government on a dower which they may not have even collected or may never collect. (FFL, 9 September 2007)

A similar point was made by some of the revisionist interviewees. Parisa, who is also a lawyer, illustrates the role of dower in Iranian society: 'There is no need for *mehrieh* if there are equal rights in the family. But currently women's rights are few, and men can have many wives. In this case *mehrieh* gives women protection' (Interview with Parisa, October 2010). Similarly, Zohreh saw it as necessary in view of the general lack of rights for women. She said: 'In this situation [the lack of divorce rights for women], it is better in my opinion that women have *mehrieh* than not, because *mehrieh* can be a support for women after divorce' (Interview with Zohreh, August 2011).

The second view on taxation of dower argues against it on the grounds that dower is a religious directive and consequently of private concern. Zohreh, for instance, highlighted both these aspects:

> *Mehrieh* is an agreement between two persons, man and woman. They must decide this freely in their marriage. The [religious] regulations on *mehrieh* say the man and woman should say how much the *mehrieh* should be, both of them. They should decide it without the family, society and culture and law and regime; without any pressure; we want, just we, the man and woman; it's a deal! When a law wants to limit *mehrieh*, they influence your wishes and it is against regulations about *mehrieh*. The law cannot influence what you want. And tax for *mehrieh*, because many people don't take it and don't pay it, is also against

> regulations, because for example I didn't take it [*mehrieh*] from my husband; and he didn't pay. So [we should pay] tax for what? In the new bill, the law about *mehrieh* has a limitation in amount, which again depends on your culture, your families, and also tax. For example I sell something to you and take money, and tax is for this money, but in *mehrieh* we didn't pay and then you can't take tax! Many people just don't do it [don't pay *mehrieh*], [it is] just in *'aqd* [the marriage contract]. It's symbolic only! (Interview with Zohreh, August 2011)

In her article 'Take a dowry: the divine gift of social dilemma', Nikzad Zanganeh argues against the tax on dower in the Family Protection Bill: 'How can a religious prescription be taxed? . . . How can such religious practices that are also rarely claimed, obtain advance tax?' (FFL, 24 April 2010). Zanganeh goes on to question how the Ministry of Economic Affairs and Finance can determine the amount of conventional dowers considering the differences in wealth and income among Iranians. Further, she asserts that if the goal of the Family Protection Bill truly is to provide comfort and peace for the family, then there are other means of securing this rather than a tax on dower, for example granting women increased access to divorce (ibid.).

The lawyer Gity Porfazel and the film producer-director Maryam Rahmani also question the Islamic validity of demanding tax on dower. They write: 'Yes, substantial dower is common, but how can one say that monogamy is contrary to Islamic principles, but to set a ceiling for tax on dower is not against Islamic principles?' (FFL, 19 May 2010). Thus, these women's rights activists refer not only to the legal context of dower, but to the actual practice. First, they argue against taxation on the basis that dower in most cases refers to deferred dower and is thus not actually paid to the wife. Second, they insist that dower relates to a religious prescription and, in other words, is a matter of piety that cannot be taxed.

Against standardisation of dower

Similar arguments against taxation of dowers have been used against a standardised dower as proposed in Article 24 of the 2010 Family

Protection Bill. First of all, the suggestion for standardised amounts of dower is criticised on the basis that the amount of dower varies according to class, status and location of the married couple. According to an article on the website Zan-e Farda (Woman of Tomorrow), the average amount of dower of Iranian women is between 260 and 450 gold coins (Zan-e Farda website, 30 October 2010). The lawyer Farideh Gheyrat makes a similar point, and claims that:

> Determining an appropriate and standard amount for *mehrieh* is not an easy task. Women living in rural areas and women living in urban areas do not require the same amount of *mehrieh*. Additionally, social, economic and cultural conditions play an important part in determining the amount of *mehrieh* a woman demands. Instead of placing limits or standardizing *mehrieh*s we have to ask why it is that the *mehrieh*s demanded by women tend to be so high? Why are women likely to ask for such high amounts for their *mehrieh*? We have to give women the option of stipulating other conditions in the marriage contract, so that they feel they stand on equal footing with their future spouse in the marriage and in their life together. If we can do this, then women will have no need to stipulate heavy *mehrieh*s as part of their marriage contract. (Campaign for Equality website, 29 November 2010)

A second objection to establishing a standardised amount of dower is based on religious arguments. As dower is a religious demand defined in the Qur'an, to impose restrictions on it is thus not seen as Islamic. Gheyrat explains that Article 24: 'should be eliminated, because setting limits on *mehrieh* . . . is not in line with the law, nor is it in line with Shari'a or Islamic Jurisprudence' (ibid.).

A third argument to be found in the revisionist approach rejects a standard amount of dower on the basis that it is a matter of personal choice. This line of reasoning is connected to the previous one, treating dower not only as a religious prescription but also as a private concern. Gheyrat claims that it is not appropriate to place a limit on dower, because it is a result of negotiations over conditions inserted in the contract (ibid.). If dower is limited to a standard sum, this will undermine the contract:

> For several years now, the parliament has been seeking through a variety of means to place limits on the amount of *mehrieh* ... demanded by women. This is not appropriate. We cannot impose a limit for *mehrieh*. According to the Civil Code, marriage is a type of contract and has its own specific conditions. In order to enter into the marriage contract, the spouses must benefit from certain conditions, such as an ability to make sound decisions, sanity, adulthood, legal age, etc. Otherwise the contract will not be recognized. As such, when the *mehrieh* is specified in the marriage contract, it is based on the presumption that these conditions were satisfied, and given that the parties have agreed to this based on the soundness of their own judgment, then their agreement must be recognized under law. Therefore we cannot impose limits, when the Civil Code has made it clear that it is the parties who decide. (ibid.)

A fourth line of reasoning argues that inserting a standardised amount of dower will have adverse effects on women's rights. Gheyrat claims that the reason for women demanding high dowers is men's unrestricted and unilateral right to divorce, and that because women risk being divorced at any time for any reason they are forced to demand high dowers in order to secure their basic rights (ibid.). She also refers to the wider problem of women's rights as a reason for high dower demands: 'If women's rights are guaranteed and if the courts can decide on divorce, then many of the problems we are facing would indeed be resolved and we will no longer be faced with the problem of heavy *mehriehs* demanded by women' (ibid.).

Rather than deciding a standard for dower, there is a need to examine why women demand such high dowers, according to Gheyrat. She cites the opinion of Ayatollah Khomeini, who declared himself in favour of the use of contractual stipulations in the marriage contract in a speech on 6 March 1979 (ibid.). This speech eventually led to the 1982 amendments to marriage contracts, as Gheyrat explains:

> Ayatollah Khomeini too, believed that despite the fact that the law does not give women the right to divorce, a woman is free to stipulate this right as part of her conditions in the marriage contract and there is nothing that would limit her in doing so. (ibid.)

If women are allowed to extend the grounds for applying for divorce, the high demands of dower would subsequently be lowered, according to Gheyrat. For this reason she wants to eliminate Article 24, and to focus instead on giving women improved rights in marriage and divorce as a means of lowering amounts of dowers. Thus, she points to the contextual nature of dowers and draws a comparison between high dower demands and women's lack of divorce rights.

Similarly, the 2010 statement against the Family Protection Bill contends that Article 24 contributes to the deterioration in women's rights by leaving it ambiguous, and limiting the only means for negotiation that women had in divorce. An article published on the Fair Family Law website states: 'By law, any time they want, men can divorce their spouse, while a woman will need ten years of proving their claims by documents in court' (FFL, 15 January 2010). This argument is also referred to in the 2010 statement against the Family Protection Bill:

> The *mehrieh* is allocated to a woman at marriage and often serves as a woman's only guarantee and safeguard in case of divorce and maltreatment. The new bill has omitted the tax, but has divided the Gift Money into 'conventional' and 'unconventional' amounts without setting a standard for this, thus restricting the only legal mechanism women had within the institution of family. (Feminist School website, 3 March 2010)

As a consequence, the 2010 statement claims that women will lose their previous use of dower in cases of negotiation over divorce, or in obtaining child custody after divorce.

Faezeh Hashemi also supports the rejection of Article 24/25. In an interview with Feminist School she is asked about the Family Protection Bill:

Feminist School: Do you accept the issue of *mehrieh* or not?

Faezeh Hashemi: I don't believe in this issue.

Feminist School: Do you have any proposal for the replacement of Articles 23 and 25?

Faezeh Hashemi: I think Article 22 should be deleted, and the laws should be reformed in such a way that polygyny, except in very rare and special circumstances, could not become possible even with the permission of the first wife. About Article 25, I believe, this article should be deleted, since *mehrieh* is an agreement, and the man [the husband] gets enough support from the law to be able to reject such an agreement. Instead of this article I propose that the issues, which we include by free will in the marriage contract [*daftarcheha-ye 'aqd*], should be enforced by law. The law should be reformed to ensure justice in family affairs. (Feminist School website, 21 April 2010)

Hashemi argues in favour of deleting Article 25 and proposes that 'justice (*'edalat*) in family affairs' should be secured in the legislation. Similarly, other revisionist women's rights activists tend to argue in favour of maintaining dower in relation to its contextual framework. The practice is seen in connection with larger issues of family law and in particular women's access to divorce. The practice of dower is underlined as a means of securing women's right to negotiate in divorce cases and to keep dower as a private and religious prescription. Still, inserting limitations of taxation and standardisation on dower as proposed in the Family Protection Bill is generally not supported by the revisionists.

In favour of regulating dower

Some women's rights activists debating the Family Protection Bill see the article on dower as a necessary regulation because of the increasing and unrealistic amounts and kinds of dowers often inserted into marriage contracts. Like the revisionists, the loyalists' approach relates dower to its broader legal and societal context, although in a slightly different manner.

Maryam thought that imposing a tax on dower could have a positive effect on women's financial rights, as it would ensure that dower represented actual and payable amounts that could secure women financially after divorce. She did not believe in a rapid reform of family law, but in gradual change. As for altering the law on dower, she made a comparison with the practice of child marriages and argued that changes would come with time:

> There are rights that women can have during marriage, and for example we have also changed the law to have the payment for women and it is a kind of social security for them. Of course, you know when anybody wants to change some law, especially the family law and women's rights, we should be more careful. Challenging the norms of the society is not a very easy task and we should not change things rapidly. With the change of education and the change in the minds of the people, we could also change some of the laws. But one of the things that all of the time is in my mind is that . . . our country and our thinking is traditional. Whenever you want to enter a marriage, you have many desires, very good wedding, very good clothes, very good jewellery from your husband, and when you enter the marriage you want to have equal rights. I think that there should be some balance between the desire of a husband and the desire of a bride. And when you are more educated and step-by-step, you reach the point when there are some needs, and then I think that society would also follow you.
>
> For example some years ago we had some problem with age on entering marriage. And it has been criticised also by many scholars inside and outside Iran. But now we have a good standard for education, and you know that more than 60 per cent of university acceptance is women. And now we have the problem of age. People now have a better life, and it is very rare that they sell their daughters and only oblige them to have a marriage at an early age. In the small cities and the rural areas

> all the people want their daughters to have the opportunity to go to school, and not to oblige them to marry. The change of social situation, with the change of social economic situation, the law will also be more advanced. (Interview with Maryam, March 2009)

Leyla, another loyalist interviewee, was positive about the changes proposed in Article 25/24. She saw the need to restrict the increasing dower demands of many women. Nevertheless, for Leyla there is a discrepancy between asking for dower and wanting equal rights in marriage, as many women tend to do today:

> They ask for *mehrieh* after divorce. They say: 'I was born in 1342 and therefore I want 1342 gold coins.' This is not equality! You can't be modern and then build on these traditions! If you want modernity you should accept the whole package! (Interview with Leyla, May 2008)

Leyla is clear that the demand for a 'romantic' dower is in contradiction to the love marriages desired by many young couples. In her opinion, they should choose between 'modern' marriages and dower. Similarly, Maryam pointed out that there 'should be some balance between the desire of a husband and the desire of a bride'. To simply put forward excessive demands of dower and of equal rights was not appropriate.

Thus, Maryam and Leyla presented loyalist attitudes not only to dower, but to women's rights. Leyla advised me several times to focus my research not on contemporary Iranian law and women's rights but on marriage and the family, topics that she said would be much less controversial than women's rights. Although I knew she wished to help me, I believe her advice also reflected her own perspective on family law and women's rights. She does not build on concepts of gender equality, but on a belief in gender complementarity – the view that men and women are equal, but have very different and complementary roles and rights. Thus, she would not speak in favour of gender equality. Others who took a loyalist approach to family law, such as Maryam, agreed with gender complementarity. Unlike many of the other interviewees, Leyla focused on what she saw as gender inequality towards men's rights resulting from the increasing amounts of dowers, rather than on women's rights. She said:

> Now we have many heavy dowers in our society. I myself am completely against this dower. It's bad for the men who can go into this marriage and after the marriage only [they] should pay all this money! This is not something I could support then. (Interview with Leyla, May 2008)

For this reason, Leyla saw the provisions of the Family Protection Bill as a means of regulating these high dower demands.

Unlike the revisionist and rejectionist approaches, the loyalist view of dower highlights the positive aspects of the Family Protection Bill. Still, the practice is read contextually and the various positions intersect. Monir Nobakht, a neoconservative politician and the head of the Women's Social and Cultural Council (*Shura-ye Farhangi-ye va Ejtema'i-ye Zanan*),[1] usually takes a loyalist approach to family law. On the question of taxation and standardisation of dower, however, she has said: 'Determination of dower is a private matter and married men and women should understand this issue carefully and decide correctly' (FFL, 7 May 2010). Nobakht also stressed that inserting limits to dower is contrary to women's rights in Islam: 'Dower can not be restricted . . . Dower is the financial right of women in Islam' (ibid.). Consequently, the religious aspects of dower are enhanced in some loyalists' approaches, and are emphasised by members of the Majles and by *ulama* in the overall debate on the Family Protection Bill (FFL, 12 November 2010).

The debate on Article 25/24 in the bill on taxation and a standardised dower has revolved around six main arguments. One has been that these amendments would contradict dower as a religious prescription. As dower often remains unpaid and merely a gift, it is claimed that inserting both a tax demand and a standardised amount would contradict its religious foundation. It has also been argued that such changes would leave the two parties in marriage unable to decide their own dower, as this role would be given to a judge in the court or to the Judicial Commission of the Majles. Consequently, both revisionists and loyalists have pointed out that the kind of regulations proposed in the bill would lead to dower and the marriage contract losing their character of being a personal and a civil matter. A third argument, used by the rejectionists and the revisionists, is that dower as suggested in the 2007 and 2010 Family Protection Bill, would deprive women of their basic right to negotiate in cases of divorce and thus have an adverse effect on women's rights. A fourth argument is that dower is an outdated practice that has no relevance for Iranian society today. This is put forward mainly by the rejectionists. Fifth, a revisionist argument against a standard amount for dower claims that this would prove impossible because of variations in class, status and location of married couples.

Finally, supporters of the Family Protection Bill and the loyalists assert that the proposed article on dower represents a necessary response to contemporary challenges of unrealistic demands for dower, and also that the Family Protection Bill article would, in fact, maintain religious prescriptions in the light of these challenges. An interesting point is that whereas state-proposed limitations on dower (supported by some activists with a loyalist approach) do call for application of the principle of *ijtihad* in regulating dower by taxation or standardisation, rejectionist and revisionist women's rights activists oppose such a use of it. Rather, some revisionists maintain that a standardisation of dower is 'un-Islamic' and contravenes their religious rights. Thus, the debate over dower regulations signifies the possible intersections of arguments and principles from the various positions. It is not always the case that loyalist approaches to family law are based only on religious arguments or that revisionists necessarily advocate reform, as both sources and arguments are more fluid and can shift.

What can be drawn from these divergent views is that dower has become a very salient topic in the contemporary family law debate in Iran as a result of its many functions and the symbolic position it holds both in society and in women's rights. Besides representing a religious prescription and function, dower epitomises the diverse opinions among women's rights activists, which in turn reflect broader positions vis-à-vis family law. The different perspectives on Article 25/24 mostly seem to follow the divisions between rejectionist, revisionist and loyalist positions. There is, however, some overlapping. These divergences are also evident in the debates about Article 23 on polygyny and Article 22 on temporary marriage.

Polygyny

The issue of polygyny has been debated in various reforms of family law. Although it is only indirectly a topic in the Civil Code of Iran (Article 942), polygyny was restricted in the 1967 Family Protection Law by making it dependent on a number of conditions, such as the consent of the first wife and the court's authorisation of a man's capacity to support more than one wife (Hinchcliffe 1968). After 1979, however, polygyny was officially said to be reinstated as an unrestricted practice prescribed in the Qur'an, but in fact it continued to follow rulings according to the Family Protection Law even after the establishment of the Islamic Republic. In 1982, the option to insert conditions in the marriage contract made it possible to include reservations against polygyny (amendments to Article 1130 in the Civil Code of Iran). In the event of a husband contracting a second marriage without the first wife's consent, a judge could dissolve the marriage on the wife's behalf (by *talaq-e tatliq* or *tafriq*) if one or more condition in the contract had been broken and/or if the marriage would entail harm and difficulty for the wife (*'asr va haraj*) (Mir-Hosseini 2000a: 57).

Not until 2007 was polygyny again made a topic of family law debate. The draft of Article 23 in the Family Protection Bill that year proposed to make the contracting of a polygynous marriage dependent on court authorisation of a husband's capacity to 'uphold justice' (*'edalat-e ejrae'*) among his wives. The article thus proposed changes to the 1982 marriage contract amendments by replacing the consent of the first wife with the authorisation of the court as a sole ground for contracting a polygynous marriage. Many women's rights activists in Iran saw this as a major setback. Several protests against this version of Article 23 led to a review starting in the autumn of 2008. In the 2010 Bill, Article 23 was redefined, and ten conditions were proposed for a man to contract more than one permanent marriage, among them, for instance, the consent of the first wife, her inability to perform marital duties and her lack of obedience dependent on a court order. In August 2011, the Majles once again delayed the ratification of the Family Protection Bill because of controversies over the proposed conditions. As a result, Article 23 was omitted from the bill, and it was officially stated that the issue of polygyny would be addressed at a later stage (We Change website, 28 July 2011).

Polygyny has been among the most contentious issues of the contemporary family law debate. Many interviewees referred to the 1982 marriage contract amendment as one of the major legal improvements after 1979. Subsequently, the legal change on polygyny proposed by the 2007 Family Protection Bill, removing the demand for the consent of the first wife, was seen as a major setback, as Afsaneh explains:

> There were mainly two articles in the new bill that we reacted against. One was the proposal to remove the consent of the first wife. In 1967 it was introduced. After 1979, it was removed after two weeks. But the demand of the first wife's consent was soon reintroduced. Now they want to go back to the '50s, yes maybe even further back. They want the judge to decide if a man is capable of taking care of several wives economically and psychologically. How can a judge decide this? It is the first wife who decides if this is possible or not! (Interview with Afsaneh, February 2009)[2]

Afsaneh was among the women's rights activists who had opposed the reversal of the 1967 Family Protection Law during the Revolution in 1979 and had argued strongly for restrictions on polygyny. Thus, she regarded the 1982 amendments to marriage contracts as a significant step towards improvement of women's rights. Several other interviewees agreed, and Article 23 in the Family Protection Bill has been the one receiving most criticism and attention. For this reason, opinions on Article 23 also illustrate positions and arguments in relation to family law.

Prohibition of polygyny

Among those who have debated the Family Protection Bill, some have taken a clear rejectionist stand and advocated the prohibition of polygyny. When the bill was first introduced, many women's rights activists argued against it as a whole (FFL, 23 August 2008). While anticipating the launch of the 2010 review, a number of women's rights activists openly opposed polygyny. Several articles that they published on the Fair Family Law website dealt mainly with the consequences of the practice for family life and women's rights. Moreover, both the basis and the outcomes of polygyny were portrayed in these articles as contrary to provisions of Shari'a (ibid.).

Following a workshop on family law held by a coalition of women's rights activists in May 2010, an alternative proposition on polygyny was published on the Fair Family Law website (FFL, 8 May 2010a). It presented various perspectives on aspects of family law such as polygyny, dower, divorce, temporary marriage, custody of children and inheritance. Reference was made to the legal positions of different schools of law, and comparisons were drawn with family law codifications in other Muslim majority countries, as well as to international conventions and relevant laws. Mehrangiz Manoochehrian's alternative family law bill was taken into consideration, and the family law draft prepared by the Centre for Women's Affairs. Out of this, the 2010 workshop produced an alternative family law proposal called 'Proposal by Iranian women from different cities'. It states:

> We propose monogamy. Marriage is a relationship between two persons. Justice [*'edalat*] between two people, both financially and emotionally . . . in polygynous marriages is not possible, as it is bad for the children and for the wife. (FFL, 8 May 2010a)

It is argued that justice cannot be maintained in a polygynous marriage, which has negative effects on the wife and the children. Indirect criticism is made of the amendment proposed by the 2010 Family Protection Bill, in which the financial ability of the husband forms a ground for engaging in a polygynous marriage. The proposal also mentions that 'There are other kinds of justice than of the financial kind', and the 'mental' and 'psychological' problems that result from polygynous marriages are emphasised (ibid.). For all these reasons, the proposition states that 'Polygamy should be abolished' (FFL, 8 May 2010a).

A few months later, the statement of the coalition of women's rights activists from September 2010 was drafted into a petition called 'Prohibit Polygamy' and published on the Internet (FFL, 23 September 2010). It refers to the ten conditions for polygyny listed in the 2010 version of the Family Protection Bill, and states that:

> These conditions not only make polygamy easy, but actually give rise to the break-up of families. An important point here is that according to Shari'a, men do not need to observe any of these conditions and can marry regardless. This is reflected in the court's attitude once such an application is made, which in practice has made any challenge virtually impossible. It should also be noted that the first wife does not have the right to divorce if her husband takes on another wife. Furthermore, despite amendments to the divorce laws in 2002, proving any of the above by a woman as grounds for divorce is extremely difficult, which is a further sign of discrimination and inequality in the laws. (ibid.)

The 'Prohibit polygamy' statement criticises the 2010 Family Protection Bill on several grounds. First, the facilitation of polygyny allowed by Article 23 of the bill is underlined, and also its perceived consequences in divorces and 'the break-up of families' (ibid.). Second, the point is made that these conditions are not seen as intrinsic to Shari'a and that it thus can be ignored in practice. Third, the conditions inserted into Article 23 are held to contradict previous amendments to divorce laws enacted in Iran, in particular the

1967/1975 Family Protection Law, and as reinforcing what is seen as gender discriminatory family law legislation (ibid.).

A main reason for the rejectionist stance is the perceived adverse effects of polygyny both on women's rights and on families in general. This is made clear in a signatures campaign launched in reaction to the 2010 version of the bill. According to the Fair Family Law website (1 December 2010), the campaign gathered 10,000 signatures to a letter called 'Disallow polygamy'. The campaign statement announced that 'thirty mothers and women's rights activists' delivered the letter both to the Majles's Legal and Judicial Committee and to the Social and Cultural Committee on 1 December 2010. In addition, a 'quilt illustrating the pain women endure as a result of polygamy laws ... each narrating the story of a different woman from a city of Iran who had suffered as a result of polygamy', was delivered along with the letter (ibid.).

On the basis of these statements, it is clear that the polygyny provisions in the Family Protection Bill aroused larger protests than other aspects of the bill and have led to concrete campaigns. Also, the issue of polygyny seems to bring out more rejectionist responses than to the other issues in question.

Limiting polygyny

Although the statements of coalitions of women's rights activists openly reject the practice of polygyny in its entirety, some women's rights activists take different approaches. Nevertheless, there seem to be overlapping tendencies between the rejectionist and revisionist positions that cannot easily be distinguished. Probably some of the same activists who took part in the 2008 and 2010 family law workshops and argued for the prohibition of polygyny, have been consistent in their revisionist approach to it elsewhere. However, the revisionist stance towards polygyny is supported in several articles published on the Fair Family Law website, as well as among the interviewees. In short, the revisionist position towards polygyny would like the practice to be limited. The reasons for restrictions, however, vary. By and large, they deal with contextual grounds for why polygyny is not a suitable marriage arrangement in contemporary Iran.

Polygyny as an unsuitable practice

In addition to the petition against Article 23, background information on polygyny is available on the Fair Family Law website. The point that the Qur'an enables men to have up to four wives is discussed. The words of leading religious scholars are quoted, such as 'Ali Motahhari's 'Polygamy is Islam's honour', but the argument is rather that 'polygamy is not widely practiced in Iran and women have enjoyed greater rights and freedoms than in some other Muslim countries. At present, an Iranian man needs his first wife's permission to take a second wife' (FFL, 23 September 2010). Moreover, a survey conducted by Shahla E'zazi in 2008 is referred to, which is said to confirm 'that 96 per cent of Iranian women do not approve of allowing a man to take a rival wife' (ibid.). Likewise, statistics that show an increase in terms of education, literacy, marriage age of women and women in their working life are underlined as reasons making polygyny unsuitable for contemporary Iranian society (ibid.).

Article 23 of the bill is thus criticised in the light of contemporary Iranian society as well as the current position of Iranian women. Both the point that polygyny is not widely practised and that Iranian women are not used to the practice are stressed. That the state should promote polygyny by means of Article 23 has also been criticised. For instance, at a meeting organised by the OMSC, Faezeh Hashemi stated that:

> Maybe a few per cent of Iranian families are involved in polygamy, but women are highly sensitive to this issue. We clearly witnessed this during the signature gathering [of the campaign]. The response of women shows that this issue [polygyny] is their concern. So I think the reaction of women activists to the issue should be decisive [in the revision of the bill]. (FFL, 12 November 2010)

In the introduction to the 2007 Family Protection Bill, the reason for a new version of family law legislation in Iran was said to result from a 'consideration of certain shortcomings and defects in the applicable laws governing the institution of the family and their incompatibility with the current realities' (Introduction to the 2007 bill). The 2007 Statement against the ratification of the Family Protection Bill states that this was not in fact achieved in the 2007 Bill:

> This law has been submitted with the suggested motives of 'the need to match current law to today's issues' and 'the removal of defects in current laws of family nature', while the material in the bill rejects the statements above. Not only does this bill not have any matching to the reality of the lives of today's Iranian women, on the contrary, the bill proposes to move back women's status 42 years. (FFL, 9 September 2007)

Not only is the overall intention of the Family Protection Bill criticised, but also Article 23 in detail:

> This legislation has not only in its totality disregarded the dignity and humanity of women, but in Article 23 it proposes to eliminate a women's say in her husband's right to take on a second wife, a right currently accorded to women by law. (ibid.)

Thus, the 2007 Statement relates the rejection both of the overall content of the Family Protection Bill and Article 23 in particular to the lack of conformity for women's rights, by referring to the 1967 Family Protection Law rulings for limiting polygyny, and the bill's relevance to contemporary Iranian society.

Polygyny as contrary to women's rights

Article 23 of the Family Protection Bill is also criticised more broadly for its consequences for women's rights. Zahra Rahnavard has argued that the bill would be damaging for women's rights on the basis of Article 23, because it 'gives more power to men to have polygamy without the wife's consent and harshly discriminates against the women even further than what the women are suffering today in Iranian society according to the current laws' (Rahnavard 21 August 2010).

Rahnavard's objection to the bill, however, goes beyond the issue of Article 23 because she connects the bill's implementation to the foundation of the Iranian nation. Rahnavard writes: 'Calling off the so-called "Family Protection" bill from Parliament's agenda is not a feminine demand, but rather is a symbol of the national demand for the prosperity of the Iranian nation and the stability of the Iranian families' (ibid.).

The rejectionist position towards polygyny also makes use of arguments that the provisions of Article 23 of the Family Protection Bill are contrary to women's rights. In the 2010 statement called 'Prohibit polygamy' it is argued:

> The new version still requires the first wife to give permission, though controversially this would not be required under certain conditions, such as if she is mentally ill, or suffers from infertility, a chronic medical condition or drug addiction, in which case the husband can marry another woman. Also if the first wife does not cooperate sexually, the husband can take another wife. (FFL, 23 September 2010)

Consequently, the conditions under which the first wife loses the right to oppose her husband contracting a polygynous marriage are seen as contradicting women's rights. What is more, the general discriminatory character of Iranian family law is highlighted in the 2010 Statement:

> Under Iranian divorce law, men can split from their wives under any circumstance, whereas women must have a 'valid justification' such as the man's addiction to drugs. Married men can have as many *Sighe*s as they wish, whereas women are stoned to death if they have an extramarital affair. In most cases, men also get custody of the children. (ibid.)

As a result, the 2010 Statement illustrates how the various arguments intersect within both the rejectionist and the revisionist positions in the polygyny debate.

Against state promotion of polygyny

The state promotion of polygyny is criticised both by rejectionists and revisionists. A mixed group of women's rights activists issued a statement called 'Warning against efforts to facilitate and promote polygamy' (FFL, 12 November 2010). In a letter opposing Articles 22, 23 and 24 of the Family Protection Bill addressed to 'Ali Larijani, the Speaker of the Majles, Zahra Rahnavard wrote:

> I remember that during the war, polygamy was introduced by some involved in women's affairs to ease the [situation of] the country ... Now its time [for these issues] to be resolved in more normal circumstances than those of war. (ibid.)

Rahnavard therefore recommends that the amendments to the Family Protection Bill as presented by women's rights activists, to protect, maintain and respect the family unit as basis of society should be followed (ibid.).

In favour of monogamy

A recurrent argument made against Article 23 is that polygyny is not considered suitable for contemporary Iran. Several women's rights activists who represent rejectionist, revisionist and loyalist approaches have stressed this point and argue instead for the importance of legislation that protects the family unit and thus the practice of monogamy (FFL, 12 November 2010).

The context in which the verse on polygyny in the Qur'an is believed to have been revealed is also underlined in the debate. Jila Shariat Panahi, a women's rights activists and Qur'anic scholar, has argued that the verse emerged in a time when married men were allowed to marry an infinite number of wives, and verse 4: 3 was therefore revealed to limit this practice (ibid.). In light of this specific context, Panahi argues that 'the spirit of Islam is in fact monogamy' (ibid.).

In an article published on the FFL (19 May 2010) called 'Based on current law, any man can have a small harem', Gity Porfazel argues that the problem for family law legislation is not necessarily related to religion, but rather emerges from culture. Asked what she considers to be the criterion for family law legislation, Porfazel says: 'In Iran, our law is derived from the culture of society and therefore it is backward. Shari'a cannot come from tradition ['*urf*], or be backwards, because '*urf* is subject to change ... but Shari'a is a constant' (ibid.). She then proclaims:

> I believe in monogamy, if you assume monogamy [as basis for legislation], the second man can only marry a second wife in very special circumstances, which is not easily done ... Society should not put monogamy aside and move towards polygamy. (ibid.)

Seddiqeh Vasmaqi, a professor of law and jurisprudence and a former member of Tehran's city council, claims that the grounds for restricting polygyyny are not against Shari'a (FFL, 4 August 2008):

> At first, polygyny was limited in Islam, and having more than four women was forbidden. But at the same time, there was an emphasis on the principle of justice ['*edalat*], [and for this reason] the Qur'an explicitly proposed that to rely on one spouse was better [than several wives]. The Qur'an says that if you cannot justly treat [more than one wife] you should rely on only one ... In particular, the Qur'an stipulates that it is better to rely on one spouse, [as cases of] oppression are fewer in this case. (ibid.)

Vasmaqi primarily focuses on verse 4: 3 in the Qur'an, but stresses the relevance of another Qur'anic verse to the polygyny debate. It reads: 'You can never be equal in dealing with more than one wife, no matter how hard you try' (4: 129).

Vasmaqi claims, moreover, that introducing limitations on polygyny is comparable to the abolition of slavery in Islam (ibid.). Like polygyny, the practice of slavery is mentioned in several places in the Qur'an and has thus never been formally banned in Islam. Vasmaqi explains the reason for this:

> Such man-made phenomena should be corrected and reformed [*eslah shodan*] by the man himself. Islam is about banning enslavement of free people and bringing justice to slaves and emphasises the rights of the slaves. Gradually, humans have come to understand this, that slavery is an ugly phenomenon, and accept it. (ibid.)

As with the gradual banning of slavery in Islam, Vasmaqi recommends a move towards monogamy:

> Polygamy was a common phenomenon in previous societies, but the Qur'an actually forbids polygamy and asserts that monogamy is seen as the best ... Now some are trying to promote polygamy in Iranian society. This effort is not wise and good. (ibid.)

Vasmaqi explains her concept of family structure:

> Given the experience of most human societies, the monogamous family is the ideal, because this form of marriage offers less stress and crisis for the family members. Promotion of polygamy in the last three decades shows that crises and emotional stresses are experienced by families. The husband's renewed marriage has been one of the causes of divorce. Justice for the wife is not only provided by [financial] support. The family is [also] in need of peace and security. (ibid.)

The importance of maintaining justice (*'edalat*), support (both financial and psychological) and security for the wife in marriage as well as for the family, are reasons put forward by women's rights activists who take a revisionist approach. In general, they are more concerned with imposing limitations on the practice of polygyny than on rejecting Article 23 of the Family Protection Bill as a whole. After the removal of Article 23 in 2011, this concern was again raised. Zahra Arzani, for instance, claimed: '[if] Article 23 is removed, silence will be maintained on the subject of polygyny'

(FFL, 4 August 2011). Arzani is concerned that a simple exclusion of the article will leave polygyny as an unresolved issue in Iranian family law legislation. Rather than promoting conditions that would make possible polygynous marriages, the revisionist approach generally stresses monogamy as the ideal family structure.

In support of polygyny

Some of the views of the loyalists on polygyny overlap with those of the revisionist approach. Maryam Behrouzi, a member of the Coalition of Muslim Women and leader of the Zeynab Society, has for instance claimed that the need to secure justice (*'edalat*) among women is a reason for a modification of polygyny (FFL, 15 October 2010). Most loyalists, however, tend to support some degree of state promotion of polygyny.

Alhough many women's rights activists have criticised and opposed Article 23 on polygyny, loyalist women's rights activists look to the Qur'anic prescription and consider polygyny to be a religious practice that cannot be banned, and some even emphasise polygyny as a possible solution for the contemporary needs and challenges facing society. Maryam explained:

> The average marriage age of women is becoming so high. Many women are working and not so occupied with getting married, so the number of single women is increasing and on the other hand many people are getting divorced. So there are many women today without any husband. This is against Islamic rules; maybe the government is encouraging polygamy and *sighe* to prevent so many women from being single. (Interview with Maryam, May 2008)

Maryam's perspective is in line with the state discourse on marriage. Since 1979 the state has encouraged polygyny as a means of protection for the family, and claims that polygyny will prevent women from being single, remaining unmarried, or getting divorced. Arguments seeking to defend the role of polygyny often address problems in the family structure or factors challenging the family as such. In Indonesia,

Bowen has found that polygyny is supported as a means of avoiding high numbers of orphans and widows and of reducing prostitution, all of which are seen as threatening the family basis of society (Bowen 2003: 226). In a similar way, the activists in this study who take a loyalist approach to family law tend to project polygyny as necessary for the common good. Their mode of speech is often directed at maintaining the best interests of society, and refers to *maslaha*, a principle of Shari'a that can also be interpreted on more political lines, because the loyalist means of securing *maslaha* tend to coincide with state interests and policies.

Leyli, who was sceptical of the proposed bill, drew attention to the broad discourse on this area:

> The bill suggested that the approval of the first wife is not needed anymore, but now they have to ask the court. We are not supporting this ... Now we don't have any specific rules on polygamy, but as soon as there come some rules it is very easy to have a polygamous marriage. And now all films and TV series are talking about the benefit of polygamy ... They do this to make it part of the culture, even though it is not very common now in Iran. By having all these movies and so on, it is not a bad thing any more. Also, the economic situation today is very bad and men can't even support one family, how can they then support two! (Interview with Leyli, May 2008)

Zohreh Elaheyian, who is a member of the Majles and takes a loyalist approach, has argued in support of the Family Protection Bill on several occasions. She claims that the bill, despite its bad reputation abroad, has several positive aspects that will benefit women and children and solve their problems (FFL, 19 October 2010). In particular, she points to the need for a comprehensive family law codification that is intrinsic to the Islamic Republic, as well as the introduction of new family counselling centres. Elaheyian has commented on Article 23 in particular:

> Despite the impression that some have of this article, men are not allowed to take several wives, but it rather limits this.

> The view of the Majles and Islam has always been monogamy and still is. And the debate on polygyny that is introduced in this article is only in certain specific cases. (ibid.)

Thus, similar to the revisionist approach, Elaheyian regards monogamy as the ideal form of marriage, but sees a need to revise current family laws:

> If Articles 22 and 23 will be removed from the Family Protection Bill, then we don't have comprehensive laws regarding temporary marriage and renewed marriage, and there is an open door for men to have numerous marriages. (ILNA, 25 August 2010)

She has also claimed that having no laws relating to these practices could lead to chaos (ibid.).

Laleh Eftekhari is another politician who has expressed support of the Family Protection Bill and thus takes a loyalist approach. Like the rejectionist and revisionist view, she opposes the introduction of the ten conditions for polygynous marriage in the 2010 Bill, although on different grounds (FFL, 12 November 2010). Eftekhari believes that men should be allowed to contract polygynous marriages regardless of restrictions, and that the ten conditions introduced to Article 23 are contrary to Islamic laws and rules (ibid.). She says that 'There are no conditions for polygynous marriage in Shari'a and therefore these conditions must be removed' (ibid.).

The reasons for opposing the conditions laid down for polygyny in the 2010 version of Article 23 thus vary. Whereas the rejectionist and the revisionist views assert that the conditions do not adequately secure the rights and position of women in marriage and divorce, the loyalists argue that the conditions contravene the right of men to engage in a polygynous marriage as stated in the Qur'an and thus in Shari'a. The loyalist position, however, does include perspectives on the setting of conditions for polygyny, as they are intended to limit polygyny and thus are lawful, as previously argued by Elaheyian (FFL, 19 October 2010). Still, Elaheyian maintains that opposition towards the Family Protection Bill as a whole relates to political differences, rather than to opinions over the bill as such:

> Of course Articles 22 and 23 of the Family Protection Bill have drawbacks that must be corrected and we will offer some suggestions in this field. But this is not a reason for one of two difficult and controversial details should lead to political discussions ... Those who oppose the bill have political goals and are against the system and women's rights. (ILNA, 25 August 2010)

In favour of restricting polygyny

As mentioned earlier, the approaches to polygyny seem to intersect between the revisionist and loyalist positions. Not all in the loyalist camp are wholly in favour of polygynous marriages. Some wish to see legal limitations on polygyny rather than making it illegal altogether. Elaheyian argues that it is better to have the restrictions offered by the Family Protection Bill than to leave unresolved the legal status of polygyny and temporary marriages. She says:

> Some women's rights activists and some NGOs believe that these articles must be removed, but my question to them is that if we remove these articles, [we won't have] any laws for polygyny and temporary marriage in our country. Is it better to have chaos in temporary marriage than limits? (ILNA, 25 August 2010)

Other loyalists have expressed similar reasoning. During the review of the Family Protection Bill between 2007 and 2010, the Centre for Women's Affairs introduced two sets of propositions for family law codification (FFL, 8 May 2010). The first is the draft of a commission based at Mofid University. On the subject of conditions for a plurality of marriages, both permanent and temporary, the commission has proposed a mandatory registration of temporary marriages of more than three months. In the event of lack of registration, any partner in the marriage can be sentenced to imprisonment (ibid.).

The second draft is based on Meimanat Chubak's proposition. In 1997 Chubak was the first female assistant judge appointed in Iran since the 1979 ban against female judges. Chubak upholds limiting the number of women in a permanent marriage to four, with possible penal provisions for those who violate this (ibid.). She further maintains that if a man wants to have more than one wife, he is obliged to seek authorisation and permission from the court that he is able to 'fulfil the necessary measures and has the financial ability to establish justice' in the marriage (ibid.). If a man should contract more than one marriage at the same time without the court's permission, he will be sentenced to a penalty under Article 5 of the 1931–7 Marriage Act.

Both these propositions reflect the loyalist position on polygyny. They do not introduce revisions, because restrictions on the practice are in line with previously enacted laws in the Islamic Republic.

Article 23 has undoubtedly been the most debated topic of the Family Protection Bill since its introduction. Whereas the rejectionist approach includes arguments in clear favour of prohibiting polygyny as a whole due to its adverse effects on family life and women's rights, the revisionists seek rather to limit and modify the practice, as it is not considered suitable either for contemporary Iranian society or for women in Iran. The rejectionist perspective also maintains that polygyny as defined in the Family Protection Bill contradicts previous laws, for instance the 1967 Family Protection Law. As a solution, women's rights activists with a rejectionist approach propose that monogamy should be the established basis for marriage. Revisionist activists also advocate monogamy. First, because it better serves women's rights and the family, and second, based on contextual interpretations of the Qur'an. Although there are some divergences among loyalist women's rights activists, in general it is argued that polygyny is a religious prescription legitimised in the Qur'an and thus cannot be banned. This is similar to the revisionist position, but some loyalists go further, claiming that polygyny offers solutions to contemporary social problems. Some of them also argue that the bill as a whole provides an Iranian solution to current challenges in society.

Temporary marriage

Although related to polygyny, temporary marriage has been less controversial in Iran. The main reason is the indirect treatment of the issue in family law legislation, and the dubious character of the practice. Nonetheless, the issue is dealt with in the 1928 Civil Code. In the 1931 Marriage Law, the 1967/75 Family Protection Law and post-1979 reforms, the subject is not mentioned. It was not until the introduction of the Family Protection Bill in 2007 that it emerged as a legal debate on its own terms, as defined in Article 22 in the 2007 and 2010 versions of the Family Protection Bill. The 2007 article asserts that the registration of temporary marriages is to be subject to 'rules of procedure'. The bill thus proposed to leave temporary marriage as an unsettled legal issue, without any immediate need for legal management.

Many interpret the Family Protection Bill provision on temporary marriage as an encouragement of the practice, and as a religious solution to contemporary social challenges. After some debate, Article 22 was amended in the 2010 version of the bill, which specified a legal procedure for temporary marriage. The article contains a demand for registration of a temporary marriage if the wife is pregnant, and if both parties in the marriage agree on the registration. Consequently, the 2010 version of Article 22 represents a break with previous rulings on temporary marriage, although the demand for registration remains voluntary to a certain degree.

The approach to temporary marriage in the Family Protection Bill shares similarities with its position on polygyny. Most often, temporary marriage involves more than two partners. However, there are additional consequences related to the status of the temporary wife (*sighe*), not to mention a child of a temporary marriage. Because it has been an unresolved issue in family law, the arrangement continues to be connected with prostitution.

Prohibition of temporary marriage

Similarly to their view on polygyny, those who take a rejectionist approach to temporary marriage see it as primarily serving men's sexual needs and to be contrary to women's rights. For many, there is a striking resemblance between temporary marriage as paying for a time-limited marriage and paying for the sexual services of a prostitute. Thus, temporary marriage represents a form of religious legitimisation of prostitution in contemporary Iran. The rejectionist approach mainly relates the issue to the lack of rights for women and children.

Touran pointed out the potential for temporary marriage to allow young people to live together before marriage, but commented on its limitations for the couple:

> They don't have any rights, and in Iran it is used more for just sexual relations ... many women are in *sighe* in secret. I think that is very special ... You have no rights, no love ... They [the couple in temporary marriage] don't have any rights. [Temporary marriage is used] just for sex relations. It is like prostitution. (Interview with Touran, August 2011)

Touran's description explains why many women's rights activists take a rejectionist approach. 'The 2008 Statement against the Family Protection Bill' states that 'The "Anti-Family Bill" not only does not prohibit the practice of temporary marriage for married men, it does not require the registration of such marriages' (We Change website, 18 August 2008). Thus, many activists anticipated that the practice would be restricted or even outlawed in the new family law proposal, and not left unresolved as the 2007 bill suggests.

Like polygyny, temporary marriage is seen as unsuitable for contemporary Iranian society. Elahe Amani, an Iranian women's rights activist living in the United States, wrote on the Feminist School website:

> Historically, the practice has been limited to shrine cities like Mashhad and Qum, and mostly to pilgrims who travelled. The *sigheh* or 'temporary marriage' contract should have an expiration date, varying from a few hours after the marriage up to 99 years. Many secular Iranians view legalized 'temporary

> marriage' as a reflection of the hypocrisy of clerics, who have exploited 'temporary marriage' over the years but are adamantly opposed to premarital or extramarital sex. Despite its religious imprimatur, temporary marriage has never been very popular in Iran. Many Iranians regard *sigheh* as little more than legalized prostitution. The practice of 'temporary marriage' has been debated in recent years, and advocates point out that children of such unions are legitimate and entitled to a share of the father's inheritance. The current bill will leave women who engage in such marriages and children being born from these unions without any legal protection or rights. (Feminist School website, 18 August 2008)

Thus, on the basis that temporary marriage is neither a widespread practice, nor does it guarantee the rights of the wife or child, Amani rejects the religious legitimisation of the practice. She continues:

> Temporary marriages have been encouraged in the last decade as a response to the complex social issues and restricted Islamic norms in terms of socialization of young men and women. However, in finding a 'religiously acceptable solution' to deep-rooted social issues, the legalization of 'temporary marriages' and its social consequences have not been evaluated in the context of sexuality, public health, sexually transmitted diseases, women's human rights, birth control, violence against women, and the welfare of children born within these marriages. (ibid.)

An argument made against temporary marriage is its lack of resonance in Iranian society. Amani writes:

> It should be noted that polygamy and temporary marriages have hardly become part of the fabric of Iranian society. Although the number of polygamous marriages has increased after Iran adapted to Shari'a law after 1979, it remains relatively rare in Iran compared with some Arab countries, and is frowned upon by many. (ibid.)

Among several of the interviewees there was scepticism towards the broad discourse of the state encouraging polygynous and temporary marriages in recent years. Ziba, a young female student, told me that even her professor in women's studies promoted the idea of temporary marriage in class:

> The professor says it [*sighe*] is necessary for men [and] that I am not a man to understand [this]. But he is not a woman to understand how hard it is for a wife to see that her husband has got a *sighe*! It is not good! It is not a healthy family that! (Interview with Ziba, March 2009)

Rokhana is not a women's rights activist per se, as she is not engaged in any activities or public discussions of women's rights. Rather, she represents an ordinary Tehrani woman in her late 30s. Rokhana has had personal experience of temporary marriage. She told me that she had been seeing a man for several months. Of course, dating in Iran is not socially acceptable, but they had met through work and had started a relationship. After some time, the man asked Rokhana if she wanted to engage in a temporary marriage with him. Rokhana was reluctant to accept, mainly because she didn't understand why he didn't ask her to marry him permanently. She took some time to think about his offer, and during this time she found out that he already had a wife. Rokhana was then appalled by his offer. Although she was single, she had no intention of being someone's second, or temporary wife. Rokhana was heartbroken after this episode and said she cried for days.

When she told me about the incident, though, she criticised the arrangement of temporary marriage in today's society. Particularly in Tehran, she said, an increasing number of men make use of the arrangement in order to have a mistress outside their ordinary marriage. Temporary marriages are mainly reserved for men who can afford to pay the dower in question (*ajr*). Rokhana pointed out, though, that whereas polygynous marriages are the privilege of well-off men who can afford to pay for more than one household, temporary marriages did not require the same kind of wealth. To have a *sighe* for a shorter period of time was thus seen as more affordable to a greater number of men than polygynous marriages.

The fact that there has been an increase in state encouragement of temporary marriage is also underlined by the Women's Coalition opposing the Family Protection Bill:[3]

> Unfortunately, today we witness that certain old traditions are again propagated. For example, in Iranian state television, the practice of having multiple wives is propagated, and the picture of family put forward there does not mirror what is deemed customary in society. Legal restrictions and the encouragement of faulty cultural traditions hinder the growth and development of women and can lead them toward negative or reactionary behaviour. (Feminist School website, 10 June 2009)

Thus, the state promotion of temporary marriage is seen as encouraging 'faulty cultural traditions', which also leads to the breakdown of family life.

The issue of legal solutions to temporary marriage falls under the call for prohibition of polygyny. The proposition from the family law workshop made up of 'women from different Iranian cities' builds on Mehrangiz Manoochehrian's 1963/64 alternative family law bill (Manoochehrian 1963/64). It proposes monogamy between only two persons in a marriage (FFL, 8 May 2010a), and states: 'Temporary marriage is a completely inhuman relationship that must be excluded from legal definitions' (ibid.). Moreover, the proposition spells out that registration of temporary marriages should be mandatory, and registered in identity cards of men and women in the same way as a permanent marriage (ibid.). In addition, it suggests that 'An open relationship between boys and girls is to be regarded as a personal relationship' (op. cit.). Finally, the practice is seen as acceptable only if properly registered and available for *both* men and women:

> It is better if temporary marriage is eliminated from the law ... We are 100 per cent against this ugly practice. And if this ugly act can be done it must be registered in identity cards of every

> person. If man can have temporary marriage, woman must also be able to order one. (ibid.)

Thus, the 2010 workshop sought the prohibition of temporary marriage, or its restriction to unmarried men and formally registered, and that women should be allowed the same right to take a *sighe* as men. The Fair Family Law website demands full gender equality in the matter.[4]

Limitation of temporary marriage

Many of the rejectionist arguments figure also in the revisionist view of temporary marriage, which elaborates on the many aspects of temporary marriage in Iran. Just as the rejectionist approach to temporary marriage addresses the lack of mandatory registration, so does the revisionist one. 'Ali, a male member of the OMSC, explained: '*Sighe* is from one second until 99 years.[5] Now it should be registered, but in the bill it is suggested that it does not need registration' (Interview with 'Ali, February 2009). Many of the interviewees opposed the article on temporary marriage because of the lack of registration. The demand for it reflects the side-effects that temporary marriage might have for women and children. Most of the reactions provoked by Article 22 in the Family Protection Bill were made on the basis that it sought to continue temporary marriage as an unresolved legal issue. Like most other areas of family law debate, the consequences of temporary marriage go beyond the actual legal practice. These were emphasised in the 2007 Statement opposing the Family Protection Bill:

> We don't yet know what this directive will entail, but surely until its issuance we will be witness to increased numbers of women, who cannot legally prove that they have a husband and we will be witness to the birth and suffering of children resulting from temporary marriage, who will not be allowed to obtain birth certificates. (FFL, 9 September 2007)

The rights of children from a temporary marriage have been addressed. In theory, the children of temporary marriages are considered legitimate and enjoy the same rights as children from permanent marriages (Haeri 1989: 2). In practice, however, they are often stigmatised because they lack the social recognition of children from permanent marriages. Also, women in temporary marriages frequently experience a decrease in social status after divorce. They do not enjoy the financial security of divorce in a permanent marriage, and often suffer social stigma and gossip as they are still considered divorcees (op. cit.: 66).

Bahareh, one of the interviewees, thought of temporary marriage as useful in some ways. She claimed, however, that the current practice took advantage of women. She said: 'Sometimes it works like prostitution, it makes prostitution legalised . . . Temporary marriage can sometimes be a good way, but in Iran it is not good. It doesn't have a good function now, because men are abusing women' (Interview with Bahareh, November 2002). In theory, she continued, temporary marriage allows women a freer position than in permanent marriage. But as the woman is often left without any form of financial security after divorce, it has adverse effects on women's lives. Bahareh's description illustrates various aspects of temporary marriage today. She explains why the practice has become widespread in Iran in recent years:

> There is no system of girlfriend or boyfriend in Iran, like the one you might have in Europe. So for example if you want to go to another city and take into a hotel, you should be married. Therefore the *mut'a* marriage is the best way. Therefore they can go to a registration office and they marry temporarily and then they can be together. (Interview with Bahareh, November 2002)

The increase in temporary marriage is thus not only the result of state encouragement, but because of new forms of gender relationships. Some may choose temporary marriage because they cannot afford a proper marriage, or they want to try living together before deciding to get married. Some would also use temporary marriage as a sort of test marriage. Many of the interviewees had quite ambiguous attitudes towards the practice. As Leyli commented:

> Sexual relations in Iran are not permitted outside of marriage, so it's a way to have relation between young people. And it can be a winning card for men who want to have several wives. It is not used much by young people, but more often by men who already have a wife. (Interview with Leyli, February 2009)

Thus, for young and unmarried couples in particular it was seen as having advantages. But because of its close resemblance to prostitution and the lack of rights of the wife and child, the practice was for the most part condemned by revisionist interviewees.

Shahla Sherkat is a well-known women's rights activist in Iran.[6] Although she opposes the practice, she has pointed out that temporary marriage could have various functions:

> First, relations between young men and women will become a little bit freer ... Second, they can satisfy their sexual needs. Third, sex will become depoliticized. Fourth, they will use up some of the energy they are putting into street demonstrations. Finally, our society's obsession with virginity will disappear. (Scioloino, 4 October 2000)

In a similar way, Muhammad Javad Larijani, a conservative politician and *'alim*, asked 'What's wrong with temporary marriage? You've got a variation of it in California. It's called a partnership. Better to have it legal than have it done clandestinely in the streets' (ibid.).

The contentious character of temporary marriage is clearly illustrated by the reactions to Article 22 of the Family Protection Bill. The alternative proposals have a connection with those for polygynous marriage as a whole. Namely, that monogamy is the basic unit of Iranian society, that temporary marriage is unsuitable for contemporary Iran and degrades the rights of women and children. Therefore, the same provisions for polygyny are suggested for temporary marriage. That is, the mandatory registration of temporary marriage in the identity papers of both the man and the woman, and that it should be available only for unmarried men (FFL website, 8 May 2010b).

Promotion of temporary marriage

The loyalist approach to temporary marriage as defined in the Family Protection Bill generally resembles the opinions on polygyny. Moreover, some loyalists portray temporary marriage as an 'authentic' expression of Shi'a Islam that can provide solutions for contemporary Iranian society.

Maryam supported the state promotion of both polygyny and temporary marriage, as well as the Family Protection Bill's definition of temporary marriage. As quoted above, she considered polygynous and temporary marriages to be necessary for contemporary society in order to limit the number of single and unmarried women (Interview with Maryam, February 2009). Her point of view relates to finding solutions that are in line with the broader policies of the Islamic Republic, and thus with Shi'a Islam. Temporary marriage is a Shi'a Islamic instruction that can be seen as providing such 'authentic' solutions. However, some loyalists do call for certain restrictions on the practice.

As mentioned in the previous chapter, Zohreh Elaheyian claims that if Article 22 is not ratified, temporary marriage will continue to be an unresolved issue in Iran (ILNA, 25 August 2010). On this basis, some supporters of this kind of marriage argue for legal provisions that would restrict the practice, such as mandatory registration if the wife in a temporary marriage is pregnant. This would be on the basis of securing the rights of a child born into a permanent marriage. The proposal by the Mofid University commission, for instance, states that registration of temporary marriage for more than three months should be mandatory, and a lack of registration for any part of the marriage would result in imprisonment (FFL, 8 May 2010b). Meimanat Chubak does not, however, address the topic of temporary marriage directly, but states that in a permanent marriage the number of wives should be limited to four, and that authorisation of polygynous marriage should depend on court authorisation as defined in the 1931 Marriage Act Law (ibid.).

The issues of polygyny and temporary marriage share many similarities, because temporary marriage most often involves a plurality of wives in the same marriage. For this reason, the conceptions of temporary marriage are quite similar to those of polygyny. The rejectionist approach seeks a prohibition of polygyny as a whole. Because of the legitimisation that temporary marriage provides for prostitution, according to the rejectionists, they want to prohibit the practice once and for all.

The revisionist approach shares several of the rejectionist claims, but seeks to limit and modify polygyny and temporary marriage rather than a total prohibition. The issue of temporary marriage in particular, though, has a mixed perception among revisionists. Although they partly agree with the rejectionists that it serves to legitimate prostitution, they also see it as having other functions. For instance, the possibility for young couples to contract trial marriages or to be girlfriends and boyfriends is underscored. The revisionists do, however, seek to restrict the practice to unmarried men alone. The loyalist position on temporary marriage also shares similarities with the revisionist one, but they argue strongly that polygyny cannot be banned because of the Qur'anic references to it, and that it constitutes a religious prescription. The same goes for temporary marriage. Both are considered religious practices that offer solutions to social problems. Moreover, the loyalists do not argue for unrestricted temporary marriages, but see the Family Protection Bill as offering an Iranian solution to contemporary problems.

Pevious chapters have presented the arguments used in the debate over Articles 22, 23 and 25/24 in the Family Protection Bill, and have shown that the women's rights activists included in this study draw on various aspects of Shari'a and women's rights. Rejectionist women's rights activists contest the mere existence of polygynous marriages on the basis that they contravene women's rights. Revisionist activists have argued in favour of restricting the practice, both as an unsuitable marriage arrangement in contemporary society and as violating women's rights. The loyalist activists have maintained that polygyny cannot be abolished because of the Qur'anic references to it, but it could be limited to safeguard the common good. The debate over temporary marriage and dower likewise draws on differing understandings of what Shari'a and women's rights entail. All the approaches tend to rely on degrees of safeguarding both women's rights and Shari'a, and this dual challenge was stated both in the introduction to the Family Protection Bill (formulated as 'rights of the family', *Hoqoq-e khanevadeh*), and has been prominent in the larger public debate.

In preceding chapters, the commitment of Iranian women's rights activists' to debating family law legislation has been manifest. Not only do they argue decisively in favour of women's rights, but they are also dedicated to the scrutiny of Islamic legal principles and concepts. Yet it should come as no surprise that the activists present clear and well-defined arguments in relation to the family law bill. Women's rights activism in Iran has a long and rich history that has formed the basis for the various claims and ideas put forward in this study. Thus, in order to understand present-day activism, the most significant aspects of women's rights activism in Iran are reviewed in the next chapter.

CHAPTER 6

WOMEN'S RIGHTS ACTIVISM IN IRAN SINCE 1900

For nearly a century, women's rights activists have played a small but significant role in Iran. This brief historical overview illustrates the deep roots and complex character of women's rights activism in Iran through the Pahlavi era (1925–79) and into the Islamic Republic of Iran (1979–2005). The period during the Islamic Republic is divided into four parts: the 'First' Islamic Republic (1979–89), the 'Second' Islamic Republic (1990–96), the 'Third' Islamic Republic (1997–2004) and the 'Fourth' Islamic Republic (2005–13).[1]

Women's rights activism in the early 1900s

The contemporary debate on women's rights in Iran goes back to the early 1900s, and increased with the development of the Constitutional Movement.[2] Until the early twentieth century, public debate on the position of women was consistently male-led. Studies by Parvin Paidar, however, show that women took part in nationalist activities such as the Constitutional Movement, the Tobacco Movement, and protests against the presence of the British in Iran (Paidar 1995). Eliz Sanasarian also discusses the participation of women in the Constitutional Revolution and gives an account of violent and non-violent activities and campaigns organised by women (Sanasarian 1982).[3] Despite women's involvement in support of the Constitutional Revolution, they themselves acquired no rights under the new Constitution and had little influence on the drafting of its text. As a result of the increased personal freedoms and rights that the constitution offered to every citizen, however, it was mainly after 1906 that women were able to establish their own organisations (op. cit.: 21).

Sanasarian argues that women's groups in the early 1900s were incorporated into the contemporary nationalist movement, as they supported both the idea of having a constitution and the opposition to the presence of foreign countries in Iran. Consequently, claims for women's rights were closely linked, but still secondary, to nationalistic demands at the time. The women who took part in the early women's movement were also active in either the constitutionalist or the nationalist movements, and their families (mainly their fathers) were intellectual nationalists (ibid.).

The first women's rights activists in Iran were from the upper class and elite families, and mainly from urban areas.[4] Most were literate; illiterate women – who had participated in the early constitutional movement – did not take part in the emerging women's movement. Sanasarian further claims that it is probable that the average Iranian was unaware of the rising women's movement at the time. Even so, quite a few men played an important role in the early stages of the women's movement, especially in debates on women's right to vote (op. cit.: 24). In general, though, there was a lack of a solid common ideology among the early women's rights activists.

There is also a need to look into the international influence on women's issues in Iran. Although the women's movement emerged at the same time as those in neighbouring countries, it progressed quite differently. The Iranian debate on women's rights lacked the intensity of the one developing, for example, in Egypt and Turkey at the time.[5] This was partly due to Iran's linguistic isolation from the Arab world, and partly because it was never in the Ottoman Empire, or colonised by European countries. Thus, Iranian intellectuals did not have the same links with and knowledge about contemporary nationalistic, political and feminist ideas in Europe as did Egyptian and Turkish intellectuals (Hoodfar 1999: 5). Another probable explanation is that only a small number of women received education in Iran at the time, reflected in their low political and intellectual contribution in general. Sanasarian points out, however, that there was increasing contact between Iranian women's groups, the Russian delegation and British suffragettes after World War I (1982: 21). In Britain, the suffragettes led the campaign for women's right to vote and in 1918 gained results. Two years later women in the United States also won the right to vote, and news of these achievements spread to Iran through women's journals. Because of the presence of foreign powers in Iran, translations of British and American articles about women's rights were widely distributed. For example, an article published in *'Alam Nesvan* stated that western women were 'two centuries ahead of Iranian women' (op. cit.: 39).

There are also signs of influence from other countries on the Iranian debate. At the time, the uprising against the British in Egypt took place, and Qasim Amin's book *The Liberation of Women* (1899) was important in the debate that followed in Egypt. Similar ideas did not immediately emerge in Iran, but some reformist thinkers took intellectual inspiration from Egypt. In particular, Jamal al-Din Al-Afghani (1838–97) drew on the ideas of Muhammad 'Abduh (1849–1905) when hoping to reform Iranian society (Paidar 1995: 45). Al-Afghani was an anti-imperialist, but sought reforms in Iran by what he called 'Pan-Islamic reformism'. Some women's rights activists were attracted by Al-Afghani's ideas and began to argue for women's education as a condition for the progress of an Islamic society. In doing so they drew parallels between Iran and Egypt, a country that the Iranian state usually compared itself to and where women had easier access to education (ibid.).

In 1919, Huda Shaar'awi established the Egyptian Feminist Union (EFU). The EFU participated in the Oriental Women's Congress in Tehran in 1932 hosted by the Patriotic Women's League. The congress also has participants from Iraq, Turkey, Lebanon and India. One of the main themes was the need for women's education and the abolition of polygyny (Sanasarian 1982: 67–8). During the Pahlavi era, when the prevailing influence of feminist thought came from Europe, these contacts were lost (Hoodfar 1999: 17).[6] From the

1920s until the 1930s, Atatürk initiated a range of educational and social reforms in Turkey that improved the status of women. These would prove to have a major impact on future reforms instigated by Reza Shah Pahlavi, showing that the outside influence on the women's rights debate in Iran at the time was considerable.

Women's rights activism in the Pahlavi era

From the first days of Pahlavi rule, the debate on women's rights changed. The participation of women in public life and particularly the promotion of women's education were now seen as preconditions for developing a modern society. Women were more active in public debates and contributed to a change in the official discourse. On 7 January 1936, Reza Shah introduced the first official day for women to be unveiled in public. Later the same year, women gained admission to Tehran University (Paidar 1995: 108).

At the same time, the Pahlavi era was a period of strict censorship and government control. During World War II, however, the regime was weakened and censorship loosened. When Reza Shah Pahlavi was forced to leave Iran in 1944 as a result of his support for Germany, a political vacuum developed and led to greater freedom of expression. Some women's organisations benefited from this for a short time. New associations surfaced and some women's journals first published in the early 1900s were relaunched, such as *Zaban-e Zanan*. In addition, new organisations and journals were established with links to political parties. In 1943, a women's faction of the Tudeh party started the journal *Bida-ye Ma* (Our Awakening), which expressed anti-clerical and communist opinions. In 1944, *Hezb-e Zanan* (Women's Party) was founded and then *Zan-e Emruz* (Woman of Today), only to be banned a year later.

In 1952 the Pahlavi regime regained control after the struggle with Prime Minister Mosaddeq and strict censorship continued. The restrictions affected women's organisations, and a period of assimilation of women's issues was initiated (Sanasarian 1982: 78–9). Princess Ashraf, the Shah's sister, had established the Council of Iranian Women's Organisations (*Shura-ye Sazeman-e Iran*) together with political allies in 1949. The council enjoyed state support and sought to control all women's organisations in the country. Within a few years this was accomplished. All organisations that did not become part of it were dissolved and Iranian women's organisations in general lost their independence. Ashraf's organisation then took the name Women's Organisation of Iran (WOI, *Sazeman-e Zanan-e Iran*) in 1966. WOI worked for family welfare centres, literacy classes, legal counselling and professional training for women (Hoodfar 1999: 19). Its biggest success was lobbying prior to the 1963 ratification of women's right to vote and to run for public office and later for the Family Protection Law of 1967. The debate about women needing their husband's approval to travel abroad followed shortly (op. cit.: 20).

Sanasarian traces the decline of the women's movement in Iran by the 1930s and even announced the end of the movement by 1932 (Sanasarian 1982: 47). Although such a conclusion seems premature, it is evident that women's movements in Iran were different from those, for example, in Egypt. According to Hoodfar, there is no clear explanation why they did not develop in the same way. Part of the reason, she writes, can be found in the Pahlavi regime's strict censorship and the fact that the state included many of the politically active women in its institutions. Both created difficulties for an independent women's movement (Hoodfar 1999: 17). The project of transforming Iranian womanhood that took place during the Pahlavi era can thus be seen as a kind of state feminism (Amin 2002: 1). The project was an integral part of the 1963 White Revolution (*Enghelab-e Sefid*) and a precondition for the modernisation of Iran. It left little room for an independent women's movement to develop, however.

Despite the lack of such a movement at the time, some women's rights activists were still able to operate. Mehrangiz Manoochehrian (1906–2000) was the first female senator in Iran (1963–72). She was a lawyer and among the first women to study at Tehran University's Faculty of Law. Manoochehrian founded the Association of Women Lawyers (*Anjoman-e hoqoqdan-e Zanan*), which was active in debating the Family Protection Law prior to 1967. The association was part of a broader campaign initiated by the WOI and together, in 1956, they submitted demands to the Shah on political rights for women, equality of rights in employment, divorces to take place in courts, and the abolition of temporary marriage and polygyny (Paidar 1995: 138). Manoochehrian is today best known for drafting an alternative family law bill in 1963. Her certificate to practise law was made invalid after the Revolution in 1979, and Shirin 'Ebadi, another well-known female lawyer, was also no longer allowed to practise. Manoochehrian's alternative family law bill would, however, prove to play an important role for women' rights campaigns later on.

During the Pahlavi's reign there was growing discontent against Muhammad Reza Shah and a religious and political oppositionist movement was initiated. Many Iranians were not content with the modernisation projects. Despite all the reforms introduced as part of the 1963 White Revolution, most people did not experience a country in progress. From the outside, however, the socioeconomic reforms during the late 1960s and early 1970s were considered a success. Keddie writes that the image presented abroad was of a country with a great increase in GNP and a remarkable growth in industry, agriculture and infrastructure (Keddie 2003: 148–9). On the surface, the future looked promising, as numerous social welfare projects were established. Another side of the story, not so obvious from outside Iran, was the growing dissatisfaction of the many opponents of the regime who saw the downside of the reforms. Many considered the White Revolution as fraudulent and benefiting mainly the rich. According to leading oppositionists, the reforms did not represent real change, but only contributed to widening the differences between the masses and the elites. Keddie labels the divide within the Iranian population, the split between the popular bazaar culture and the educated elite culture, as the 'two cultures' phenomenon (op. cit: 170). This distinction was significant among Iranian women's rights activists as well. Although it gives a simplified picture, it helps to understand the contradictions existing in Iranian society at the time.

The anti-Shah movement that emerged included many women. The question of women's rights was, however, seen as secondary to anti-imperialistic and anti-Shah sentiments (Paidar 1995: 213). For many women who took part in the anti-Shah demonstrations, women's issues were never declared aims. The Shah's regime had been so closely linked to women's rights through the implementation of the Family Protection Law that demands for women's rights were seen as signs of support of the Shah. Instead, many supporters of the anti-Shah movement made use of the oppositional force of religion. Keddie states that 'Islam appeared, to those who rejected both liberalism and Marxism, as the natural ideological base from which to fight the West and the Pahlavis, especially as Islam was believed by, and familiar to, the great masses of Iranians' (Keddie 2003: 212).

The Islamic opposition movement recruited many women, and even well-educated and literate women, previously in charge of women's organisations, now supported the religious opposition. Sanasarian questions this tendency, which she considers a contradiction to women's rights activism as such. She asks why the legal consciousness of women's rights activists did not change along with the reforms enacted in the country, and finds an explanation in the fact that most Iranian women had not been active in advocating the legal reforms concerning their own rights in the 1960s and 1970s. The many reforms introduced had come from above, and were not in line with the legal awareness of most women at the time (Sanasarian 1982: 109–10). Although the White Revolution had opened up new rights and possibilities for some women, these were considered arguments in support of the modernisation of Iran, rather than a particular motivation for women's rights (Najmabadi 1998: 60). Thus, women's rights were never declared aims in the demonstrations prior to 1979 and many women were reluctant to raise women's issues because of their close association with the Shah (Hoodfar 1999: 22).

In 1971, 'Ali Shari'ati (1933–77), an Iranian intellectual educated in France, published a book, *Fatemeh Fatemeh Ast* (*Fatemeh is Fatemeh*), that would prove to have huge influence on women's rights activism in the years to come. The activism inspired by Shari'ati's writing looked to a different starting point than the one encouraged during the White Revolution. Rather than building on notions of a modern society, it made references to a Shi'i Islamic past. Shari'ati presented the story of Fatemeh, the daughter of Prophet Muhammad and the wife of 'Ali, the first Shi'a Imam. His book was directed towards Iranian women who had different role models. Instead of choosing western idols, Shari'ati encouraged women to look to Shi'i Islamic history and to the model of Fatemeh. He presented her as a leading star for modern Muslim women due to her political talent, her views on the Qur'an and her sense of responsibility towards her family, known as 'the holy five' in Shi'i tradition (Hermansen 1983).

Shari'ati enjoyed excessive popularity before his death in 1977 and inspired many women and men to engage in the Revolution in 1979. The ideals presented in his work were taken both from western philosophy and science as well as the Shi'i tradition. Parvin Paidar refers to this trend as a 'radicalisation of Shi'ism', in which new generations combined state and religion together in ways that had not been seen since the formative years of Islam (Paidar 1995: 178). The radicalisation of Shi'ism also had a particular impact on understandings of genderhood, and especially of womanhood. Undoubtedly, the Shi'a idols provided many women with answers they had not been able to find in the ideology of the Pahlavi government. In particular, Shari'ati sought to confront what he called *zan-e hich va pouch* (a woman in her nothingness) (Moallem 2005: 92). Shari'ati describes her as a 'frightening creature ... who sits at home and is good for nothing' (Shari'ati 1980: 113). In contrast to the *zan-e hich va pouch*, Shari'ati presents Fatemeh as signifying ideal womanhood, 'the woman that Islam wants a woman to be' (op. cit.: 224–5). Shari'ati thus encourages Iranian women to dismiss the model of *zan-e hich va pouch*, which according to him is unproductive, passive and useless, and to adopt the ideal of Fatemeh as productive, active and useful for the society in which they live.

Shari'ati's writings were influential not only for the rising anti-Shah movement, but also for women's rights activists at the time. One of the women who joined the anti-Shah movement and adopted Shari'ati's ideal notion of womanhood was A'zam Taleqani (1944–). Today she is known as a prominent politician, women's rights activist and as the daughter of Ayatollah Taleqani.[7] Prior to 1979, A'zam Taleqani was active in pursuing women's issues from a religious point of view. Neither her views on women's rights nor her political opinions, however, corresponded with those dominant in Iran at the time. During an interview with Taleqani in May 2008, she explained the problems of engaging in women's rights activism outside of WOI. She projected a religious activism and had ideas for women's rights that were seen as radical at the time, and which had consequences for her:

> I was imprisoned for two years. Actually, I was sentenced for life, but after a lot of work from a human rights group, I was released after two years. It was a military prison. The hardest part for me was to be without my children. How would they manage without their mother? . . . They accused me of being a member of the Mujahedin,[8] but I wasn't. I was politically active, but I think it was really because of my family name. (Interview with A'zam Taleqani, May 2008)

Although A'zam Taleqani represents a particular position of women's rights activism related to her family background and political affiliations, many women's rights activists shared her views and a large number of women initially supported the coming of the Islamic Republic.

Women's rights activism in the Islamic Republic

The 'First' Republic: 1979–89

During the 'First' Republic, women's rights activism underwent a process of institutionalisation and self-definition that took place at the same time as the establishment of the Islamic Republic. The amendments introduced after 1979 were met by protests and demonstrations by women. On 13 June 1979, for instance, women employees at the Communication Corporation protested against the closure of day-care centres for children (Tabari and Yeganeh 1982: 235). During the Islamic Republic's first year the issue of wearing hejab was also a recurrent topic of debate. On 7 March 1979, Khomeini declared that women should take jobs, but also make sure that they were properly dressed in public by wearing the hejab (op. cit.: 233). The next day, 8 March, women gathered in Tehran to celebrate International Women's Day and to protest against Khomeini's declaration on dress codes. And on 10 March, a sit-in protest against the imposition of the hejab was arranged. The demonstrations against enforcing the hejab continued. Another wave of demonstrations began in October, when the Council of the Revolution declared that all family law rulings should be made according to Shari'a. As a result, the Family Protection Law was abolished. Women's rights activists responded by arranging demonstrations against the new family law rulings on 30 October 1979 (op. cit.: 236).

The legal changes affecting women were followed by a series of more or less organised protests and demonstrations during the first years of the Islamic Republic.[9] According to Yeganeh and Tabari,[10] women's organisations in this early phase represented three main ideological directions – Islam, nationalism and Marxism (op. cit.: 203). These three trends, however, did not necessarily represent separate movements (ibid.).

The political and ideological disagreements over women's issues were highly visible at the time. In particular, discord between religious- and secular-oriented women's rights activists was evident. Many secular-oriented activists were accused of supporting western-inspired views on women's rights and of defying Islam. By contradicting the official view on women, they were seen as disagreeing with the foundation of the Islamic Republic, which limited their possibility of cooperating with religious-oriented women's rights activists (Najmabadi 1998: 61). There were, however, some common topics of debate. Among the most recurrent were the issue of celebrating International Women's Day on 8 March, clothing (hejab) and the bill of Retribution. On all three issues, religious-oriented women's rights activists proved to have better potential for speaking their mind and being heard than secular-oriented women. In addition, the question of women's rights to education, work and financial independence started to emerge.

The protest against the enforced use of hejab on 8 March 1979, which was also International Women's Day and therefore considered a western invention unsuitable for the Islamic Republic, was eventually dissolved by the police. In April 1980 it was decided that the birthday of Fatemeh should be celebrated as Muslim Women's Day on 6 May and replace 8 March (Kalinock 2003).

The issue of women's clothing was a hotly debated topic in this first phase of the Islamic Republic. In July 1980, a seminar addressing Ayatollah Khomeini's message on the issue of the hejab was arranged. A'zam Taleqani, Shahin Tabatabai, Zahra Rahnavard and Ansieh Mofidi delivered a speech called 'Instead of Compulsory veiling, public decency for all should be compulsory' (later published in the newspaper *Ettela'* (Information), quoted in Tabari and Yeganeh 1982: 194). A common idea among these women's rights activists at the time was that appropriate and modest dress codes should apply to both men and women, and that the use of the hejab should be voluntary. During the 'First' Republic, however, not all women's rights activists necessarily spoke in favour of women's rights. Monir Gorji, a female representative in the Assembly of Experts, addressed gender roles from a different perspective. She is reported to have said:

> I feel ashamed to talk about 'women's rights'. Have any of our brothers in this assembly mentioned 'men's rights'? . . . In Islam we do not have separate women's and men's questions and rights. We only have the rights of the 'human beings.' (op. cit.: 55)

The view of gender proclaimed by Gorji did not, however, seem to represent women's rights activists at the time. The general trend among them during the 'First' Republic was rather a gradual decline of support for the government and for state-defined models of womanhood, as well as increased opposition towards the enforced legal amendments.

In 1980, the bill of Retribution (*Layehe-ye Qisas*) was ratified in the Majles. Article 5 received the most attention. It states that 'If a Muslim man wilfully murders a Muslim woman, he will be sentenced to *qisas* [retaliation] but the woman's guardian must pay the murderer one half of a man's blood-money before he receives *qisas*' (Shahidian 1994: 226).

Several women's rights activists considered the new law to be highly discriminatory towards women, as it requested only half the amount of a man's blood money (*diyeh*) for a murdered woman. The bill led to protests from women's rights activists, and in May 1981 the article 'The Place of Women in the bill of Retribution' was published in the women's journal *Zan-e Ruz* (*Woman of Today*). The article exemplifies the strategies and lines of argument in use during the first period of the Islamic Republic. It highlights a different approach to Islam and women's rights than the one presented in the bill of Retribution:

> Women's place in the Retribution Bill is problematic and in need of discussion. Its discussion of gender is one of its brilliant points. Each sex has its own particular sociology and psychology and, importantly, the division of labour and tasks which Islam assigns to men and women demands different treatment of them by law. Yet the criticism of the place of women in the bill of Retribution turns on the important point that Islam considers men and women, in the words of martyr Shari'ati, as 'dual humans'. Is it the case that what is entailed in this duality is a spirit of oppression, superiority, discrimination? Never! In an Islam which calls the most pious the most valuable, the criterion of judgement is piety. Being men and women as dual, different, does not mean comparing them as superior or inferior. Does Islam consider women who, under oppressive decaying systems, turned into 'dolls' or household objects the same as those who follow the Zeinab's ways and looks upon each category in the same way? A woman who is a mother, a wife, an active member of society, and a pious devotee of her God; a woman who is serving the Islamic republic under the hardest conditions in far-away places with courage, competence, and belief – can her understanding, intellectual awareness of the problems be the same as a woman who only thinks of her appearance and her household possessions? Which of these categories is the subject of treatment by the retribution Bill, and do these two categories deserve the same treatment? (Tabari and Yeganeh 1982: 198)

The above passage from *Zan-e Ruz* refers to Ali Shari'ati's view of men and women as 'dual humans'. It points to the role model of Zeynab[11] as a pious Muslim, a mother, wife, and an active member of society. On the basis of this understanding of Islam, women's rights activists contested the bill of Retribution. Similarly, any law seen as discriminatory towards women at the time was debated from an Islamic point of view. For example, a document issued by women's rights activists in the Mujahedin-e Khalq movement discussed discrimination against women with references to the concept of *tawhid* (monotheism) in Islam. In it, the basis of gender discrimination is eliminated on the basis of this principle:

> The reality of discrimination between women and men can be approached in another way and that is, in our opinion, a realistic and *tawhidi* (divine and non-antagonistic) one, namely an approach which is employed towards any social discrimination in the *tawhidi* world outlook. As we know, *tawhidi* is against any class, racial, national, and sexual discrimination. It cannot, therefore, accept the discrimination between women and men as a holy matter and approve it. (Tabari and Yeganeh 1982: 113)

Both the references to Shari'ati and the concept of *tawhid* refer to changes in rhetoric over women's rights in this phase of women's rights activism. The three main debates that took place at this time signify the prevalence of religious-oriented women's rights activism over the secular-oriented one. Arguments made on the basis of secular sources were dismissed as being 'western' or 'un-Islamic' and thus lacked legitimacy. Rhetoric situated within the religiously accepted language of the Islamic Republic, though, gradually formed the basis of the women's rights activism evolving throughout the Islamic Republic. Already, though, there are signs of their conceptions of Islam and womanhood departing from officially defined models. Steadily, the debate on women's rights that took place within the framework of Islam would gain authority and bring results over time.

In the first period of the Islamic Republic the organisation that unified the mostly religious-oriented women's rights activists was the Women's Society of the Islamic Revolution (*Jam'e-ye Zanan-e Enghelab-e Eslami*, WSIR). The WSIR consisted of women from the higher social strata, many of whom held doctorates from universities in Europe and the United States and belonged to respected religious and political families. Despite similarities in background, Tabari and Yeganeh claim that the WSIR was not a formally organised body, but rather a loose association in which most activities were conducted by and under the name of individual members (op. cit.: 224). A'zam Taleqani, the head of WSIR, says:

> The organisation was established in 1978. While I was in prison I got the idea that we should establish a women's organisation where the main agenda was women's rights. After I was released I invited 30 women to my home and we discussed how this could be done. The goal was just to have an organisation dedicated to women's issues. Then we rented a room in a human rights office. We wrote down the rules and declarations of the organisation. Under the Shah there was a women's organisation led by the Queen, for women. After the revolution the temporary government asked me and three other women to be responsible for this organisation. We worked for five months considering the needs [of women], wrote a budget and so forth. But when we presented the budget to the government they refused to accept it. So this group was dissolved. Then we went back to the first organisation. We arranged courses in philosophy and ideology for women, and we also had weapon training. All courses were free. The students asked for weapon training ... These were revolutionary times and no one knew what would happen! At this time we were known as the Women's Society of Islamic Revolution. We also arranged free counselling for women, and judicial help. And we offered women the assistance of a lawyer in family court cases. Another important activity was that we provided work for women. We started a clothes factory in this building!

> But during the years the activities changed. (Interview with A'zam Taleqani, May 2008)

Because of the political affiliations of some of its members, WSIR had significant influence on the contemporary debate on women's rights.[12] It did not, however, represent a unified opposition to the state, and it could be said that WSIR members worked both within and in opposition to the state. On 15 March 1980, A'zam Taleqani and Monir Gorji, both members of the WSIR, were elected to the Majles.[13] According to Taleqani, her family background was significant:

> Before the war I was elected MP. In the first parliamentary election I got over two million votes! I was very popular, probably because I was my father's daughter ... When I was in the Majles I worked on and proposed many bills, but only two of them were ratified. Some of my rejected bills were used later on. They were about better conditions for women in case of divorce and taking care of widows after the war. (Interview with A'zam Taleqani, May 2008)

WSIR also conducted international activities and participated in a conference in New Delhi in 1979, in the Copenhagen International Women's Conference in 1980 and in the Inter-Parliamentary Union in Havana in 1981. Taleqani confirmed this and said that a report from these seminars was published in *Payam-e Hajar* (*The Message of Hajar*), a journal published by the WSIR from 1982 until it was shut down in 2000. *Payam-e Hajar* covered both national and international objectives, and stated that it was 'introducing the Islamic Revolution, women's role within it, and its gains for Iranian women's position to women around the world' (Tabari and Yeganeh 1982: 223). Taleqani explained that the journal was dependent on state authorisation and was constantly subject to state control:

> We started to publish *Payam-e Hajar*. After eighteen years this journal became illegal. The first time it was closed down was in 1995, but it was republished in 1997. It was closed down in

> 2000 we were not able to republish. We have asked for permission, and I got an oral permission, but it was never written and formal. (Interview with A'zam Taleqani, May 2008)

According to the anthropologist Homa Hoodfar, Taleqani continued the work of WSIR and maintained the organisation's independence after her term in the Majles was over, in spite of the difficulties (1999: 29). Taleqani explains how even the choice of name was a challenge:

> Another change before 1980 was that the government decided that we could no longer name ourselves a 'society' [*jam'e*]. They said we had to take the name 'council' [*shura*]. We started all over again, considering the needs of women. I travelled all around the country to gather information about Iranian women before I was a member of the Majles. As I mentioned, there were no parties back then, and because we wanted to work legally, we changed our name from society to Institute [*mo'assese*] ... In 1983 we were finally a legal institution ... After twelve years we were finally registered as a party. (Interview with A'zam Taleqani, May 2008)

A'zam Taleqani's recollections are significant for understanding women's rights activism during the first phase of the Islamic Republic. Although many activists maintained a secular-oriented approach to women's issues and some were even forced to go into exile abroad because of the tense political situation, Taleqani is an activist who has worked both inside the state and in opposition to it since the early stages of the Islamic Republic. Although a supporter of the 1979 Revolution and a member of the first Majles, she both supported and challenged the new government's policies on women. She is also a typical example of a women's rights activist during these early years of the Islamic Republic in regard to her family, personal and political background, which gave her the opportunity to engage in this kind of work. Nonetheless, she experienced difficulties in doing so.

The 'Second' Republic: 1990–96

At the beginning of the 1990s, Iran faced a range of new challenges. In 1989, the death of Ayatollah Khomeini had left a void in the political and religious leadership that was not easily filled. Ayatollah Ali Hossein Khamenei was appointed as the new leader (*velayat-e faqih*), and despite some controversies with other *ulama*, he gradually took the place of his predecessor (Keddie 2003: 260–2).[14] As a result of the Iran–Iraq war, Iran also faced urgent challenges of reconstruction and re-institutionalisation. In 1989, Ayatollah Akbar Hashemi Rafsanjani was elected President and embarked on the postwar reconstruction of the country. In order to rebuild the Iranian economy, Iran was in need of help from the international community and Rafsanjani embarked on a new phase of openness.[15] Other challenges in Iran at this time were family planning, population control and the rising numbers of divorces. All three issues became the cause of rising dissent in the early 1990s.

At the same time a 'new religious thinking' (*now-e andishi-ye dini*) emerged gradually from the 1990s and presented challenges to both the traditional and ideological structures of Shari'a (Mir-Hosseini 2006).[16] In general, the advocates of the new thinking held a more flexible view. Their main thrust can be explained by the concept of dynamic jurisprudence (*fiqh-e puya*). It builds on the idea that while Shari'a is regarded as unchangeable and sacred, jurisprudence (*fiqh*) is seen as a result of human thought and is therefore temporal and changeable (op. cit.: 636).[17] Despite the emergence of the 'new religious thinking' at the time, most of the Shi'i *ulama* and intellectuals involved in this trend were reluctant to deal with the issue of women's rights in detail.[18]

Iranian women's rights activists, however, have been important for pushing the debate forward and demanding a gendered discussion of Shari'a. They were involved in arguing for the amendments on divorce in 1992 and on dower in 1997, and their lobbying increased generally during the 'Second' Republic in three main areas. These were the publication of three women's journals, the political participation of women and the increased internationalisation of the demand for women's rights. Although these areas of activism resembled previous periods, they now took a new direction and began to develop into what is often referred to as 'Islamic feminism'. This was a new kind activism. Whereas during the Pahlavi era women's rights activities were largely centred in a secular defined framework, in this second phase their activism shifted to a religiously defined context. The definitions that developed set a new agenda for women's rights issues in Islam, not only in Iran but also internationally.

The three journals that played a significant part of women's rights activism, *Zan-e Ruz* (*Woman of Today*), *Zanan* (*Women*) and *Farzaneh* (*Wise Wo/man*), were intimately connected by a common past history, a current ideological self-definition and by location (Najmabadi 1998: 62). *Zan-e Ruz* was established in 1964 but has adopted various ideological profiles since then.[19] In 1984, Shahla Sherkat was appointed editor. In 1991, however, she left this position 'because of unresolved disagreements' (Mir-Hosseini 2002: 75). Shortly after, in 1992, Sherkat published the first issue of the journal *Zanan*, which contained articles relevant to contemporary debates on family law (custody rights, women as judges, etc.), new views on the concept of 'feminism' and heterodox perspectives on who, how and on which basis the Islamic sources could be interpreted. In 1995 and 1996, *Zanan* held a series of round-table discussions on the so-called 'woman question' (*mas'ale-ye zan*) and a series of interviews with religious intellectuals who represented the branch of *fiqh-e puya* (Farhi 2001: 319).

Farzaneh was first published in 1993 and was the third women's journal of significance for women's rights activism at this time. As a scholarly and academic journal, *Farzaneh* differs from both *Zanan* and *Zan-e Ruz* and has not had a feminist profile. However, it has clear links to the Institute of Women's Studies and Research (*Mo'assese-ye Mottal'at-e va Tahqiqat-e Zanan*), a semi-state-controlled NGO in Tehran. Articles in *Farzaneh* vary from discussing Islamic feminism in Iran (Abbasgholizadeh 2000) to dealing with Fatemeh Zahra as a contemporary role model (Gorji and Ebtekar 1997). Like *Zan-e Ruz*, *Farzaneh* has also gone through major ideological shifts since its inauguration. Although representing various outlooks on feminism, both *Farzaneh* and *Zanan* carried articles that discussed the patriarchal character of religious interpretations in Iran. *Farzaneh* underlines the importance of the link between the women's movement and academia, as seen in the development of women's studies programmes during the 'Third' Republic.

The three women's journals have been significant in raising issues of women's rights not only in Iran, but also internationally. In a 1993 article in *Zanan*, Mehrangiz Kar declared that 'It is time for *ijtihad*' (Ahmadi 2006: 37). *Zanan,* in particular, broke new ground for women to engage in the interpretation of Islamic sources and law. *Ijtihad* was no longer seen a process reserved for *ulama*, but as a struggle in which ordinary Muslims, and even women, could participate. *Zanan* is often seen as founding 'Islamic feminism' in Iran as a result of its approach both to Islam and feminism, and its unifying of them. It is recognised as carving out a new route for women's rights in Islam in the Muslim world (Najmabadi 1998).

Women's rights activism has been shaped and conditioned by developments intrinsic to Iranian society and history. From the early 1900s, however, it has had connections with activists both in other Muslim countries, as well as in the United States and Britain (Sanasarian 1982: 21). According to Nayereh Tohidi, local and global intersections have been of three kinds since 1979. First, there was a missionary approach seeking to export the Islamic Revolution and the Iranian model of 'Islamic' womanhood; second, a more pragmatic approach that built on connections and cooperation with activists in Muslim countries and in Europe; third, the development of secular-oriented, religious minorities and gender-egalitarian activists who sought to move away from feminism defined within a religious framework (Tohidi 2002).

Increasingly from the 1970s, links have been established with the so-called global feminism initiated by the United Nations (op. cit.: 277). Networks such as Women Living Under Muslim Laws, and later Musawah, have drawn attention to the women's rights situation in Iran. The later internationalisation of women's rights corresponds to the promotion of Islamic feminism as a common strategy for women in Muslim countries. Although seen as important for highlighting the specific situation of discrimination against Muslim women, such global feminist endeavours have also been criticised for enforcing a universal form of feminism that runs the risk of being exclusionary and ignoring local variations (Tohidi 2002, Basu 2010, Badran 2011, Bøe and Tønnessen 2011). Moreover, Iranians scattered abroad have had a major influence on the international connections of women's rights activism. On the one hand, diaspora communities have facilitated contacts between women's rights activists inside Iran and internationally. In particular, personalities such as Shirin 'Ebadi and Mehrangiz Kar have been significant in raising international awareness about the state of women's rights in Iran. On the other hand, there are some unfortunate consequences from the involvement of Iranian diaspora communities, who may risk exporting an imagined notion of Iranian womanhood that is not necessarily consistent with contemporary realities in Iran. Afsaneh, one of the interviewees, expressed this concern over the portrayal of women in Iran in some research literature, and claimed that the fascination with Iranian women 'and everything they could do within the framework of the Islamic Republic' overshadowed the realities under which most women in Iran live (Interview with Afsaneh, April 2008). Thus, there is a dual consequence of the diaspora engagement with local Iranian women's rights activism.

During the 'Second' Republic the representation of women in politics increased to new heights. Nine female representatives were elected to the fourth Majles in 1992[20] and the political participation of women increased dramatically during this period. A total of 350 women announced their candidacy for the fifth Majles election, and 14 female MPs were elected in 1996.[21] Faezeh Hashemi, the daughter of former President Hashemi Rafsanjani, was one of them and gained a high number of votes. She said:

> I was there [in the Majles] for four years. I was the first MP from Tehran. It means [I received] the largest vote from Tehran. In the second period I was not re-elected by the people. I failed to gain the vote of the people. (Interview with Faezeh Hashemi, May 2008)

As the daughter of Rafsanjani, Faezeh Hashemi is an example of a female politician with prominent political affiliations. She was also important in promoting women's issues during the 'Second' Republic, and in 1992 she founded the Islamic Countries Women's Sports Solidarity Council, of which she is still president.[22] She also founded and edited *Zan*, the first daily women's newspaper in Iran:

> I published *Zan*, a daily newspaper that focused on women's issues. It only lasted for 10 months before being shut down in 1997 ... These publications are important for information and awareness among women. The media do not pay any attention to women's issues. Therefore we need our own publications for this. It will increase knowledge about discrimination and what is important. And women can exchange experiences. (Interview with Faezeh Hashemi, May 2008)

Prior to the Law of Amendment to Divorce Regulations passed in 1992, female politicians in Iran played a significant part in promoting it. One of them was Faezeh Hashemi, who explained her involvement:

> Before providing a bill we must gather a minimum of signatures. For example about women's rights that, we as reformists think this is the right of women, but other women from conservative parties think that women should not have this right. And they think they are against Islam. But I think it is not. Maybe it is against a special interpretation of Islam, not real Islam. These are differences between ideas you find everywhere in Iran. For example, the right of divorce, or the right of custody. These women didn't agree that it must be for women. And they think this it is a right for men only. Because they were conservative ... And in my time, a women's commission was established in the Majles. I wanted to be a member of this commission, but the head of the Majles didn't agree. Because they had to choose. They had to approve who could be in this commission. So they didn't choose me, or my friends in my party. Instead they sent those

women who talked conservatively. Yes, you could say there were some problems, but they were not very hard, not very difficult. Because I like struggling. Struggling is not difficult for me! I like challenges! (Interview with Faezeh Hashemi, May 2008)

During Rafsanjani's presidency there was increased contact between Iran and the international community. The policies of internationalisation also affected women's issues, and women's delegations from Iran were sent both to the UN conference on Population and Development in Cairo in 1994 and to the Fourth World Conference on Women in Beijing in 1995. The Beijing conference in particular represented a change and initiated a new phase for women's rights activism, as new ideas and strategies were adopted from women's movements worldwide.

In June 1994, Shahla Habib and Massumeh Ebtekar were appointed organisers of the Iranian delegation to Beijing and arranged the first meeting of women's NGOs in Tehran in preparation for the conference. In Beijing, new ideas relevant to women's rights activism emerged. For example, the plan to initiate women's studies at universities in Iran developed after this conference. The promotion of women's rights both through women's journals and women's greater political participation had proved successful in strengthening the lobbying efforts of women's rights activists, for the 1992 divorce reform in particular. And with the increasing internationalisation of women's rights, Iran's 'Islamic feminism' gradually spread to other Muslim countries (Mir-Hosseini 2006).

The 'Third' Republic: 1997–2004

The 1997 election marked a turning point in Iranian politics. In May of that year, Muhammad Khatami was elected President. His election campaign had promoted a new direction for the Islamic Republic with regard to democracy, civil society, women's rights, economic development and foreign policy. The result was a landslide election and Khatami won 69 per cent of the votes, with women and young people constituting the majority of the voters (Keddie 2003: 270). The reformists also triumphed in the parliamentary election of May

2000. Many Iranians hoped that these elections would lay the basis for a number of new reforms. The Guardian Council,[23] however, blocked most of the numerous amendments suggested by the Majles (Keddie 2003: 278). In 2002, the sixth Majles ratified amendments to Article 1133 of the Iranian Civil Code, which allowed women to apply for divorce on the same basis as men. The bill, however, was rejected by the Guardian Council (Payvand, 28 September 2002). Nevetheless, the proposed amendments on divorce signify attempts by the sixth Majles to bring about legal reforms on such issues as inheritance, divorce and child custody, and also for Iran to ratify CEDAW. Although there was still significant opposition to the reformists' plans, the period of the 'Third' Republic opened up new possibilities for women's rights activism, and women's participation in civil society and politics continued to gain ground.

One relevant event was the renaming of the Women's Bureau in the Presidential Office (*Edar-e Zanan dar Daftar-e Ra'is-e Jomhuri*) established in 1988. In 1997, the Bureau became the Centre for Women's Participation (*Markaz-e Mosharekat-e Zanan*).[24] Along with the name change, its scope was extended. The Centre was a government organisation set up to facilitate connections between NGOs, government organisations and international institutions.[25] According to the anthropologist Arzoo Osanloo, the Centre also helped to define the government's reformist agenda in focusing on women's economic, political, social and legal status (2009: 43). The Centre's staff represented Iran before the UN, and played a significant part in securing the ratification of CEDAW by the sixth Majles, although the Guardian Council would later block the CEDAW approval (ibid.). Zahra Shoja'e was appointed as the Centre's first director-general. The Centre had close collaboration in particular with the Women's Commission in the Majles, which played a significant role in promoting family courts in 1997. Also, the Centre lobbied for women's increased rights in divorce, post-divorce alimony, domestic violence laws, greater equality in inheritance, employment, pension laws and criminal sanctions (op. cit.: 43). Parvin, an interviewee, used to work at the Centre and explained its objectives of the Centre as of 2002:

> Considering the women's necessities and what they need, we try to adopt some strategies. We have a thorough plan for the amendment of the legal structure regarding women, in which we are thoroughly considering women's problems. And we hope ... [to] present some bills to the Parliament. At the same time we have some direct contact with the religious scientists, these *ulama* that have very new ideas about women. And considering the ideas of these persons we try to come to a better position of women in the society, so they can achieve their legal rights and a more favourable position ... We have some very close relations with the women's factions in the Parliament and we try to make use of our ideas. But unfortunately the processes for changing the laws are very slow, but we continue step by step. (Interview with Parvin, November 2002)

Another significant event took place in 2003, when Shirin 'Ebadi was awarded the Nobel Peace Prize on the basis of her work for women's, children's and human rights. Not only was this important for raising awareness of women's rights and position in Iran, but it also drew increased attention to reformist interpretations of Islam.

In 2001, women's studies programmes were established at universities. This was the result of the initiative from several Iranian NGOs that had participated in the 1995 International Women's Conference in Beijing. The process of establishing women's studies programmes took some time, however. It was promoted by the Institute for Women's Studies and Research (*Mo'assese-ye Mottal'at-e va Tahqiqat-e Zanan* / IWSR) in Tehran. Arezoo, one of their employees, explained the inordinately long process:

> In 1995 Iranian NGOs participated in an international conference for the first time after the revolution, in Beijing. Afterwards, 20 lecturers from universities in Iran were invited here to establish a programme for women's studies in Iran. The programme included religious issues ... We invited religious leaders to underline the necessity of this study. The result was sent to the Ministry of Education. The Minister would not

> accept it. The argument was: 'Why should we focus on women? What about men?' We continued for two more years. It was mainly two women behind this work, *Khanom-e* Ebtekar and *Khanom-e* Shoja'e. They were both Khatami's advisers. After two years the proposal was passed due to their work and the support of Khatami. (Interview with Arezoo, May 2008)

Once established, the women's studies programmes would prove to be long-lasting and had a significant impact on women's rights activism in Iran. Several of the young women's rights activists I met in Tehran had studied in one or more women's studies courses since 2001 and some high-profile activists, like Shahla Sherkat, had joined the courses. Since 2008, however, the courses have been gradually limited, as university administrations have begun to interview prospective students and to exclude those with an activist background. The final nail in the coffin came in the autumn of 2008, when sociology professor Shahla E'zazi, who had taught women's studies at Tabatabai University for years, was replaced. Some women's studies programmes continued at the Centre for Women's Studies at the University of Tehran. But according to previous students at Tabatabai University, the Tehran University course focuses on so-called family studies, rather than on women's studies.

Among the activities and debates during the second and third phases of the Islamic Republic, three changes were particularly relevant to family law: the 1997 amendments on dower, revision of the custody of children in 1997 and the establishment of Special Civil Courts in 1998. However, not all efforts by women's rights activists during this period resulted in amendments. During the 'Third' Republic the question arose of women's participation in public and political life and whether a woman could become president in the Islamic Republic. In 1997, A'zam Taleqani launched her candidature for the presidency for the first time. This campaign was characterised by a more open public debate than for many ears, and women's rights activists used the opening to promote the question of women's political leadership. In *Payam-e Hajar*, Taleqani published the article 'Why I can be a Presidential Candidate in the Republic?' (Taleqani 1997). Her main argument was based on her view that the Constitution is unclear on the topic of female political leadership. In Article 115 it states:

> The President must be elected from among religious and political personalities [*rejal-e mazhabi-ye va siasi*] possessing the following qualifications: Iranian origin; Iranian nationality; administrative ability and resourcefulness; a good past record; trustworthiness and piety; firm belief in the fundamental principles of the Islamic Republic of Iran and the official *madhhab* [school of law] of the country.

For Taleqani, the Arabic word *rejal* is a key to understanding these criteria, and its meaning has become a question of debate. Some claim that *rejal* refers to males and means *men*, while others believe that it refers more generally to the word *human*. This is a matter of interpretation, according to Taleqani. She stresses that the Persian language does not distinguish between the genders of the noun, and claims that *rejal* does not necessarily refer only to men. She has therefore taken Article 115 as permitting members of the religious and political elite to become president, and not necessarily only men. She writes: 'From the Islamic viewpoint men and women enjoy equal rights in Iran, which sets the example for all Islamic societies, and should not ignore the rights of half of the Iranian population, which is composed of women' (Taleqani 1997: 48).

What is more, Taleqani asserts that the word *rajul* (singular of *rejal*) appears 15 times in the Qur'an, and in five places has been used as a general term and not a gender-specific one. She writes:

> I did the research, and without the least doubt I can say that females have never been barred from assuming the top posts of administration in Islam ... It is a divine and humanitarian duty to make clear whether a female can assume to an administrative post or not. (ibid.)

Taleqani has said that she considers it her duty to run for election, and that she cannot justify to her God that half of the population should be excluded from this position. Therefore she sees no other option other than to present herself as a presidential candidate. Since the 1997 election her candidacy has had a contagious effect and other women have followed her lead. Even before that election, nine women announced their candidacies. In the 2000 election, the number rose to 47 and in 2005 it was 89. Every one of the female candidates has, however, been disqualified before each election, as the Guardian Council must approve all registered candidates in advance. Prior to the presidential election in 2009, 475 candidates registered as candidates. Only four were approved, however, and not surprisingly none of them was a woman.

Women's rights activism as expressed through the work of the Centre for Women's Participation, the setting up of women's studies programmes and a growing number of female presidential candidates underlines the same trend. During the 'Third' Republic there was an increasing correlation between state policies on women and the work of women's rights activists. The link can be explained, first, by a reformist turn in politics, not only on women's issues, but more generally. Second, and as a result of this shift, women entered new fields of policy making as members of parliament, formed state-acknowledged NGOs and published legitimate women's journals. These new conditions for women's rights activism laid the foundation for new initiatives like the women's studies programmes and presidential candidacies. With regard to family law, though, no significant legal amendments took place, although many topics relevant to women's rights were thoroughly debated and addressed in public during this period.

The 'Fourth' Republic: 2005–13

A new change in politics and women's rights activism emerged with the presidential election of Mahmoud Ahmadinejad in 2005. Ahmadinejad was a relatively unknown political figure before being elected mayor of Tehran in 2003, and even before the 2005 presidential election he did not receive much attention. The first round was a rather close race, but Ahmadinejad defeated Rafsanjani in the second round with 61.7 per cent of the votes.[26] Many have claimed that it was Ahmadinejad's populist politics directed at poor people and his promises of tackling social justice and corruption that led to his election (Ehteshami and Zweiri 2007: 46). Ironically, it is said that it was the reformists who prepared the ground for the massive number of lower-class and rural votes for Ahmadinejad, by opening up the issues of political rights, civil society, democracy, freedom of speech, freedom of the press and women's rights. After 2005, political rights were overtaken by the so-called basic needs of the people (op. cit.: 74).[27] Ahmadinejad's election is also claimed to have led to the disempowering of the intellectual elite. The neoconservatives adopted a 'Chinese model of development' and political debates over political rights, civil society and democracy were no longer seen as necessary (op. cit.: 88). The neoconservatives saw subjects such as democracy, civil society and women's rights as irrelevant for the *mustaz'afin* (the oppressed) and thus the need for an intellectual elite disappeared (op. cit.: 90). In general, Ahmadinejad's presidency brought a new political direction that focused on economic and social justice rather than political rights.

The neoconservative turn in politics brought about significant changes, as women's rights were no longer seen by the government as relevant. After 2005, the intentions for women were rather to bring them in line with the so-called 'principles' of the Islamic Republic (op. cit.: 88). Women's rights organisations and journals have been closed down and banned and women's rights activists are subject to surveillance and imprisonment. This increasingly conservative and harsh treatment has had unpredicted results. In response to the apparent crushing of women's rights activism, it has moved into new directions. During the 'Fourth' Republic, women's movements and activism have developed into campaigns that seek a broader basis than ever before. In particular, two changes have taken place since 2005. First, the attention in the 1990s to women and women's rights has diverted into an emphasis on the family and family issues. Second, new forms of women's rights activism have come to the fore.

One of the important changes was the renaming of the government's Centre for Women's Participation (*Markaz-e Mosharekat-e Zanan*). The

Centre was first established as the Women's Centre (*Markaz-e Zanan*) in the presidential office in 1988 during the presidency of Ayatollah Rafsanjani, and was later transformed into the Centre for Women's Participation in 1997 during Khatami's presidency. After Ahmadinejad's election it was renamed the Centre for Women's and Family Affairs (*Markaz-e Umur-e Zanan va Khanevadeh*). Thus, women are once again officially defined by their roles within the family. In spring 2006, Ahmadinejad appointed Zohreh Tabibzadeh Nouri as the Centre's new director. Under Nouri, its profile has changed even more. Previously, the Centre was active in promoting Iran's ratification of CEDAW. Shortly after her appointment, however, Nouri announced that Iran would not ratify CEDAW as long as she was in charge (Aftab News, 30 May 2007), although she did not deny that there were some 'gaps in the [Iranian] law when it comes to protection of women's rights'. She announced:

> As long as I live and remain in charge of this Centre, I will not let anyone sign international charters [or] declarations of international conferences on women's rights, since we can [fix] the gaps and existing problems through the Islamic faith. I see no reason to follow the unsuccessful western model. (ibid.)

Since 2005, several NGOs promoting women's rights have been closed down, and the control of women's rights activists has reached a new high.[28] In February 2008, the Iranian government shut down the women's journal *Zanan* after 16 years of publication. The closure was a watershed for women's rights activism in Iran, as the journal had vigorously advocated strategies of combining the discourses of women's rights and Islam (Najmabadi 2005). Now, the journal was accused of 'offering a dark picture of the Islamic Republic ... [and] compromising the psyche and mental health [by publishing] morally questionable information' (Learning Partnership website, 8 February 2008).

The increasingly harsh treatment of women's rights activists since 2005 has had unforeseen results. Activism has not ceased, but has taken new forms. On the one hand, there are women's organisations that comply with the policies of the neoconservative government, as represented by the Women's *Basij*, the female branch of Iran's paramilitary volunteer militia and 'morality police'. On the other hand, organisations and initiatives protesting the policies of the neoconservative government have emerged and represent new forms of activism. In between these two positions is the Zeynab Society (*Jam'e-ye Zeynab*), a conservative and loyalist women's rights group. It is headed by Maryam Behrouzi, and relies on definitions of women's rights that correspond to a Shi'a Islamic framework. The Zeynab Society is sometimes associated with Iran's neoconservative government, but at other times Behrouzi has spoken out against official policies on women's rights. In particular, she has participated in the debate over the content and revision of the Family Protection Bill, not always in support of the proposed amendments (FFL, 12 November 10).

The Women's branch of *Basij* deals specifically with women's issues.[29] According to its deputy head, Minoo Aslani, 3.6 million women have joined *Basij* nationwide and there were 350 female commanders in the Women's *Basij* Resistance Headquarters. Other sources report a substantially smaller number and point out that recruitment to *Basij* is often related to seeking job opportunities or university admission (Telegraph, 21 June 2009). The size and support of *Basij* is thus widely contested. The Islamic Republic News Agency (IRNA) reported in 2007 that the organisation had 12.5 million members, of which 5 million were women (IRNA, 26 November 2007). Despite disagreements about its size, Aslani has asserted that the Women's *Basij* is the largest women's organisation of the country and that one of its main responsibilities is to defend the ideals of the Islamic Revolution and ensure the continuity of Ayatollah Khamenei's instructions. She has stated that: 'Women *Basij* plays a crucial role in fulfilment of this cause. Becoming equipped with knowledge and scientific, cultural and political insight along with commitment, *Basij* helps thwart the enemies' plots' (Iran Daily, 30 December 2005).

A quite different form of women's rights activism has emerged with the One Million Signatures Campaign (OMSC).[30] On 8 March 2006, a number of women gathered in Daneshju-ye Park in Tehran,[31] to protest against what they saw as general discrimination against women in legislation. The police broke up the demonstration after a short time, and several protesters were beaten and arrested, including the famous writer and poet Simin Behbahani (Hoodfar 2009: 12). On 12 June 2006, over 1,000 women gathered in front of Tehran University to protest against laws they considered discriminatory towards women (Payvand, 13 June 2006). They had prepared posters with slogans like 'We women want our human rights' (*Ma zanan khahan hoqoq-e ensani hastim*), and chanted similar slogans. The police soon arrived and started to break up the demonstration by force. According to eyewitnesses, the police acted violently and arrested about 50 people, and there were also fights between women protestors and female police officers.[32]

In the following weeks, women's rights activists gathered to discuss the road ahead for women's rights activism. Their aim was to draw attention to the discriminatory laws and the recent change in policies towards women. These discussions led to the creation of the OMSC, which was officially launched on 27 August 2006,[33] during a seminar entitled: 'The Impact of Laws on Women's Lives' (Tohidi 2006). In its initial stage, the members of the OMSC were primarily occupied with gathering signatures, but over time they extended their activities. In spring 2008 one of their activists, Leyli, explained:

> When the campaign started we thought it would last two to five years. We wanted to present a bill and then end the campaign. But now we have started to see the real potential of the campaign. I therefore quit *Hastia*,[34] and now I use all my time on the campaign. It is always a major problem for NGOs to find a place and equipment, but in this campaign everything is so easy! Every week we have workshops and training of new members. Usually we meet in the homes of members in Tehran. Even housewives arrange these courses in their house! The solidarity of women in different cities is important. We have new groups, new programmes, and see new potentials all the time. (Interview with Leyli, May 2008)

The challenges confronting the OMSC were more complex, though, and the Leyli's story highlights the danger of being a women's rights activist:

> On 4 March last year [2007] we, a group of women, went to the trial of one of the women who was imprisoned on 22 *Khordad* [12 June]. We said that she was not alone, but that we were all responsible. All 33 women were arrested. I spent two days in prison. They told us that we could not have any demonstrations, but that we could work as a women's organisation. They asked no questions about the signatures. One month later two other women were arrested in *Park-e* Laleh. Then we first realised the importance of the campaign. [From then on] ... all mobile phones were watched and we lost many members. But then some new members also came. And we know we can trust them because they joined after the difficulties. Before maybe 40–50 people came to our meetings. It was difficult to have the meetings in our houses and we needed more room, but then the meetings would be so visible. We therefore started smaller groups. They do the same work, but they can still meet in people's houses. (Interview with Leyli, May 2008)

Most of the laws addressed by the OMSC are found in the Iranian Civil Code and pertain to marriage, divorce, custody rights, honour killings, age of criminal responsibility, blood money, citizenship, inheritance and bearing witness. The OMSC focuses on their discriminatory effects (Sign 4 Change website, 28 August 2006). For example, OMSC activists question a husband's permission to kill his wife if she commits adultery (Article 630 in the Iranian Penal Code), and that a woman is only recognised as a citizen after being married and becoming a mother. Similarly, the citizenship of a mother is not transferrable to the child, because the child's citizenship is decided by the father's nationality alone (Tohidi, 12 December 2007).[35]

Members of the OMSC whom I have met have focused on its broad support and that it was simple to run.[36] Shahla, one of the OMSC's founding members, said:

> First of all this is a strange campaign, but in a good sense. It is easy to organise, easy to participate in, and does not require a lot of economic support. And second, all the laws we want to change are basic laws. Everyone who supports equality will support our campaign. You can maybe see the difference betwen those who are very active and those who are not so active. Even women who cooperate with the government support the campaign. Two groups are against us: those who support the Republic. They say: 'You just oppose the Republic.' And those who are against the Republic, they say: 'You want this Republic and you just demand marginal changes. You don't want to change the Republic'. (Interview with Shahla, May 2008)

Shahla points to the opposition faced by the OMSC in Iran. Intriguingly, she asserts that the campaign is criticised both for opposing the Islamic Republic, and for not being oppositional enough. Generally, the OMSC can be said to present revisionist views on family law reform, and it is thus challenged by activists from both loyalist and rejectionist camps. It is also interesting to note that according to Shahla, the idea behind the OMSC originated in Morocco. In 1992, the Union de l'Action Feminin (UAF) launched a signatures campaign that contributed to the 2004 Moroccan family law reform (Mudawwana). When women's rights activists in Iran learned about the success of the Moroccan campaign, they decided to launch a similar one in Iran.

The OMSC consists of several sub-groups. Although the overall campaign claims to represent broad factions of women's rights activists and not to be linked to any political, religious, or ideological positionings, these sub-groups are founded on different criteria. One of them is *Madrese-ye Feministi* (Feminist School).[37] According to Shahla, one of the founders of the Feminist School, the various groups play an important role for the OMSC:

> Now we have different groups with different websites, which makes it difficult to monitor . . . I think the Feminist School is one of the campaigns biggest achievements. We represent common

points of view. No matter what will happen to the campaign this group will continue. (Interview with Shahla, May 2008)

Despite this claim that there are common points of view, there seems to be a clear difference between the profile of the OMSC and the Feminist School. Whereas the OMSC does not declare a 'feminist' stance and refers to 'equality' as a basis for their work, the Feminist School openly adheres to 'feminism' as a founding principle. The members I met did not want to focus on this. Shahla said: 'The Feminist School is a neutral group. We have different opinions, both religious and secular participants. And we do practical work, not theoretical' (Interview with Shahla, May 2008). The concept of 'feminism', however, denotes a clear position on women's rights. The Feminist School openly refers to European feminists such as Simone de Beauvoir, as well as to Iranian women's rights activists from the Pahlavi era like Mehrangiz Manoochehrian and Forough Farrokhzad (Feminist School website, 25 August 2008 and 29 December 2010). Such references are not explicitly made by the OMSC. Despite some variations, the Feminist School takes a clearer and more outspoken position on women's rights than the OMSC.

Another significant feature of women's rights activism during this period has been the emergence of ad hoc or issue-based campaigns. These have included demands for equal citizenship, changes in Iran's penal code, and women's access to public places. For example, the Campaign for the Nationality of Children addressed the Iranian Civil Code's ruling that the nationality of a child is passed on from the father. In recent years, many Iranian women marrying husbands of Afghan origin have suffered the consequences of this, as the child is restricted to Afghan nationality. The law is considered an example of women's second-class citizenship. Another initiative is the Campaign for Women's Access to Football Stadiums. Women have been banned from access to football arenas since 1979. Despite some attempts to reduce the restrictions by allowing women to attend if accompanied by their families, or permitting the access of foreign female football fans, the prohibition still exists. Iranian female football fans consider this ban yet further proof of the everyday discrimination against women. Since 2005, women's rights activists have campaigned to repeal this prohibition by demonstrating and 'breaking into' stadiums during matches. Despite signs of success in 2006 when Ahmadinejad announced the repeal of the ban (which was later overruled by Khamenei), the campaign has so far been unsuccessful.

According to Hoodfar, the many campaigns initiated since 2005 show that no single 'correct strategy' existed (Hoodfar 2009: 10). What the ad hoc campaigns have in common, however, is, first, they take on very specific cases of discrimination against women. Second, they often emerge in reaction to a proposed amendment or situation that women's rights activists see as discriminatory towards women. Third, many of them relate to legal discrimination and require a high degree of legal knowledge. All the campaigns have been launched under the heading of the OMSC.

The Stop Stoning Campaign represents an issue-based campaign that takes on both the subject of stoning in the Iranian penal code and a specific case where the stoning penalty was applied. In spring 2006, news spread about a man and a woman being stoned to death in Mashhad. Mahboubeh and 'Abbas had been accused of adultery and sentenced to stoning. According to Shadi Sadr, the initiator of the Stop Stoning Campaign, no Iranian newspaper reported the case because it was considered taboo to talk about stoning or to write about it would be extremely risky for journalists and editors (Sadr 2010). In the Iranian Penal Code (Article 83) it is stated that adultery is to be punished by flogging or stoning. Sadr, however, notes that:

> Although stoning exists as a punitive act in the rules and regulations of Iran, governmental authorities announced that the judiciary had stayed the enforcement of the 'stoning' execution as a death penalty while in Human Rights negotiations with the European Union in 2002. (Sadr 2007: 2)

Thus, it came as quite a shock to Sadr and other lawyers when they discovered that the application of stoning for adultery was increasing in Iran. The Stop Stoning Campaign was then established by a group of women's rights activists and, together with the Volunteer Lawyers

Network, they discovered that a total of 11 women had been sentenced to stoning in recent years (op. cit.: 4). The campaign has worked mainly to collect signatures against this form of punishment and to raise international awareness about it. The activists have also drawn attention to the gendered dimension of the punishment of stoning and elaborated on how women, due to their general position in family law, are more likely to receive sentences of stoning for adultery than men. Sadr writes that 'If women had the right to divorce they would never betray their husbands or kill them and then wait to be stoned' (ibid.). The campaign has thus focused on the complex legal situation of women and how it results in gender-based punishments, for which they see no legal basis in the Qur'an.

The punishment of stoning for adultery has gained increasing international attention in the past few years. In 2010, the story of Sakineh Ashtiani, who was sentenced to stoning for committing adultery and murder, received massive coverage in the world media. The sentence against Ashtiani was suspended in 2010 and the Iranian media reported that her case would be reviewed at a later stage (Press TV, 29 August 2010). The case of Ashtiani has illustrated that international attention drawn to a case by the Stop Stoning Campaign, among other initiatives on issues like stoning, can have an impact, and also that stoning sentences are not always carried out.

Another initiative, run by different women's rights activists, is Towards a Fair Family Law (*Ta Qanun-e Khanevadeh-ye Barabari*).[38] This project is also affiliated to the OMSC and the Feminist School. Towards a Fair Family Law consists primarily of a website that collects and publishes articles, analysis and news about the Family Protection Bill. Coalitions of women's rights groups that oppose the Family Protection Bill and work in favour of 'women's human rights' (*hoqoq-e ensani-ye zanan*) and 'gender equality' (*barabar-e jensiati*) also publish articles and reports on the website.

Changes and continuities

Although women's rights activism in Iran has existed in quite different political periods, several connections may be found in the kinds of activism and activities. It is striking, in fact, that there seem to be more continuities and similarities than differences throughout very diverse phases of Iranian history. Generally speaking, women's rights activists have published designated women's journals, taken part in official legal debates and had links to the broader international debates on women's rights throughout the different periods. Moreover, the awareness of and aspirations to address family law issues have been persistent. Although political limitations have been imposed on such debates both under the Pahlavi dynasty and the Islamic Republic, the debates have not ended but have rather been adjusted to contemporary circumstances and taken on new forms and directions.

In this regard, however, there is a noteworthy shift to be found in the kinds of people involved in women's rights activism in Iran now and before. Until quite recently, it has been a more or less elite phenomenon involving mostly women from the bigger cities, often educated abroad, and coming from the upper strata of society and from renowned political families. Since 2005, however, a new kind of women's rights activist has appeared. With the many ad hoc campaigns launched after 2005, the new women's rights activist tends to be younger, often a student at an Iranian university, either male or female, and often originating from a rural area and from the lower or middle social strata. These differences were obvious among the younger and older activists interviewed for this study, and are significant features among women's rights activists in Iran more generally.

Women's rights activism in Iran has developed from the context of constitutionalism and nationalism in the early 1900s, to the context of the Islamic Republic of Iran since 1979. Moreover, it has moved from state opposition to state dependency throughout different periods. The activism has been progressively more religiously oriented. Contemporary activism, however, is not confined to either religious or secular frames of references. An interesting aspect is the continuing coexistence of both secular and religious-oriented women's rights activism since the early 1900s. Muslim women's rights activism is often depicted as a uniform group representing unanimous claims on what the combination of Islam and women's rights should entail, sometimes under the label of 'Islamic feminism'. Margot Badran has expressed concern over the promotion of a 'holistic Muslim feminist project', which in her opinion may lead to an exclusionary identity politics (Badran 2011: 82–4). Based on the present study, I share Badran's concern. There is a risk of ignoring both rejectionist and loyalist women's rights activism when promoting the 'Islamic feminist' project in Iran. To present a homogenous form of Iranian women's rights activism under the label 'Islamic feminism' not only disregards the complexities that have characterised both its past and present forms, but may also set normative guidelines for what kind of women's rights activism may exist and develop in contemporary Iran.

CHAPTER 7

SHIFTING PARADIGMS ON GENDER AND SEXUALITY

The debate over issues on family law – and thus on women's rights and Shari'a – has been persistent throughout the modern history of Iran. Sigificant to these debates have been topics of gender and sexuality. The ways underlying paradigms of genderhood and sexuality have been constructed, negotiated and transformed throughout Iran's modern history are presented in the following.

Towards heteronormative monogamy

In the early 1900s, the Constitutional Revolution and the drafts of both the first Constitution of Iran in 1906 and the Iranian Civil Code in 1928 contributed to alter the character of the country from the period of the Qajar dynasty (1794–1925).[1] During the Pahlavi era (1925–79), steps towards codified heteronormative monogamy took place that had a particular effect on gender relations and sexuality. The 1931 Marriage Law introduced registration of all marriages in courts and enabled women to initiate divorce proceedings in civil courts. Consequently, the practice of arranged marriages declined and young people increasingly took part in choosing their own spouses.

During the Qajar period, the practices of having multiple wives (polygynous and temporary marriages) and keeping boy concubines were common among men from the upper class (Afary 2009: 8). Despite religious prohibitions, homosexuality was a fairly common, but discreet practice (op. cit.: 14). The early Qajar era had a different conception of gender and sexuality. In the book *Women with Mustaches and Men without Beards* (2005), Afsaneh Najmabadi shows how notions of beauty during the Qajar dynasty were not based on gender differentiation, at least among the upper classes. The markers of female and male beauty were not constructed in binary opposition, but rather represented ideals of beauty that blurred the male/female dichotomy. Carla Serena, an Italian woman who travelled in Iran in the late 1800s, wrote about her experience when invited to dinner by the Qajar Princess 'Esmat al-Dawlah in 1877:

> The princess expressed interest in making me up... First she covered my eyebrows across the forehead with mascara and turned each of them into a bow-shape, then she dyed my eyelashes, covered my cheeks with white powder and red blush, and finally made my lips red without forgetting to draw a thin shade of a mustache over my lips, which is apparently considered one of the beauty marks for an Iranian woman's face. (op. cit.: 232)

As this story implies, portraits of hairy women with moustaches and Qajar kings showing off their slim waists were perceived as symbols of beauty among the upper classes (op. cit.: 59). Consequently, femininity and masculinity were not perceived as binary oppositions of beauty, but men and women were portrayed with very similar facial and bodily features (op. cit.: 59).[2] Within a short period of time, however, female beauty as expressed through a moustache was transformed. Najmabadi places the shift of the moustache as a mark of beauty and femininity into a mark of female ugliness and masculinity at the end of the Qajar era in the early 1920s (op. cit.: 232). At the same time, sexual politics in Iran in the nineteenth century developed into a 'heteronormalisation of love' that would ultimately come to signify modern Iran and also women's emancipation projects (op. cit.: 7).

Increasingly during Pahlavi rule, support for formal polygyny and status-defined homosexuality declined and heterosexual monogamy became the new norm (Afary 2009: 9). This corresponded with broader steps towards a modernisation of society, and between 1936 and 1941 the Pahlavi state also enforced unveiling (op. cit.: 13). Both women and men were encouraged to wear 'European-style' clothing, and it is said that hats were the only headgear allowed. In terms of family policies, a major change was enforced as part of the White Revolution initiated by Muhammad Reza Shah in 1963. In general, these reforms introduced two major changes that affected gender relations and sexuality. First, with the ratification of the Family Protection Law in 1967, polygyny and men's unilateral right to divorce (*talaq*) was restricted. The 1975 amendments to this law also brought increased rights for women to have custody of children. Second, the law introduced monogamy, heterosexuality and companionate marriage as norms for sexual relations. Increasingly during the Pahlavi period, support for formal polygyny and status-defined homosexuality declined, and heterosexual monogamy became established as the new norm (ibid.).

The Pahlavi project of establishing a modern Iran was mainly conducted from above. The increased rights for women were introduced without the direct influence of the already established women's movement. Under the Pahlavis strict censorship was enforced. The restrictions also affected women's organisations and a period of assimilation of women's issues began (Sanasarian 1982: 78–9), as described in the previous chapter.

Encouraging heteronormative polygyny

During the late 1960s and early 1970s, the policies initiated by Muhammad Reza Shah as part of the White Revolution divided the Iranian people. According to the historian Nikkie R. Keddie, the Iranian population was separated by a 'two-culture' system represented by a secular-oriented, educated middle and upper class and a religious, pious and uneducated *bazari*[3] class (Keddie 2003: 102). These two cultures represented quite different perceptions of gender relations, and the differences between them became increasingly visible with regard to implementation of the Family Protection Law in 1967. Whereas the upper and middle classes mainly supported the reforms, the *bazaris* by and large were sceptical of the imposed changes. The core of the conflict was the law's compatibility with the principles of Shari'a. After the 1979 Revolution, policies on gender again shifted. The Family Protection Law was abolished, and policies seen as consistent with an Islamic Republic and principles of Shari'a, such as child marriages, polygynous and temporary marriages, were again enforced. Furthermore, new restrictions and harsh punishments with regard to homosexuality were introduced.[4] Thus, the new policies on gender and sexuality in the Islamic Republic maintained the hetero-normative character of marriage, but represented a change with regard to encouragement of polygynous and temporary marriages. Furthermore, the state attempted to reverse contemporary trends in love and marriage such as dating and companionship that were seen as expressions of 'western modernity' (Afary 2009: 12).

Universalisation of marriage

Since 1979, the Iran is said to have hosted one of the most successful family planning programmes in the non-western world (Hoodfar 2008: 80). Family planning policies have, however, gone through different stages. Different socioeconomic factors have led to a revision of their religious and political justifications and content. In the early phase of the Islamic Republic and during the Iran–Iraq war (1980–88), new policies were established. The sociologist Parvin Paidar has claimed that the Islamic Republic introduced a policy of 'universalisation of marriage' after 1979, as attempts were made to extend the legal boundaries of marriage to the furthest extent possible in Islam (1995: 282). The policies of 'universalisation of marriage' involved clear-cut gender roles. During the Iran–Iraq war, the official state rhetoric referred to men as martyrs and to women as mothers, with references to the history of Shi'a Islam and to the day of 'Ashura' in particular (Afshar 1998: 120–1 and Moallem 2005:

Chapter 3).[5] Consequently, the dichotomy of martyrdom and motherhood led to discourses of masculinity and femininity, and in the early days of the Islamic Republic the state discourse on gender had clear references to these binary gender roles as a foundational element of the nation.

In the 1980s, a new challenge emerged in the high number of widows because of the growing number of fallen soldiers in the Iraq–Iran war. The widows of the war martyrs were classified as 'unprotected' and viewed as a 'social problem' that the state had to solve. It was thus seen as necessary for widows of martyrs to remarry fast and continue to reproduce in accordance with their primary role as mothers (Afshar 1998: 122). Although the problem of widows was increasing, the '"problem" of single girls' was seen as even worse. Ayatollah Rafsanjani[6] referred to the phenomenon of unmarried women as 'western-style urban depravity' (ibid.). Because family and motherhood was considered to represent the centres of nationhood, the increasing numbers of single and unmarried women challenged the foundations of the Islamic Republic. The solution offered by the? state was to encourage women either to marry disabled war veterans, or to engage in polygynous or temporary marriages. The government encouraged small dowers in order for men to be able to engage in polygynous marriages, and referred to religious rhetoric claiming it was a man's duty to do so. On the same lines, temporary marriages were encouraged as a means of providing for widows and single women. For instance, the opinion of Ayatollah Motahhari, who once claimed that polygyny was a 'social necessity', was invoked (op. cit.: Chapter 8).

Returning to heteronormative monogamy

In turn, however, the 'universalisation of marriage' led to a social crisis within a few years as the population growth rate increased and the economy stagnated. The problems of the dramatic population growth and its political effects reopened the debate on polygynous marriages and also on abortion during the second phase of the Islamic Republic (1989–97). In due course, the official attitude towards polygynous marriages shifted in favour of restriction as soon as the government became aware of the problems of family planning and population control (Paidar 1995: 285). As Paidar notes, 'once again economic and political imperatives defined which practices in relation to the family were or were not acceptable "Islamic"' (op. cit.: 289).

During the late 1990s, state policies towards gender and sexuality once again underwent changes. Although Iran is often portrayed as a static and conservative Muslim society unable to adapt to social changes, there have been noticeable demographic, social and cultural shifts over recent decades (Abbasi-Shavazi et al. 2008: 217–18). For instance, improvements in literacy and education (for women in particular) have been associated with larger transformations of family life (ibid.).[7] A shift in gender policies was introduced with the election of Seyyed Muhammad Khatami to the presidency in 1997. Iran now experienced an opening up of civil society, and the question of women's rights was intensely debated both in the Majles and in public. In turn, the new policies gave women new roles and opportunities for social, cultural, religious, educational and political participation (Keddie 2003 and Mehran 2003). These led to greater changes in society with regard to sexuality and genderhood more generally. Young couples' expectations of marriage changed gradually, moving from dependence on parental approval towards love-defined relationships (Afary 2009: 326). Dating and cross-sex friendships became more common, and Valentine's Day, for instance became an increasingly popular celebration among many young couples, and also signified more openness to the West (ibid.).

Ambiguous policies on sexuality

The broader discourses on gender relations are also visible in the perception of different sexualities. Sex reassignment surgeries are allowed and frequently carried out. The background to their religious legitimation is significant with regard to how sexuality is treated in Shi'a Islamic legal theology. Homosexuality in Iran is considered *zina* (unlawful sexual intercourse) and is punishable by death. Transsexuality, however, is perceived differently. Sex reassignment surgeries are even encouraged. The idea is that people can be born with a 'wrong' sex, in which case it is recommended that the person undergo surgery rather than be 'caught in the wrong body'. Interestingly, Ayatollah Khomeini published a book on the issue of transsexuality in 1963, and in 1987 issued a fatwa based on the case of Maryam Khatoon Molkara[8] endorsing sex reassignment surgery

The documentary film *Be Like Others* portrays how the practice is legitimised in Shi'a jurisprudence (Eshaghian 2008). According to *Hojatul* Kariminia, a Shi'a *'alim* (a religious scholar),[9] the issue poses no problems in Shi'a Islamic jurisprudence. In the film, he compares the process of transforming one sex into another to making a chair or a table from a piece of wood. The operation involves only one simple change. Similar changes are made all the time and therefore 'it is not illegal' (*haram nist*), he asserts.

Sex reassignment surgeries can help transsexual people in need of a sex-affirming operation. The reasoning behind their religious legitimation, however, projects condemnatory views on sexuality. The surgeries are justified as a means of altering the genitalia of those who feel they have been born with a 'wrong' body. Consequently, the operations strengthen the view that sexualities other than heterosexuality and the male/female sex division are abnormal and must be overcome. In *Be Like Others*, we follow the destiny of some young men who might have settled for being 'just' homosexuals if it had been an alternative. Living in Iran, however, offers them few options other than going through sex reassignment surgeries, because practicing homosexuality is punishable by death. The state policy towards transsexuality thus contributes to reinforcing heteronormative views on sexuality by eradicating all other forms as *haram* (forbidden). Yet, despite the strict legal punishment for homosexuality, the perception of same-sex relations has been ambiguous. Minoo Moallem notes that a homosocial world was in effect normalised during the Iran–Iraq war in the 1980s. She writes that 'The war zone is a place between life and death, a land without women, enabling the expression of homoerotic desire. In this homosocial world, men live without women, enabling the expression of homoerotic desire' (2005: 115).

Moreover, Janet Afary affirms that homosocial expressions of love were also allowed outside the battlefield (2009: 289). In Iran, it is quite common to see boys holding hands and kissing each other on the streets and the same goes for girls. Many of these relationships may work as a kind of substitute for heterosexual relationships. Afary also argues that the state policies on sexuality promote gender hierarchical relationships:

> In matters of sexuality (both heterosexual and homosexual), the Islamist state rejected many modern gender constructs but endured and often encouraged other, premodern ones. Polygamy, temporary marriage, and covert sexuality – that is, hierarchical social relations where one partner is subservient to the other – were allowed and ... promoted, while more egalitarian heterosexual or homosexual relations (feminist and gay/lesbian rights) were pushed back. (2009: 290)

Policies towards sexual differences have thus been somewhat ambiguous. Although secret homosexual relationships and the existence of transsexuals (as long as they are willing to undergo surgery) have been accepted, official policies still promote and accommodate heteronormative and gender hierarchical relationships.

A new direction in the politics of gender and sexuality

In a speech at Columbia University in New York in September 2007, President Ahmadinejad stated that 'In Iran, we don't have homosexuals like you do in your country.' These words not only brought attention to his rejectionist attitudes towards homosexuality, but also signified a shift in policies on gender and sexuality that emerged after he came to power in 2005. This change echoed the early principlist (*usual garan*) policies (referring to the principles of Ayatollah Khomeini) enforced in the first phase of the Islamic Republic, when a policy of 'universalisation of marriage' prevailed. Once more, polygyny and temporary marriage were encouraged, discourses on martyrdom and motherhood reappeared, there was an increased focus on the collectivity versus the individual, and an upsurge in gender segregation and stricter dress codes took place.

Elections in the late 1990s changed the political climate and laid the ground for an imbalance of power between so-called traditional conservatives, neoconservatives and reformists (Etheshami and Zweiri 2007: 33).[10] The terms 'reformist' and 'conservative' are not all-embracing, but are starting points for understanding the polarisations in Iranian politics. 'Reformist' refers to sympathisers with Khatami, who sought to introduce changes mainly with regard to democracy, a more open civil society and increase in women's and human rights. The label 'conservative' can be divided into two branches – traditional conservatives and neoconservatives. A distinction between these can be traced to the municipal elections in 2003. According to Etheshami and Zweiri, the neoconservatives at this point 'had found a new rallying cry: economic justice – one that resonated favourably with the masses' (op. cit.: xv). The differences between them and the traditional conservatives are, first, that the neoconservatives, led by Ahmadinejad, prioritise the needs of the impoverished masses in order to win back their political support, and focus on social justice and the welfare of the oppressed masses (*mustaz'afin umma*) (op. cit.: 45–6). Second, the neoconservatives want a more interventionist state, while the traditional conservatives favour a more 'privatised' state.

The neoconservative turn in Iranian politics was illustrated in *Letters to the President*, a documentary by Petr Lom from 2009. A film crew follows Ahmadinejad in his presidential election campaign of that year. Many people lined up to talk to him on his day trips to the country and wanted to meet him personally, but most passed on letters to him in which they express their needs for financial or medical help. In the film, Ahmadinejad has a team of mainly female *Basiji* members who read and handle the requests. According to the documentary, the neoconservative government openly called for people to send such letters to Ahmadinejad, but of course the demands for help exceeded the available means, and people tell the film crew how their cries for help were left unanswered. The documentary demonstrates the populist aspect of Ahmadinejad's election campaign, the class differences in the Iranian population and the problems of poverty and rising inflation.

Another division that became evident in the 2009 presidential election campaign was between two kinds of principlists. On the one hand, the hardline principlists believe that the only future for the Islamic Republic is in following the original principles of Ayatollah Khomeini. On the other hand, the reformist principlists assert that the principles of 1979 must be reformed and adapted to current needs. Ahmadinejad belongs to the first camp and Mir-Hossein Mousavi and Hassan Rouhani – who was elected president in June 2013 – to the latter. All of them support the principles of the Islamic Republic, but represent different solutions for adjusting to today's Iranian society.

During Ahmedinejad's first presidency (2005–9) there was growing discontent among both reformists and traditional conservatives. His opponents criticised him for spending too much time confronting the United States and Israel, and too little on fixing Iran's inflation and deteriorating economy. This reached its peak in the 2009 elections. Although Ahmadinejad was officially declared the winner, masses of people took to the streets of and challenged the results as fraudulent. Many of the protesters were women. Neda Agha-Soltan, who was shot dead in the street during a protest, became a symbol of the Green Movement (Jombesh-e Sabz), which had emerged during the 2009 protests. Neda's death was filmed and the video went viral and spread internationally. She was declared a martyr by election protestors for sacrificing her life in the demonstrations (Bøe, 25 June 2009, Erdbrink and Branigin, 27 June 2009, and Strobel-Dahan, 23 June 2009).

As mentioned, 'principlist' refers to a political position advocating a return to the principles of Ayatollah Khomeini and the early Islamic Republic. After returning to power in 2005, the neoconservatives brought in significant changes to policies on women's rights in particular. Whereas the question of women's rights had been highly debated both in the Majles and in public during the presidency of Khatami (1997–2005), the neoconservative government no longer saw the subject as relevant. Lip-service to women's important role continued to be made, but it was gradually transformed into the issue of the wellbeing of the family. In addition, Ahmadinejad resumed the previous rhetoric of the Islamic Republic by referring to martyrdom as a foundation of the nation (Tabnak, 24 April 2008). Thus, there were signs that the dichotomy of martyrdom and motherhood had reappeared, along with discourses of masculinity and femininity that had been used in the early phase of the Islamic Republic. Ahmadinejad also recalled Shi'a rhetoric by stating that the real ruler of Iran was the Twelfth Imam (Vali Nasr 2007: 133–4). Unlike Khomeini, who was seen as adapting Shi'ism towards Sunnism, Ahmadinejad's policies helped to underscore a Shi'a revival. Thus, Ahmadinejad not only attracted voters who felt deeply attached to the core values and piety of Shi'ism, but he stressed the difference between Sunnism and Shi'ism in promoting Iran's position (op. cit.: 225–6). The differences between different branches in Iranian politics serve to illustrate that it does not consist of singular authorities and cannot be considered one-dimensional. Instead, it constantly changes in accordance with the influence of various participants. The direction that President Rouhani will choose remains to be seen, but as long as Ayatollah Khamenei remains as Supreme Leader no substantial changes are likely to occur.

In 2006, new policies on gender, new policies on dress codes were implemented. Although Islamic dress codes had been adopted after the 1979 Revolution, compliance had varied at different times. During the 1990s, the reformist turn in Iranian politics brought signs of a more relaxed attitude, but after 2005 dress codes were again enforced. A new law on them was approved by the Majles in May 2006. It stated that the government, the private sector and Iranian society in general must uphold Islamic morals by implementing dress codes for both men and women (Boghrati, 2 May 2006). In April 2006, Mortazee Tala'e, the police chief of Tehran, is reported to have said that police officers would deal with those who did not comply with 'the Islamic dressing values'. The 'non-compliants' who wore short or tight *manteau* (coat), *bad-hejabi*, capri pants, or those who refused to wear socks in public would be 'confronted' (ibid.).

The restrictions imposed in recent years not only addressed women's clothing. In 2010, the Department of Culture introduced new guidelines for men's hairstyles (Norwegian Broadcasting Corporation, NRK, 6 July 2010). Several hairstyles were suggested in the new state-approved guidelines, which were said to be inspired by 'Iranians' facial colour, culture, religion, and Islamic law' (ibid.). Among those disapproved were, for instance, ponytails. Men's creative hairstyles have been under attack in recent years in Tehran in particular, and in the summer of 2008 I heard stories of young men being forced by the morality police to soak their hair in buckets of water in order to remove styling products.

In addition, new steps towards enforcing gender segregation have been implemented since 2005. Laleh Eftekhari, a member of the seventh Majles, stated in 2008:

> Gender separation in public places, including offices, parks, cinema theatres, trains, elevators, universities and other public places to protect women is implementable. This type of separation is part of Ahmadinejad's cultural policy which is viewed as the most important element in public demands. (Roozonline, 18.8.08)

One example was the establishment of a park for women only in Iran's capital. During the summer of 2008, Tehran's Mayor Qalibaf opened this park, which was given the fine-sounding name of *Behesht-e Madaran* (The Heaven of Mothers). The park is reserved for women, where they are allowed to cycle, jog and play tennis without hejab. Tall green fences prevent men from looking in and visitors are not allowed to bring cameras or mobile phones into the park. It was an attempt to ease women's lack of freedom to be outside without hejab and to exercise in a public place, and similar parks followed in other cities. Nevertheless, gender segregation remains very visible in Iran. Men and women are allocated separate zones in the metro and in buses, and there are designated workout centres for men and women. A few years ago women-only taxis were introduced, although most women in Tehran still squeeze into the backseat of a *dar bas* (open and shared taxi), which is cheaper than the private ones.

The paradigms of gender relations and sexuality in Iran's recent history have shifted between projecting heteronormative monogamy and polygyny, as well as ambiguous policies on sexuality. Models of genderhood are highly contested issues. Although the paradigms on gender and sexuality do not represent linear developments, they have been part of larger state projects at the time. Women's rights activists have been active in constructing, maintaining and negotiating official paradigms for women's rights and womanhood, and we have seen the ways in which concepts of gender, nation and religion are closely interlinked. The quest for genderhood in Iran's contemporary history can thus be conceptualised within the framework of religion and nation.

Family law is a key in this intersectional relationship. Suad Joseph has defined family law as a main site of dispute in the making of state and nation (2000: 20). Not only that, but legislation pertaining to personal status and family law is often seen as the last bastion of Shari'a. While other areas such as penal and economic law have been reformed and codified in most Muslim majority countries, family law often remains the sole area of legislation controlled by *ulama* and the principles of Shari'a. Family law involves regulating gender relations and sexuality. Through rulings on marriage, divorce, inheritance and custody of children, it remains a major symbol of how gender relations and sexuality are defined. In Iran, family law and models of genderhood have emerged as primary parameters of not only national identity, but also of the 'Islamicness' and 'authenticity' of various state projects.

CHAPTER 8

SOURCES OF LEGITIMACY

Family law is a divisive topic that attracts wide public attention in Iran. A vast number of participants take part in these discussions, including religious scholars, politicians and women's rights activists, but the positions clearly differ. They represent different degrees of authority in the debate depending on factors such as gender, social status, political affiliation and religious proximity. Accordingly, their respective arguments have different kinds of legitimacy. Rather than measuring the actual level of legitimacy and authority gained by the diverse women's rights activists, attention in this chapter will be on the sources of legitimacy they use.

'The new Muslim woman'

Codifications of family law in Iran have meant an ongoing search for models of genderhood and have had particular consequences for what is considered the ideal womanhood. The Islamic Republic is known to uphold an ideal model of a woman who is both active in society and maintains a central role in the family as mother, daughter and wife – referred to as 'The new Muslim woman' (Mehran 2003: 273). This ideal model corresponds to the dual call of maintaining both women's rights and Shari'a in family law codifications. The tension between these two demands, however, is not easily resolvable and remains a tug-of-war at the heart of family law debates.

Several of the interviewees referred to the project of defining genderhood that was conducted after the revolution in 1979. Two of them described a contemporary model of womanhood. Maryam portrayed women in Iran as 'projectors of Islamic values' but emhasised their diversity:

> Despite the image many people from the West have of Iranian women, all they have in common is the way they dress. Iranian women are as diverse as Iran itself. They have different ideologies, different cultures and backgrounds. But they have one other thing in common: namely the power of command. They are all powerful and demand their rights. Contrary to women in Afghanistan and Iraq for example, Iranian women are not invisible. In Palestine for example, you never see any women throwing stones or demonstrating, but in Iran it is different. Women are always participating and are very visible. (Interview with Maryam, March 2009)

Maryam sees Iranian women as active, powerful and visible, in contrast to women in other predominantly Muslim countries. Minoo takes a different approach to women's rights and family law and says that Iranian women require their own solution:

> I am first and foremost a nationalist. My country comes first and I am very proud of my country. We can find a solution for our women. But it takes time. Before we would take one step forward and two [steps back]. Now we move one forward and one back, but we keep what we have achieved. In the future I hope we will move two [steps] forward and one back and gradually reach our goal. We must first agree on what we want and how we want to achieve it. But I am optimistic about the future of Iranian women. Just look at the universities; who do you think will rule the country in the future? (Interview Minoo, May 2008)

Maryam and Minoo represent a loyalist and a revisionist perspective on family law. Nevertheless, they both refer to notions of the Iranian woman in which they see Iranian-ness as intrinsic to the future of family law in Iran. They seem to agree that there is a common sense of nation that unites 'Iranian women'.

Sources of legitimacy that are quintessentially Iranian form the basis of and justification for the concepts of Shari'a and women's rights used by the women's rights activists interviewed for this book. Such forms of justification can be seen as an expression of *Iraniyat* (Iran's cultural and historical heritage). Shabnam J. Holliday maintains that the concepts of *Iraniyat*, *Islamiyat* (Islamic culture and heritage) and *gharbzadegi* (westoxification) lie at the heart of identity in contemporary Iran (2011). The construction of these, however, is subject to dispute. In particular, the formation of *Islamiyat* and *Iraniyat* has been contentious throughout Iran's history.[1] As Holliday notes: 'The cause for contestation with regard to how Iranian national identity should be constructed is what is considered to be authentic and legitimate, also contested, and how it is justified' (op. cit.: 2). Although some prioritise one concept over the other in their understanding of what is authentic and legitimate, both concepts are fundamental elements in contemporary Iranian identity. Accordingly, *Iraniyat*, *Islamiyat* and *gharbzadegi* are to be seen as shifting and contested issues.

The new models of genderhood after 1979 were based on the ideas of influential figures such as Ayatollah Khomeini and 'Ali Shari'ati. The content of these models has, however, been subject to negotiations, continuation and disputes, particularly in relation to the family law debate. Ayatollah Khomeini, however, still appears to hold a favoured position among some of the women's rights activists. Arezoo, for instance, referred to Khomeini as a guiding star for women, and explained:

> After the revolution there has been a change in a way of thinking about women. Ayatollah Khomeini believes that ... He looks at the issues of women, Islam and religion in another way, different from the religious thinkers before the revolution; I mean the clerics and also the authorities in the Shah's regime.

> If you can follow what Ayatollah Khomeini said about women, then there is progress and advancement for women. (Interview with Arezoo, November 2002)

In general, Arezoo presented a revisionist approach to family law, stressing in particular the need to distinguish Khomeini's teachings on family law from previous codifications. She said:

> Before the revolution women were discriminated because of certain laws. For example men could get divorce without the permission of the woman or a judge, or an office that registers marriages and divorce. When the revolution happened, the past 20 years, there is always a changing look towards the civil law and there is a lot of endeavour to change the law. For example, Ayatollah Khomeini had a better attitude towards women's issues in jurisprudence. (Interview with Arezoo, November 2002)

In claiming that the position of women has improved since 1979, Areoo mentioned the 1982 amendments to marriage contracts and the 1997 Family Courts Law. She argued that since 1979 a new approach towards Islam has been adopted that is suitable for the contemporary needs of society:

> Islam is not a reactionary religion; it is a religion of all ages with a lot of potential that can make it change according to the necessities of time and place. That is why there are a lot of endeavours from the religious elites. They would like to reform the situation according to a new approach to Islam. New thinking is what it is called. Since the revolution there has been a change in the way of thinking about women. (Interview with Arezoo, November 2002)

'The new religious thinking' (*now-ye andishi-ye dini*) that Arezoo refers to is the renewed perspective towards Islamic jurisprudence that developed in Shi'i legal theology after 1979, particularly during the 1990s in Iran (Mir-Hosseini 2006). It draws on the work, for instance, of Ayatollah Morteza Motahhari, who spoke of gender equality in terms of what he describes as innate and conventional gender differences (Halper 2005: 134). The former are expressed in the Qur'an and in the family, whereas the latter are evident in society. Motahhari states that some innate differences are part of the unchangeable nature of Islam, but conventional differences can be subject to reform and transformation. His ideas have formed the basis for the official discourse on gender in the Islamic Republic (Mir-Hosseini 2000a: 19). His view on polygyny, for example, has been challenged in revisionist approaches that seek to prove that the practice is unsuitable for contemporary Iranian society (FFL, 23 September 2010). Arezoo, though, highlights Motahhari's perspective on Shari'a, which according to her contains possibilities for reform of women's rights, and for family law more generally. On this basis, there are signs of established religious authorities being both referred to and disregarded in order to justify family law amendments.

The political scientist Fatemeh Sadeghi has drawn on the writings of 'Ali Shari'ati for the contemporary debate on family law legislation. In a paper presented at the Sociology Association's conference, entitled 'Doctor Shari'ati's relationship with women in Iran today' (Fair Family Law, 21 June 2011), Sadeghi asserts that even though Shari'ati is a controversial figure, some of his ideas are still inspiring for women in contemporary Iran. She elaborates on Shari'ati's impact on 'our mothers and sisters' and considers his highly ideological writings to constitute a considerable part of the history of Iran because they inspired women to take to the streets in 1979 (ibid.). Thus, Shari'ati is an important part of Iran's inheritance. Sadeghi further claims that whereas many intellectuals and religious scholars are silent on the subject of gender, Shari'ati is one who has directly addressed the situation of women. On this basis, she calls for a critical dialogue with his writings and ideas: 'because he has affected us whether we approve or reject him' (ibid.). Sadeghi does not relate Shari'ati directly to Islam or to aspects of *Islamiyat*, but tends to connect his writings to the historical heritage of Iran and to addressing the position of women within the framework of national identity (*Iraniyat*).

Shari'ati's writings on Fatemeh Zahra, for instance, have clear links to Shi'i Islamic history and this has been pointed out by other women's rights activists. In an article in the journal *Farzaneh,* Monir Gorji and Massmoumeh Ebtekar elaborate on why they think Fatemeh Zahra provides an excellent model for womanhood (1997). They stress that Fatemeh Zahra, according to Shari'ati's depiction, symbolises morals and strength, and her role as a politically active woman is of particular importance. Gorji and Ebtekar refer to her as 'the leader of the world's women' and for them she serves as a good role model with regard to the rights, roles and status that a Muslim woman can achieve (ibid.).

Laleh Eftekhari is another example of defining a model for womanhood firmly within Shi'a Islamic history. Eftekhari, an Iranian MP and loyalist women's rights activist, has emphasised the role of Fatemeh Zahra and Zeynab for Muslim women today.[2] She said: 'The figures such as *Hazrat* Zeynab are the paradigms for all Muslim women around the world, especially at this time when the role of women is getting more and more obvious than before' (Rohama, 6 April 2011). In her opinion, Fatemeh and Zeynab are more appropriate role models than the one provided by 'some conventions about women that have been signed till now but these conventions cannot meet women's needs' (ibid.). The conventions that Eftekhari has in mind are probably first and foremost CEDAW, which she considers unsuitable for Muslim women, because it and other conventions 'obviate women's needs and the only thing they do is that they make them tired of the modern ignorance' (ibid.). Instead, she points to role models in Shi'a Islamic history. Eftekhari contrasted the role models provided by Shi'a Islam to those, for instance, of western role models, and said: 'Women in Islam have an important role and Islam defines specific roles for them ... but unfortunately western and Zionist media turn woman into an instrument and tool' (ibid.). She also suggested that Muslim women follow the suggestions and guidance provided by the current *velayat-e faqih*, Ayatollah Khamenei.

Eftekhari's references are thus in line with the role models for womanhood promoted by the Islamic Republic. Both Ayatollah Khomeini and Ayatollah Khamenei orientate the 'new Muslim woman' according to role models in Shi'i Islamic history in particular. The writings of Shari'ati on Fatemeh are also central here, and provide grounds for which 'the new Muslim woman' may follow the demands for protection and decency within the family through their roles as mothers, daughters and wives, as well as requirements for being active both in society and religious life. The ways in which Arezoo, Sadeghi and Eftekhari make use of notions of *Islamiyat* are important for their ideas of womanhood. Not only do they refer to aspects of Shi'i Islamic history and theology, but they also relate to concepts of *Iraniyat* through their emphasis on Khomeini, Shari'ati and Shi'ism.

Mehrangiz Manoochehrian

Conceptions of family law among many women's rights activists in this study tend to reflect the history of women's rights activism in Iran and represent an aspect of *Iraniyat* different from the one signified by 'the new Muslim woman'. Minoo and Maryam emphasised facets of *Iraniyat* as decisive for their understanding of Iranian womanhood. Another reference often made, both by the interviewees and on websites such as Fair Family Law and Feminist School, is to a female senator serving in the final years of Pahlavi rule. Mehrangiz Manoochehrian (1906–2000/1285–79) was one of the first women to study law in Iran and was appointed the country's first female senator (1963–72). With the introduction of the Family Protection Bill in 2007, her work received renewed attention among women's rights activists. Manoochehrian was brought into the debate as a symbolic figure of the history of women's legal struggle in Iran. Two leading women's rights activists, Parvin Ardalan and Noshin Ahmadi Khorasani, published a biography of Manoochehrian in 2002.[3] In it, they emphasise her role in studying law and as the first female senator. They acknowledge her work for women's legal rights both in the Senate and in public debates and present her as a feminist and human rights activist (BBC Persian, 3 December 2003). By referring to

Manoochehrian, Ardalan and Khorasani thus relate to aspects of the cultural and historical legacy of women's rights activism in Iran.

On the website of several women's rights groups, Manoochehrian's life and career are mentioned on various occasions in connection with the Family Protection Bill. Both on the Feminist School and the Fair Family websites, the text of a bill drafted by Manoochehrian in 1963/64 has been published in its entirety in connection with discussions of the 2007 Bill (Manoochehrian 1963/64). Manoochehrian's draft bill also serves as a major frame of reference for the current work and debate of different groups of women's rights activists affiliated to the OMSC (Change for Equality website, 27 December 2007). Moreover, Manoochehrian is credited with publishing the first draft of an Iranian family law bill and referred to as a pioneer in the quest for women's legal rights in Iran (ibid.).

Manoochehrian's proposal was initially published as an appendix to her book, *Legal Status of Women in the World*.[4] The following year, the bill was republished as a stand-alone pamphlet called *Proposed Draft of Family Law Based on the Equality of Women and Men* (*Layehe-ye Pishnahadi-ye Qanun-e Khanevadeh dar Barabari-ye Zanan va Mardan*). The bill then came out in four consecutive issues of the women's journal *Ettela'-e Banouvan* (Women's Information). It was not well received, however. The Minister of Justice at the time called it 'a product of her own conclusions' and made clear that 'in the Judiciary, no proposed law which is deemed to be incompatible with the enlightened religion of Islam would receive any consideration' (Change for Equality website, 27 December 2007).

Despite the disapproval of the bill, Manoochehrian continued to push for its introduction in the Senate. In October 1964 she succeeded and was able to present it to the Senate, but it was seen as premature and hasty and did not receive serious examination at the time. Shortly after, though, in February 1967, the Family Protection Law was introduced and within a few months was ratified and signed into law (ibid.). According to the Change for Equality website, Manoochehrian failed to receive credit for the work she had put into preparing the new law and her contribution was not even mentioned in its final version (ibid.). Manoochehrian herself is said not to acknowledge the Family

Protection Law in its 1967-enacted form, and published a criticism of it in a book, *Inequalities of the Rights of Women and Men in Iran and the Methods to Correct Them* (*Nabarabai-ye Hoqoq-e Zanan va Mardan dar Iran va Raveshha-ye be Toshih Anha*), which was published by the Iranian Women Lawyers' Association. Here, she addressed issues such as housing, divorce, women's access to travel abroad without the husband's permission,[5] citizenship of women, custody of children, inheritance, blood money, polygynous and temporary marriage, among others (ibid.). She saw all of these areas as receiving inadequate treatment both in the 1967 and 1975 editions of the Family Protection Law. For this reasons, contemporary women's rights activists do not regard Manoochehrian as being directly linked to the Pahlavi regime. Although appointed senator during the reign of the Shah, many rejectionist and revisionist women's rights activists see her as representing an oppositional force in terms of women's rights and as a genuine expression of activism during this period. Not surprisingly, with the establishment of the Islamic Republic in 1979 Manoochehrian lost her licence to practise law.

Manoochehrian's draft addressed several different areas of family law such as inheritance, marriage, divorce and custody of children, and resembles a revisionist approach. It relates to the 1928 Iranian Civil Code and revises some areas. In Book 7, for instance, the marriage arrangement as described in the Iranian Civil Code is redefined. Whereas the Iranian Civil Code classifies marriage as either permanent or temporary (Articles 1075–7), and as monogamous or polygynous (Aticle 942), Manoochehrian's draft takes a different approach. It states:

> (A) Marriage consists of two spouses and their children;
> (B) Marriage is only of one kind, and it is permanent;
> (C) No one in that unit can have more than one wife.
>
> Note: this law will be valid and replace all previous laws from the date of ratification (Manoochehrian 1963/64).

Manoochehrian's definition of marriage thus excludes polygynous and temporary marriages. Also, the draft revises Article 1133 in the

Civil Code on divorce.[6] Whereas the Civil Code allows a man unilateral divorce rights, Manoochehrian's draft states that a divorce should be issued in court and introduces certain conditions under which it can be granted.[7] On the subject of dower, Manoochehrian's draft refers to Articles 1078 to 1101 as defined by the Iranian Civil Code. Although the draft bill clearly relates to existing family laws and was introduced at a time when they were being reformed, there was a strong view that any changes adopted should be in accordance with existing laws. This was also a prerequisite for implementation of the 1967/75 Family Protection Law, not only in terms of adjusting laws to the 1928 Civil Code but also to Shari'a prescriptions in regard to divorce (*talaq*).

Nonetheless, contemporary women's rights groups and activists applaud Manoochehrian for taking the first initiative to change family laws in Iran. She was also mentioned by some of the interviewees. Shahla, a member of the Feminist School, referred to her as a major source of inspiration for family law reform, and her ideas of what should constitute appropriate family law legislation were largely based on Manoochehrian's draft bill:

> Manoochehrian was a senator during the Shah's period. She gave a bill to the parliament before the Family Protection Law [was ratified] that was very good. It would even be good now. But it was suspended then as well. She was a member of *Dokhtaran-e Sangeman* [The Association for Women Lawyers in Iran]; an independent society. She was the first person [woman] who studied law in Iran. It [the draft] is based on human rights, but it is also according to Shari'a ... The bill she introduced was better than the Family Protection Law. Her bill was considered offensive for her time ... She was against polygyny. But the Family Protection Law didn't reject it, only limited it. And the whole idea that the husband was the boss of the family, she was against. (Interview with Shahla, March 2009)

Shahla presents Manoochehrian's draft as laying the basis for legislation in which 'human rights' and 'Shari'a' are combined.

Moreover, Shahla underlines the draft's parallels to Shari'a. Such a link might be considered far-fetched, considering that Manoochehrian's draft bill proposes the abolition of temporary marriage, of men's unilateral divorce right, and recognises only monogamous marriages. Nor does the draft make explicit reference to either Islam or Shari'a. It is Shahla's own interpretation of the text that portrays Manoochehrian's bill as being 'according to Shari'a'. Shahla's view of family law has some similarity with the revisionist approach to polygyny and temporary marriage, which is that monogamy is an expression of being 'in accordance with Shari'a'. Thus, Manoochehrian's draft is seen an authentic, contemporary version of women's rights and as reflecting *Iraniyat*.

The concept of *Iraniyat* may, however, refer to quite different aspects of Iran's culture and history, depending on who is using it. Another aspect of *Iraniyat* that differs from the one Manoochehrian represents can be found in references to the ancient and pre-Islamic heritage of Iran. The Cyrus Cylinder, for instance, has been referred to as an ancient declaration of human rights in the Persian Empire in the sixth century BC (Farsinet website). In 1967, Reza Shah Pahlavi first introduced the idea of the Cyrus Cylinder as the original charter of human rights, and in 1971 compared himself to Cyrus at the opening of celebrations for the 2,500th anniversary of the Persian Empire (Garthwaite 2005: 251). Later, this claim was dismissed as propaganda. The British Museum, which holds the cylinder, has stated that 'This cylinder has sometimes been described as the "first charter of human rights", but it in fact reflects a long tradition in Mesopotamia where, from as early as the third millennium BC, kings began their reigns with declarations of reforms' (British Museum website). Despite this statement, it is still being referred to as 'an ancient declaration of human rights', for instance by the UN, which has kept a copy of the cylinder in its New York headquarters since 1971 (Schulz, 15 July 2008).

The Cyrus Cylinder has been a marker of various notions of *Iraniyat* throughout the last century, but is also a divisive symbol in contemporary Iranian politics. The Pahlavis identified their dynasty with nationalism and Iran based on references to Cyrus. Ayatollah Khomeini, on the other hand, identified *Iraniyat* with Islam and the

Islamic Republic and dismissed remnants of Iran's pre-Islamic heritage such as the festival of Nowruz.[8] President Ahmadinejad, however, took a different approach. In 2010, the Cyrus Cylinder was lent by the British Museum to the National Museum in Tehran. Considering the tense relationship between the two countries at the time, the loan was highly unexpected. Ahmadinejad visited the National Museum in Tehran and is reported to have praised the cylinder 'as the embodiment of human values and a cultural heritage for all humanity' (Press TV, 12 September 2010). He added that 'talking about Iran is not talking about a geographical entity or race ... Talking about Iran is tantamount to talking about culture, human values, justice, love and sacrifice' (ibid.). In addition, Ahmadinejad used references to the concept of *mellat* (nation) rather than *umma* (Muslim community), which is interpreted as a sign of claiming a national Iranian legitimacy over an Islamic one (Taheri, 8 January 2011). He also referred to the cyclinder as a charter for human rights and human dignity, and a sign that 'the Iranian nation has always been the flag-bearer of justice, devotion and human values throughout history' (Press TV, 12 September 2010).

Such quotes have been interpreted as an attempt to regain legitimacy for his policies after the 2009 demonstrations (Taheri, 8 January 2011), but have been criticised for praising pre-Islamic Iran, and not Islam (Payvand, 18 September 2010). Nevertheless, the mention of Cyrus and Iran's pre-Islamic history in different political periods and by diverse actors signifies a broader trend in which their cultural and historical legitimacy is validated on the basis of Iranian nationalism.

Contemporary women's rights activists have also made reference to the Cyrus Cylinder. Shirin 'Ebadi, in her Nobel Prize speech in Oslo in 2003, referred to both *Iraniyat* and *Islamiyat*. Although her address was in no way directly linked to the issue of family law or the Family Protection Bill, she stated:

> I am an Iranian. A descendant of Cyrus the Great. The very emperor who proclaimed at the pinnacle of power 2,500 years ago that 'he would not reign over the people if they did not wish it. And [he]

> promised not to force any person to change his religion and faith and guaranteed freedom for all.' The Charter of Cyrus the Great is one of the most important documents that should be studied in the history of human rights. ('Ebadi, 10 December 2003)

The mention of the cyclinder by figures as diverse as 'Ebadi and Ahmadinijad illustrates an ongoing tug of war about what the concept of *Iraniyat* may signify. Aspects of *Iraniyat* may also be taken to relate to Iran's modern history, as shown by the references to Manoochehrian and the 'new Muslim woman'.

Forough Farrokhzad

The women's rights activists in this study draw on different constructions of *Islamiyat* and *Iraniyat* in their approaches to family law. Yet another aspect can be found in contemporary women's rights activists' references on the Feminist School website (29 December 2010) to the female poet and film director Forough Farrokhzad (1935–76). Farrokhzad was considered to represent the variations among Iranian women, because she was far from the stereotype of a poor, suppressed, unfortunate woman that is held by many outside Iran.

Farrokhzad published several collections of poetry, of which *Tavalod-e Digar* (*Another Birth*) from 1963 is the best known.[9] During her life she claimed to be influenced by the Iranian poet Nima Yushij (1896–1960) and also drew on the poetic and intellectual heritage of Hafez (1325/26–1389/90) (Javadi 2010: 195). There are, however, noticeable shifts in her writings. The collections published in her early career explore her identity as a woman who feels trapped in a society of traditional values, and love, sexuality and romance are the main themes of self-expression and social protest (op. cit.: xiii). With *Osian* (*Rebellion*) in 1958, however, she starts to question dominant religious beliefs. With *Tavalod-e Digar* (*Another Birth*) in 1963 she moves her attention towards society as a whole (ibid.), and to spiritual rebirth and a deeper understanding of the human condition (Zubizaretta 1992: 425).

Farrokhzad is a controversial figure both for her life story and her work, which still receives attention in Iran. As a divorced female poet and film director, she stands out from her contemporaries in more ways than one. In particular, she was noted for the personal character of her poetry and for dealing with issues of politics and sexuality. Critics, both in her own lifetime and later, disliked her openness over issues like female sexuality and emotions that were considered unsuitable for the public eye. Farrokhzad's work was banned in Iran for a decade after 1979, but during the 1990s several new editions of her work were published, although her life and work continue to arouse great controversy. She is often linked to contemporary social issues, and has for instance been portrayed as 'One of the forerunners of the Iranian Women's Movement of recent years, whose daring and heroic examples we have witnessed as part of the Green Movement' (Javadi 2010: xxii).

Farrokhzad continues to be a significant figure for some contemporary women's rights activists. She has been described as 'an example of the poetry of resistance, perseverance and courage against the explicit discourse dominated patriarchy' on the website of the Feminist School (29 December 2010). After the divorce from her first husband, Farrokhzad lost custody of her only son. This experience is shared by many women in Iran and may explain why many seem to identify with her. Farrokhzad is seen as a character who transgresses the constructed gap between the two concepts of *Iraniyat* and *Islamiyat* and *gharbzadegi*. For many, she represents an authentic voice of Iranian identity that goes beyond the two extremes of 'liberalism' or 'fundamentalism' (Forough Farrokhzad website), in that she was both assertive of her national heritage and critical of the traditions of patriarchy in Iranian society.

Afsaneh Najmabadi has noted that Farrokhzad not only transgressed socially legitimate boundaries of male–female sexual relations, but also celebrated her sexuality openly, which made her an outcast among contemporary intellectuals (1993: 680). For this reason, Iranian-American artists and writers have also looked to Farrokhzad's life story and work (Darznik 2010). For both the filmmaker and visual artist Shirin Neshat and the playwright Maryam Habibians, Farrokhzad's work challenges the 'reductive representations of Middle Eastern and Muslim women', as well as the boundaries between Iranian and American literature (op. cit.: 105). Farrokhzad's work has also been linked to the construction of a modern Shi'i identity. Hamid Dabashi finds aspects of Shi'ism in Farrokhzad's poem *Someone who is like no one* (2011: 49–53):

> Forough Farrokhzad was no theologian, and for all people could tell had no particular religious faith up her sleeve. But in this single poem she planted in the inner innocence of a young girl's voice the very seed of expectation [*intizar*] at the heart of Shi'ism, a waiting, a yearning, a longing for an everlasting sense of justice that has been historically denied humanity at large ... No one was reading learned theological treatises that bearded men wrote in Qom, except for younger men at the mercy of their benevolence in secluded seminaries. Everybody, including those in the seminaries, was reading Forough Farrokhzad. (2011: 52)

Because of the immense popularity of her poems, Farrokhzad gained a large audience. Dabashi has argued that in a similar manner, Farrokhzad and 'Ali Shari'ati brought a 'renewed claim on a much wider spectrum of senses and sensitivities, allegiances and observances, pieties and politics' in Iran (Dabashi 2011: 54). He asserts that Shari'ati and Farrokhzad alike contributed to the line of Shi'is who are 'falsely branded "secular" and the other "religious"' (2011: 311). The different interpretations of Farrokhzad's life and poetry point towards the construction of imagined identities and the complex intersections of categories of nation, gender and religion through the concepts of *Islamiyat* and *Iraniyat*.

A dual aspect of feminism

Although there are different notions of *Iraniyat* and *Islamiyat*, they are always defined in relation to what is seen as un-Islamic or un-Iranian. A concept that often signifies their opposite is *gharbzadegi* (westoxification), which originated from a book of the same title by Jamal Al Ahmad in 1962, and was often used in public in Iran in the

1970s and 1980s (Moghadam 2003: 158). In contrast to *Islamiyat* and *Iraniyat*, *gharbzadegi* denotes a negative category, a loss of Iranian cultural and historical identity through the adoption of western ideas and models. *Gharbzadegi* is often connected to issues that concern women's rights, and women have been seen as being the most vulnerable to its influences (op. cit.: 159).

Feminism is often portrayed as the ultimate expression of *gharbzadegi*. Despite this, there is a dual aspect to feminism in Iran. One side perceives feminism as merely adopted from western ideas, and thus as alien to Iran. The other, though, involves what can be seen as Iran's own history and tradition of feminism. In the former view, feminism is portrayed as a foreign idea that implies imperialistic and elitist attitudes – and is thus an extreme expression of *gharbzadegi*. Feminism in Iran tends to be seen as a western and bourgeois phenomenon, and as contrary to an indigenous women's movement (Afary 1989: 66). For this reason, many of the women's rights activists in this study avoid the feminist label. Leyla was the most outspoken, stating: 'I am not a feminist. Feminists believe that men are their enemies. In Iran we are not up to date with feminism abroad, but abroad feminists are not updated either. They hate men and they want to be lesbians' (Interview with Leyla, May 2008). Later she elaborated: 'They [feminists] want similarity, and not equality. I am not similar to men. I am equal or maybe I am superior, but I am not similar!' (ibid.).

While Leyla's opinion comes across as rather extreme and may represent an outdated attitude, it shows how feminism can be seen as an expression of *gharbzadegi*, a 'plague from the West' (Moghadam 2003: 159). However, this perception seems to have reappeared in recent years. In the debate on the Family Protection Bill, arguments opposing the bill more generally have been linked to imperialist and elitist notions of women's rights. Moreover, Zahra Rahnavard has argued that the government makes use of constructed notions of the West in relation to the attempts to pass the Family Protection Bill. She says: 'The current government is trying to create a national image of the Islamic family with a fundamentalist stance just to create an image of male/female relationship that is different from the West'

(Radio Zamaneh, 17.11.10). Rahnavard continues: 'The Islamic Republic government is trying to insinuate that the western man is "loose and lustful" but the Islamic Republic system has religious frameworks to contain man's urges' (ibid.). Such notions relate to *gharbzadegi* as something to be sceptical about, and to official rhetoric that creates stereotypical images of the West. Some of the rhetoric reduces critique of the Family Protection Bill to representing anti-Iranian and anti-Islamic sentiments, and thus renders illegitimate many of the claims of women's rights activists for family law reform.

There are also several other examples of this kind of rhetoric being used towards women's rights more generally. Shirin 'Ebadi has had her national and religious legitimacy questioned for years. She is at once a controversial lawyer and a woman's rights activist. After receiving the Nobel Peace Prize in 2003, however, her work became even more controversial. The Norwegian Nobel Committee announced that: "Ebadi represents reformed Islam, and argues for a new interpretation of Islamic law which is in harmony with vital human rights such as democracy, equality before the law, religious freedom and freedom of speech' (Nobel Peace Prize website, 10 December 2003). This was not well received by the government in Iran. For them, 'Ebadi's work and ideas are regularly seen as presenting western ideas of women's and human rights and as being associated with the interests of foreign countries. Consequently, the Iranian government has made several efforts to silence 'Ebadi by imprisoning her, putting her office under surveillance and interrogating her family members. As a result, 'Ebadi has not returned to Iran since the demonstrations after the 2009 presidential elections.

The sceptical attitude towards 'Ebadi is also to be found among some women's rights activists in this study, mainly among those holding loyalist positions on family law. Leyla, for instance, said: 'I don't agree with *Khanom-e* 'Ebadi. She has avoided so many issues and did not deserve the Nobel Prize. She is really occupied with human rights, and not genuinely with women' (Interview with Leyla, May 2008). Later, Leyla expressed a more indirect critique of 'Ebadi and women's rights activists affiliated with western countries generally:

> Women activists in Iran have a political agenda. They promote the woman question with money from abroad, and then they want to go to the US and be on . . . Voice of America! They are damaging everyone who works for women in Iran! The government think that everyone who works for the woman question has this agenda. Therefore activities that are founded from abroad are banned. This is one of the Achilles heels of the women's movement. They are more occupied with being popular [*mashhur*] than with woman's rights! They talk about women, but not about men. (Interview with Leyla, May 2008)

Leyla here refers to what she sees as the lack of legitimacy of 'Ebadi and other women's rights activists who are affiliated with western countries. Her scepticism underlines the need to establish authentic roots for women's rights activism in Iran. In the light of this, 'Ebadi's mention of Cyrus and her later references to important characters in Iranian literature such as Rumi, Hafez and Mowlavi in her Nobel Prize speech, indicate aspects of *Iraniyat* that she draws on in order to categorise her work and ideas as intrinsically Iranian.

This critique of the West and of feminism is not unique to Iran, or even to Muslim countries. Feminism is still a highly controversial term. There has, however, been a tense relationship between the secular-liberal foundation of feminism and religion in general (Sharma and Young 1999: 3–4), and Islam in particular (Mahmood 2005). Thus, according to Leila Ahmed, Muslim women speaking in the name of feminism have had the choice 'between betrayal or betrayal' (1984: 122).

The second aspect of feminism, though, relates to Iran's own history and culture. Women's rights activism in Iran has a particular historical and cultural background that is frequently overlooked in the view that merely relates feminism to western culture. This aspect has been significant for Muslim women's rights activism elsewhere as well. In Egypt, for instance, the secular and feminist-oriented heritage of women's rights activism was predominant (Badran 1995 and 2009), and the women's rights movements emerged as part of nation state building processes (Baron 2005: 9).[10] Similarly, women's rights activism in Iran has nationalistic roots that go back to the early 1900s. The first organised forms of women's rights activism took place during the Constitutional Revolution in 1906, where some women played central roles in the different revolutionary campaigns. Although inspiration for the 1906 Revolution can be said to derive, for instance, from the French Revolution, forms of activism were soon adopted into the Iranian context. Shortly after the Revolution, women instigated their own campaigns for women's rights (Afary 1989: 82). Influence came not only from western women's movements, but also from Egypt and India. But from the first days of the Pahlavi dynasty, the conditions for Iran's emerging women's rights movement changed. Women's participation in politics and society was now considered a precondition for a modern Iran and the model used was mainly that of western countries (Paidar 1995: 118). Because of this history of women's rights activism, ideas pertaining to feminism are often associated with the policies of the Pahlavis or to a foreign and often western agenda.

In spite of this, both secular-oriented women's rights activism and feminist ideas are visible in contemporary Iran. The secular-oriented and rejectionist approaches towards family law among contemporary women's rights activists are not, however, widely held in the public debate on the Family Protection Bill. Examples are more often to be found where outspoken secular-oriented and feminist positions are combined with a revisionist approach. The Feminist School, established in 2008, has maintained a secular-oriented tradition of activism. It is closely affiliated with the OMSC, founded in 2006 for the purpose of changing 'discriminatory laws against women' (We Change website, 26 August 2006). Unlike the campaign, which seeks to reach a broad audience by not defining any political, ideological, or religious attitudes, the Feminist School has an explicitly feminist agenda. Its members refer both to western feminists like Virginia Woolf and Simone de Beauvoir (Interview with Afsaneh, May 2008), as well as to Iranians who have become iconic in womens rights activism such as Mehrangiz Manoochehrian and Forough Farrokhzad (Feminist School website, 25 August 2008 and 29 December 2010). Consequently, they combine notions of western and Iranian feminism in promoting secular- and Islamic-oriented legislation as the primary basis for women's rights.

Although women's studies is taught at Iranian universities, it is not a discipline that enjoys broad support. Afsaneh, who taught a course at a university in Tehran, explained that she told the students to read the official curriculum, which listed the Qur'an, teachings of famous Shi'a *ulama* and what she referred to as 'out-dated sociologists' like Talcott Parsons. In addition, she encouraged her students to read an unofficial reading list that she had put together, which included *The Second Sex* by Simone de Beauvoir, as well as writings by Virginia Woolf, Julia Kristeva and Judith Butler, among others. All the books on the unofficial list were made available in Persian, and the students could read this and other secular-oriented and feminist literature in private. After meeting several of the students, it seems clear that they related to authors like Simone de Beauvoir not just as secular, western or feminist writers, but as people whose ideas could also be relevant to women in Iran.

Moreover, there are secular-oriented positions to be found among activists in the family law debate. Although these are not evident in the official public record, it was clear that some of the interviewees held secular-oriented attitudes. Rather than seeking revisions within the framework of Shari'a, Touran, for instance, believes in a strict secularisation of family law. Mostly she refers to alternative models of law such as CEDAW as a basis for family laws:

> I think CEDAW can be a basis for equal law for family. And many countries have assented to this basis of law. We can start it and many women lawyers in Iran are researching about what we want and what we need from this law. And I know that 'Ebadi wrote a basic law for family some years ago and she brought it to parliament. But I don't know what happened with this law. I mean we have many basic papers for this, but we don't have many people in parliament with us to do it ... I believe that for gender rights CEDAW is better. And the sixth parliament accepted and confirmed CEDAW. And the *Shura-ye Negahban* deleted it. (Interview with Touran, August 2011)

References to CEDAW are also connected to anti-Islamic sentiments that are contrary to the Islamic Republic's view of women's rights. Thus, approaches to family law based on CEDAW are highly controversial and mostly excluded from the official public debate.

The sources of legitimacy used to authenticate the various conceptions of family law refer to different notions of *Iraniyat* and *Islamiyat*. In general, revisionist women's rights activists in this study related their views on Shari'a and women's rights to prominent Iranian women such as Manoochehrian and Farrokhzad. They also draw on official models of womanhood as provided by Khomeini, Shari'ati and in Shi'ism in order to legitimate their claims. Interestingly, such modes of legitimacy not only rely on framing their conceptions of family law within an Islamic and Iranian framework, but depend on being contrasted with and detached from imported ideas. This is a common strategy in regard to feminism and *gharbzadegi*, but is also used to distinguish the Iranian woman from other Muslim women. Moreover, the dual aspects that feminism entails for women's rights activists shed light on intersections of what is perceived to be secular and religious. The divide between these two concepts is not clearly defined, but seems to rely on quite subjective perceptions of what signifies Shari'a and women's rights. Touran, for instance, explained what Islam and being a 'secular Muslim' meant for her:

> Yes, the Qur'an is a base in our law. But I don't believe in it because I am secular, and I believe they should separate law and religion. This is the first day of Ramazan and I fast, but it is just this for me. You know I don't have hejab, I don't pray, and I don't anything. I just believe in one relationship between me and my God. Islam is just this for me. One energy that gives me good energy and a positive situation, and the other part [law] I think is business. The law is from the Qur'an, from Shari'a, and the other is just business. Like the other religions, I respect all religions and people to believe in it, but I don't believe it. I believe that law should be separate from Shari'a, and Islam, Christianity, Judaism and the others faiths like Bahai'ism.

> Law should be just law, just rights for people, and the people should want it. And for my country, I believe it is not important for me what Islam says about *mehrieh*. I don't believe all of them [laws such as *mehrieh*].

Although Touran considers herself to be 'secular', she still underscores the importance that Islam and being Muslim has for her life. Her sense of being secular thus relates to her view on family law legislation and to a separation of law and religions. Touran's explanation illustrates that not only does Islam play a central part in rejectionists' conceptions of family law, but also that religion is significant for her even though she refers to herself as 'secular'. On this basis, a distinct division between 'Islamic' and 'secular' is not appropriate for how Touran refers to herself. Her idea of being 'secular' does not denote a non-religious or anti-Islamic position but refers to a separation of religion and legislation. Thus, Touran's sense of being 'secular' conveys her approach towards family law, rather than a non–religious stance.

Secularism in Iran has a long history and several facets, as is the case with Iranian feminism. Although most often connected with the policies of the Pahlavis, secularism is also interpreted in regard to some of the political procedures of the current Islamic Republic (Crone 2007). Although this regime counts as a religious state, its policies are largely ruled by a secular 'state reason' (ibid.). Some have also argued that the establishment of the Islamic Republic has enabled a kind of post-Islamist society to flourish that is not anti-Islamic, but reflects a tendency to resecularise and limit the role of Islam in society (Bayat 1996: 45). The way that Touran speaks about herself as 'secular' should thus be read in terms of the various notions of secularism in Iran, and not as anti-Islamic or non-religious.

Throughout Iran's modern history, the quest for an appropriate family law has evolved around the dual call for maintaining Shari'a prescriptions and codifying appropriate concerns for women's rights. A major concern for activists has been to prove that demands for women's rights are not simply imported from outside, but are intrinsic to the Iranian context as well as to Islam. They also face a recurrent need to distance their claims from what is perceived to be western or imported. This quest for legitimacy reached a new high after 1979, when specific 'Islamic' models for womanhood and women's rights were justified within the framework of the Islamic Republic. Demands that did not fit in with the predominant models at the time were deemed 'un-Islamic' or even 'un-Iranian'. Thus, the continuing quest to legitimate family law claims is built on sources of legitimacy from a broader framework of references to Iranian history and culture, as well as to Islam. Consequently, the dividing line between 'secular' and 'religious' has been blurred, and what is regarded as 'Islamic' or 'Iranian' is not separable, but has become interactive. Hence, the quest for genderhood and family law codifications is situated within the framework of religion and nation, within *Islamiyat* and *Iraniyat*.

CONCLUSION

The relationship between family law debates and women's rights activism in Iran is complex and its intersections many. Both emerged from the Constitutional Revolution, and have since been interwoven and at the mercy of shifting political projects. A key in this intersectional relationship lies in the question of authority. Authority remains a fundamental aspect of family law debates that all participants, and not only women's rights activists, need to address. As seen in this book, women's rights activists base their arguments both on Islam and Iranian history in order to legitimate their claims. Principles of *usul al-fiqh* as well as aspects of Iranian history have been referred to as authorities for the Family Protection Bill. These sources of legitimacy are not unique to this debate, but have characterised family law debates since the early 1900s. Integral to the quest for an Iranian family law codification has been the need to define models of genderhood within the framework of religion and nation, and to contrast them with a western understanding. Within such a setting, both Ayatollah Khomeini and Mehrangiz Manoochehrian emerge as equivalent sources of legitimation for activists in relation to the Family Protection Bill.

The women's rights activists presented in this book illustrate highly diverse opinions on family law. Their differences point to several intriguing aspects of what a Muslim family law codification involves, and underlines the heterogeneous character of Iranian women's rights activism. For instance, most of those who hold rejectionist views have argued for the abolition of Shari'a-based practices in order to secure women's rights. Interestingly, such clear-cut positions are not always found in the other approaches. For those who represent revisionist and loyalist approaches to the Family Protection Bill, Shari'a and women's rights do not necessarily conflict, but are sometimes more fluid and can overlap. For instance, legal limitations on polygynous and temporary marriages are presented as being consistent both with Shari'a and women's rights. In regard to *mehrieh*, there are many interpretations. Rejectionists such as Touran see *mehrieh* as representing the sale of a woman in marriage and as a highly gender-discriminatory practice. Revisionists like Parisa and Zohreh, however, consider *mehrieh* a necessary means of protection in case of divorce, because of women's inferior legal status in the current family law legislation. Similarly, Maryam, with a loyalist view, stresses its necessity for offering women security after divorce. Other revisionists emphasise the religious foundation of the practice and bring aspects of piety into the debate. They argue that *mehrieh* is a matter of devotion, and is central to the Muslim marriage and what it means to be a Muslim. In this way, the conceptions of *mehrieh* underline both the heterogeneity and overlapping of ideas expressed by the activists.

The search for a family law codification in Iran has involved striking a balance between Shari'a and women's rights considerations since the early 1900s. The current debate not only demonstrates conflicting areas of these, but also offers examples of possible junctions in which the two demands meet. There is, however, no unanimous agreement about what constitutes 'correct' Shari'a or even acceptable definitions of women's rights. What the debates about the codification of issues of dower, polygyny and temporary marriage in the Family Protection Bill have highlighted, are the different facets of Shari'a – the ways in which it is connected to socioeconomic and gendered aspects of society and to subjective and everyday religiosity.

There are many signs that contemporary Shi'a Islam is undergoing changes, both in Iran and internationally. Discussions over family law and women's rights represent only one arena of profound religious change. The women's rights activists in this study hold varying ideas of religious legitimacy and authority, and their views of family law involve change, continuity and revision. They convey a continuation of the historical, dogmatic tradition of Islam, but also of changes and redefinitions expressed in subjective interpretations of religious authority and what it means to be Muslim. The women's rights activists' altering and combining of sources of legitimacy contributes to understanding the re-analysis of Shi'a religious knowledge at the present time. In this way, they also leave a trace on the ongoing family law debate. Hence, the intersections of family law and women's rights activism in contemporary Iran witness to a continuing religious tradition that is also being renewed.

NOTES

Prelims

1. The IJMES transliteration guide can be found at http://web.gc.cuny.edu/ijmes/pages/transliteration.html, accessed 31 December 2011.

Introduction

1. Throughout the book, I make use of the concepts 'women's rights activism' and 'women's rights activist' in order to categorise engagement in the promotion of women's rights in the contemporary Islamic Republic of Iran. The term 'women's rights' is, however, used broadly and does not signify any specific religious, political or ideological orientation. It should also be mentioned that the concept 'women's rights activist' does not presume any specific gender and may equally refer to male as well as female activists. The concept also signifies a seriality, rather than a group (cf. Young 1997: 23, and endnote 10).
2. CEDAW is the United Nation's Convention on the Elimination of all forms of Discrimination Against Women ratified by 169 countries. Iran has not ratified CEDAW and neither has the United States.
3. Polygyny refers to the practice of having two or more wives concurrently. Polyandry is a form of marriage in which a woman has two or more husbands at the same time. Polygamy is the general term for a marriage involving more than two spouses.
4. This book offers only a limited textual analysis of the Family Protection Bill. It does not aspire to providing an extensive analysis of the draft bill as such, but addresses the content, breaks and continuities of the Family Protection Bill in relation to previous family law reforms enacted both in Iran and in other comparable Muslim family law codes. Mainly, this will be done based on the legal issues of temporary marriage, polygyny and dower in the Family Protection Bill.

5. Several researchers, such as Dale F. Eickelman and John W. Anderson, have addressed these trends as the emergence of a 'new Muslim public sphere'. See for instance Eickelman and Anderson 2003, Eickelman and James Piscatori 2004, Salvatore 2007, Krämer and Schmidtke 2006, and Meyer and Moors 2006.
6. The ways in which Muslims examine and discuss their religion have received scholarly attention in recent years. Although there seems to be general agreement over the occurrence of such changes, the ways in which they should be analysed and explored are subject to debate. Eickelman and Anderson have referred to such attempts as the 'objectification of Islam' (2004: 38). Both Saba Mahmood and Lara Deeb have contested this label on several grounds (Mahmood 2005:54–6 and Deeb 2006:20–1). They do not consider the term 'objectification' as suitable for describing Muslims' endeavours to examine Islam, as the term does not locate such endeavors properly either within Islam as a discursive tradition or as contextually and situationally framed (ibid.).
7. For accounts on Egypt, see for instance Badran 1995, Al-Ali 2000 and Baron 2005.
8. See for instance Moors 2003, Buskens 2003, Sonneveld 2009, Rabo 2011 and Abu-Lughod and Rao 2011.
9. Iris M. Young suggests an alternative way of thinking of gender as a collective, and makes a distinction between group and seriality in order to provide a basic solution for the challenge of categorisations (Young 1997). Building on Jean-Paul Sartre's concept of seriality (Sartre 1976), Young suggests a way of thinking about a social collective without restricting it to a set of predefined identities (1997: 5–6). This approach 'allows us to understand them [women] as a collective without identifying common attributes that all women have or implying that all women have a common identity' (op. cit.: 13). Thus, in order to think about women as a social collective, Young distinguishes between group and series. A group is a collection of persons that recognise themselves and one another as part of a group on the basis of the actions they undertake together. They share the same goals and work towards a common objective. A series, however, is defined as 'a social collective whose members are unified passively by the objects their actions are oriented around and/or by the objectified results of the material effects of the actions of the other' (op. cit.: 23). People are bound together in a series on the basis of a shared object, but this does not necessarily entail any common identity, history or experience.
10. The categories rejectionist, revisionist and loyalist women's rights activists are discussed in Chapter Four.
11. In November 2002 I conducted an interview inquiry in Tehran with four women's rights activists as part of my master degree in history of religions at the University of Bergen.
12. The term 'Shi'a law' may refer to different directions of Shi'ism. When using the general term Shi'a Islam or Shi'a jurisprudence, I refer to the Ja'fari branch of Shi'ism, pertaining to *Ithna 'Ashari* or Twelver Shi'ism.
13. The 1967/1975 Family Protection Law is published on the Feminist School website (19 July 2009), and the Constitution of the Islamic Republic of Iran on

the Iran online website. See the list of legal codes, bills and drafts in the references section.

14. The full-text English versions of the 2007 Family Protection Bill can be found at the Meydan website and at the website of Iran Human Rights Documentation Centre. It is also available in Persian at the Fair Family Law website. The 2010 Family Protection Bill is also available there. See the list of legal codes, bills and drafts in the references section for complete url addresses.
15. The Proposition of 'women from different Iranian cities' also contains alternative proposals on the issues of polygyny (FFL, 8 May 2010a), temporary marriage (FFL, 8 May 2010b) and dower (FFL, 8 May 2010c).
16. http://www.fairfamilylaw.eu/, accessed 10 January 2012.
17. There are different names and urls to access the websites of the One Million Signatures Campaign, but a recent one is: http://we-change.org/english/, accessed 10 January 2012.
18. http://www.feministschool.com/, accessed 10 January 2012.
19. http://meydaan.org/default.aspx, accessed 10 January 2012. The names and the urls of most of these websites are changed frequently in order to avoid governmental control and censorship.
20. Not all interviews or interviewees have been cited in this book. Those cited in the book are listed in the references section.

Chapter 1 Shari'a and Family Law

1. Shari'a consists of five different categorisations of duties and obligations. First, acts that are considered obligatory are called *wajib*. Performance of *wajib* actions is rewarded, while omission of the *wajib* entails a penalty. Examples of *wajib* acts are performing prayer (*salat*), payment of religious tax (*zakat*), or performing a three-month waiting period for women after termination of marriage (*'idda*). Second, there are several actions that are recommended, referred to as *mandub*. *Mandub* acts can be both binding and non-binding in character. The main point of most *mandub* actions is that they are rewarded if performed. Marriage, for instance, is considered a *mandub* action that is recommended for all Muslims. However, refraining from marriage does not imply any specific punishment. Third, are actions that are permitted (*mubah*). The best example of this can be polygyny. In most cases *mubah* actions come with restrictions of some kind. This is also true of polygynous marriages. Fourth, deeds under the classification *makruh*, or discouraged acts. The term refers to actions that generally are allowed, but that it is better to refrain from performing. An example of *makruh* actions is divorce (*talaq*). Divorce is not, however, forbidden in Islam. On the contrary, divorce is a topic with a range of variations and regulations. Despite the possibility of performing divorce, the practice is discouraged. The fifth category defines actions that are forbidden (*haram*). Not engaging in these acts is demanded in the Qur'an. They refer to eating of carrion (Qur'an 5: 3), incest

(4: 23), or unlawful sexual intercourse (Qur'an 17: 32). *Haram* actions usually have a penalty in the present life (Khan 2010: 24–31).

2. A mufti is an Islamic scholar qualified to deliver formal legal opinions (fatawa).
3. Revisionist and Orientalist scholars of Shari'a, however, underlined the role of the *qadi* (a judge in an Islamic court) in their assessments of Shari'a. Max Weber, for instance, referred to Shari'a as *qadi* justice, because he was preoccupied with the role of the *qadi* (Rosen 1989: 59–60). The *qadi* was presented as a mythological character who would sit in the corner of a mosque and arrive at judgements almost off the top of his head. This image failed to take account of the legal process in which the role of the mufti and the methodology of *usul al-fiqh* both feature.
4. Here, I point out the inadequacies of the word 'law' and the difficulties of explaining Shari'a in terms of European conceptions or systems of law, rather than engaging in a conceptual elaboration of the various terms. For a more thorough analysis of this topic, see for instance Hallaq 2009: 2–6, Vikør 2003: 16–19, and Rosen 1989).
5. There are four basic principles or sources recognised in classical Sunni legal theory. They are known as *usul al-fiqh*, the roots of jurisprudence or the methodology of Shari'a, namely the Qur'an, the Sunna (the life and sayings of the Prophet Muhammad), analogical reasonings (*qiyas*), and consensus of opinion of *ulama* (*ijma'*). These four sources are the basis for a combined Sunni methodology of jurisprudence introduced by Muhammad ibn-Idris Al-Shafi'i (d. 819/20). Shafi'i's model of systematisation settled an ongoing dispute over methodology and sources in the development of law. In Shi'a legal theory, though, the principles of *usul al-fiqh* rely on the importance of *'aql* (reasoning) over that of *qiyas*, in addition to the sources of the Qur'an, Sunna and *ijma'*. Although these sources represent classical legal theory, there may be other sources of law interacting withand influencing how Shari'a is perceived by different actors and in different contexts, as is discussed later in this book.
6. *Furu'* refers to the branches of Shari'a or practical rules of law.
7. Examples of the so-called 'wave of Islamisation' can be found in the 1979 Revolution in Iran (which lead to the establishment of the Islamic Republic), the 1983 imposition of Shari'a in Sudan, or in the Algerian Family Law Code introduced in 1984.
8. Disagreements over the sources of Shari'a led to the establishment of several distinct schools of law. In the Sunni branch of Islam, four major schools developed that were named after their founding fathers. The Hanafi School of Law follows the rules of Abu Hanifa (d. 767), and evolved as the dominant school of law in the Ottoman Empire. In short, the Hanafi School relies on the principle of *ra'y* (reasoning) and relates to the so-called *ahl al-ra'y* (people of reasoning). The Maliki School of Law is named after Malik ibn Anas (d. 795), and is established in North Africa (Algeria, Tunisia, Morocco, etc.). The Maliki School of Law is mainly known for referring to Medina practices, and is placed as part of the *ahl al-hadith* (people of *hadith*). The Shafi'i School of Law is called

after Muhammad ibn Idris al-Shafi'i (d. 820) and exists mainly in South-east Asia and East Africa. The Shafi'i School generally depends on a combination of reasoning and tradition, and is often placed between the *ahl al-ra'y* and *ahl al-hadith*. The Hanbali School of Law derives its name from Ahmad ibn Hanbal (d. 855), and is the dominant school in Saudi Arabia and most of the Arabian Peninsula. The Hanbali School relies solely on hadith transmitted from the Prophet and his earliest companions. Hanbalis are seen as representing the strictest version of the four Sunni schools of law, and belongs to the *ahl al-hadith* tradition. These schools of law have mutual respect towards each other, but still differ in terms of what they consider to be the major theological principles of deducting rules with regard to either *ahl al-hadith* or *ahl al-ra'y* (Vikør 2003: 89).

9. In addition to Sunni and Shi'i schools of law, the Ibadi School of Law represents a third branch. It is believed to derive from the Kharijite tradition and is found today in Oman and Zanzibar.
10. A fatwa is a legal statement made by an Islamic scholar (mufti) in response to a question posed by a judge (*qadi*) in an Islamic court, or by an ordinary believer.
11. There are, however, signs that point to Shi'a and Sunni Muslims sharing the view of the legitimate caliphate during the first two centuries of the history of Islam (Arjomand 1988: 3).
12. The division between the so-called *akhbari* and *usuli* movement in Shi'ism entailed a theological disagreement over what kind of source should be the basis of religious interpretations and jurisprudence. Whereas the *akhbaris* demanded that any religious interpretation should be based on the tradition of the Prophet and the 12 Imams (*ahadith*), the *usulis* relied on the principle of independent reasoning (*ijtihad*). Since the late eighteenth century the *usuli* branch has been dominant in Shi'a Islamic jurisprudence. The *usuli/Akhbari* divide can be said to be equivalent to the *ahl al-ra'y/ahl al-hadith* division with Sunni Islamic jurisprudence (see endnote 29).
13. Appelros makes use of the concept as part of an intersectional approach to highlight the many ways gender and religion can be interrelated (2007). Thus, she introduces an analytical approach in which not only the religiosity of a person is analysed intersectionally, but rather the person's access to religious authority and legitimacy.
14. For more on female *ulama* see Umar 2004, and Künkler and Fazaeli 2012.
15. Although female judges and *ulama* were outlawed immediately after the 1979 Revolution, seminaries for training female *mujtahids* have been established in Qom in recent decades. The Fatemeh Zahra *hawza* was founded in 1988 (Kian-Thiébaut 2000), and today there are more than 270 schools across Iran that train female *ulama* and *mujtahids* (Tajali 2011: 454).
16. A'zam Taleqani is the daughter of the late Mahmoud Taleqani and Faezeh Hashemi is the daughter of Aliakbar Rafsanjani. Both have served as members of parliament and been in charge of women's organisations and journals in Iran.

17. In 2003, a special issue of the journal *Islamic Law and Society* was published on contemporary family law debates. In addition to other publications, the topic of family law reform has been covered in Mali (Schulz 2003, Soares 2009), Yemen (Würth 2003 and Dahlgren 2008), in Morocco (Buskens 2003, Bargach 2005, Salime 2009), Palestine (Moors 2003 and Welchman 2000a and 2000b), Syria (Rabo 2011), Iran (Mir-Hosseini 2000a and 2010, and Moghadam 2011), Egypt (Sonneveld 2009) and Sudan (Tønnessen 2011).
18. The so-called *khul'* law refers to Article 20 in The Law on Reorganisation of Certain Terms and Procedures of Litigation in Personal Status Matters (Sonneveld 2009).

Chapter 2 Marriage in Muslim Family Law

1. The term 'dower' denotes *mehrieh* or *mahr* and is not to be confused with 'dowry', which refers to the possessions that a bride brings into the household when she marries (Berger and Sonneveld 2010: 85). Moors claims that terms such as 'brideprice' and 'bridewealth' are misleading with regard to *mahr* as they refer to payments *for* rather than *to* the bride (1995: 87).
2. In general, jurists agree that *nafaqa* should cover food, clothing, and lodging. In addition, many support claims that it should also include other goods, not necessarily vital, but still important for maintaining a comfortable life, such as spices, makeup, henna, etc. (Tucker 2008: 50–1).
3. According to Article 1108 in the Iranian Civil Code, the lack of obedience of a wife towards her husband (*'adam-e tamkin*) is also identified as a reason for men to seek divorce (Mir-Hosseini 2000a: 59).
4. The doctrine of *nushuz* could in theory be applied both to the wife's or the husband's responsibilities towards each other, but according to Tucker most jurists have discussed the issue with regard to what was expected of the wife alone (Tucker 2008: 53).
5. The woman is not allowed to contract a new marriage during *'idda*. The purpose of *'idda* is to determine whether the woman is pregnant or not.
6. Other forms of financial maintenance that a woman can claim during marriage are *nafaqa* (financial maintenance during marriage) and *ujrat al-mithl* (wages for housework), implemented in Iran after the 1992 Divorce Reform.
7. In the Pakistan Muslim Family Law Ordinance from 1961 dower is utilised as a means of discouraging polygyny, because it states that a man who contracts a plurality of marriages without the permission of the Arbitration Council shall immediately pay the entire dower to existing wife or wives (Khan 2010: 9). The Syrian Code of Personal Statues from 1953, amended in 1975, brought in measures to control and distinguish 'fictious' and 'fraudulent' dowers from 'real' dowers (ibid.).
8. CEDAW Article 15 gives men and women equal rights on all matters related to civil rights, freedom of movement and choice of residence. The CEDAW Article

16 allocates men and women the same rights in marriage and with regard to choice of spouse.

9. A *raji'* divorce is a suspended form of divorce that comes into effect after the fulfilment of three menstrual cycles (*'idda*). *Talaq al-bain* is an irrevocable form of divorce, the opposite of *talaq al-raji'* (Mir-Hosseini 2000a: 38).
10. Iran has experienced major inflation in recent decades. This has had different effects on dower. To mention but one, the amount of dower has increased. In 1974, 9 per cent of women who married in Tehran had a dower of more than 100,000 tomans (1000,000 rials (the toman was the official currency prior to 1932, but is still commonly used in Iran. The rial is the official currency today)). In 1981, the same amount of dower applied to 52 per cent of women marrying in Tehran (Mir-Hosseini 2000a: 74). Although the amount of dower has increased, it does not mean a higher amount on paper. Because of the decline in value of the Iranian currency, dower is nowadays often stipulated in the value of gold coins to prevent a loss in value due to economic developments (ibid.). In 1974, one US dollar was equivalent to seven tomans (70 rials). In 1981, it was 70 tomans (700 rials). In 2013, the same amount is equivalent to approximately 1,000 tomans (10,000 rials).
11. The first quote is from Mu'allami, a Majles representative from Qaim Shahr, and the second quote from an unnamed Majles representative from Bandar 'Abbas. Both are taken from Halper 2007: 1184.
12. *Chandzani* is frequently used in the debate on the 2007 and 2010 Family Protection Bills. Also the term *ta'adod-e ezdevaj* is used in Article 23 in the 2007 Bill. The term *Ezdevaj-e mujadad-e dayem* is used in Article 23 in the 2010 Bill. *Ezdevaj-e mut'aded* is, however, the correct legal term for polygyny according to Ziba Mir-Hosseini (conversation at SOAS, London in March 2011).
13. Having these circumstances in mind, there are some country-based statistical reports on the topic. One is a governmental survey from Malaysia claiming that 1.4 per cent of all Muslim marriages contracted between 1995 and 2004 are polygynous. However, the women's rights group Sisters in Islam (SIS) is sceptical towards these numbers and believes that they in reality are higher, as many husbands will keep their polygynous marriages a secret from their first wife and families. Zainah Anwar, the director of SIS, announced a few years back that they would conduct interviews with 6,000 members of polygynous households, and thus create the largest survey on this area so far (Sisters in Islam, 28 December 2006). Another survey is from Morocco and reports that polygynous marriages decreased by 3.75 per cent between 2005 and 2006 (Musawah website on Morocco). The report is made by l'Association Démocratique des Femmes du Maroc, which was involved in lobbying prior to the reform of the Mudawwana in 2004. Thus, both surveys are produced on the initiative of women's rights activists. Reviewing family courts' documentation of reasons given for divorce can be another way of accessing information on the extent of polygyny. Mir-Hosseini, for instance, refers to

statistics saying that 11 per cent of divorces in Morocco were effected as a result of polygyny (Mir-Hosseini 2000a: 117).

14. Among the conditions stated in the 1974 Indonesian Marriage Act for court permission of polygyny are: (1) If the wife cannot fulfil her marital duties; (2) The wife suffers from an incurable illness or physical disease; and /or the wife cannot give birth (Otto 2010: 467). Additional conditions mentioned are: (1) The consent of the wife (if the court deems it necessary); (2) The financial ability of the husband to provide for more than one wife must be proved; (3) The declaration of the husband that he will treat his wives and children equally (op. cit.: 467–8).
15. The five conditions were that: (1) The husband had the financial means; (2) Could guarantee equal treatment of the wives; (3) No harm would be caused to the existing wife/wives; (4) The additional marriage was 'just and necessary'; (5) The proposed marriage should not directly or indirectly lower the existing wife's and dependants' standard of living (Hamza and Othman, 14 January 2010).
16. Polygyny has also been outlawed in the former Soviet Union, although the practice still remains common in countries like Turkmenistan, the Kyrgyz Republic, Tajikistan and Uzbekistan (WLUML website).
17. The website of WLUML has published a report that includes an overview of polygyny in Muslim family law codes. The report can be accessed at: http://www.wluml.org/sites/wluml.org/files/import/english/pubs/pdf/knowing%20our%20rights/kor_2006_en.pdf, read on 10 February 2011.
18. The Family Protection Law did not, however, introduce amendments with regard to temporary marriage, but left it unresolved (Paidar 1995: 114).
19. Another example relates to the marriage contracts of women who had married between 1967 and 1982. According to Mir-Hosseini, these contracts were still recognised as valid in practice by the courts after 1979, despite what Ayatollah Khomeini declared shortly after the Revolution (Mir-Hosseini 2000a: 56).
20. In the original text there is no reference to the *'asr va haraj* principle, but the article listed the grounds on which a woman could ask for divorce, as seen above (Mir-Hosseini 2000a: 210, note 8).
21. There were two main stipulations that the husband could choose to sign or not in the contract: (1) If the divorce had not been initiated or caused by the wife, the husband had to pay his wife up to half of the assets he had acquired during their marriage. It was up to the court to decide if the wife had any fault in the divorce. (2) If one of the following conditions in the marriage contract was broken, the wife had the delegated right to obtain a divorce: the husband's failure to support her financially or fulfil other marital duties for six months minimum; the husband's maltreatment of the wife; if the husband has an incurable disease; the insanity of the husband; the husband's inability to abstain from an occupation that detracts from the wife's reputation; if the husband is imprisoned for five years or more; if the court finds that a husband's addiction to anything harms family life or the marriage, or that he has deserted family life

for six months or more; if the husband is convicted for a crime that detracts from the family's reputation; the husband's failure to father a child after five years of marriage; or the husband's second marriage without the consent of the first wife or his failure to treat them equally (Mir-Hosseini 2000a: 57).

22. To refer to *nekah* as 'permanent marriage' is, however, somewhat misleading because *nekah* may be terminated according to different procedures of *talaq*, as explained previously.
23. This term is rarely used by Shi'a *ulama,* who refer to the practice as *ezdevaj-e movaqat* (temporary marriage) in contrast to *ezdevaj-e dayem* (permanent marriage) (Haeri 1989: 50). In the 2007 Family Protection Bill, temporary marriage is referred to as *nekah movaqat* (Article 22).
24. There are also differences in terms for 'wife' in the two forms of marriage. A wife in a permanent marriage is referred to as *zawjih*, but in a temporary marriage she is simply called *sighe* (Haeri 1989: 51).
25. Whereas dower in a permanent marriage is referred to as *mehrieh*, dower in a temporary marriage is called *ajr* (wage or reward). On a general basis, however, contemporary Shi'i *ulama* have referred to dower in both kinds of marriages as *mahr* (Haeri 1989: 220). This is also the case in the 1928 Civil Code of Iran, where dower is referred to as *mahr* both in relation to permanent and temporary marriage.
26. Article 940 in the Iranian Civil Code states: 'A married pair, married permanently, and not restrained from inheriting, take inheritance one from the other.' (Article 940)
27. As in permanent marriages, interfaith temporary marriages are allowed for men, but not for women (Haeri 1989: 60).
28. There are resemblances between temporary marriage and prostitution in particular when performed outside the legal system. Still, Haeri claims that the arrangement differs from prostitution, because it is dealt with in terms of Shi'a Islamic jurisprudence and the Civil Code of Iran as a legal topic regulated in the areas of dower, custody rights, and rulings of a waiting period after divorce (*'idda*).
29. I have not found sources confirming that the Zaydi and Isma'ili branch of Shi'ism bans the practice of *mut'a* as such, but it seems to be maintained and advocated mainly by the *Ithna 'Ashari* or Twelver branch (cf. Haeri 1989: 1). Also, during the Fatimid Caliphate (909–1171), which was governed by the Isma'ili branch of Shi'ism, *mut'a* marriage was not part of the legal system (Vikør 2003: 125).
30. *'Urfi* derives from the Arabic word *'urf*, which can be translated as custom or common practice (Vikør 2003: 366).
31. Jessica Carlisle has also written about the relation between state policies and what she refers to as 'irregular marriage practices' (for instance, temporary marriage) in Syria (2008). Moreover, there are reports of *misyar* marriages (marriages contracted without the formal requirements of conventional Islamic marriages) being increasingly performed in the United Arab Emirates and Saudi

Arabia alongside so-called friend marriages (Welchman 2007: 102–5). Alternatives to conventional marriage contracts are being carried out in the form of *'urfi* and *misyar* marriages in order to ease the high costs of conventional marriages, as well as allowing men and women to engage in lawful sexual relations (Singerman 2010).

32. In Article 83 in the penal code of Iran from 1991, extramarital sexual relations (*zina*) are defined as *hudud* (borders or limits) and punishable by stoning or flogging. An entire chapter in the Iranian penal code deals with punishments for extramarital sex (Chapter Three). In addition, Chapter Two is about how such relations can be proved and verified in court, and Chapter One deals with definitions of extramarital sex.
33. The discourse on 'universalisation of marriage' is discussed further in Chapter Six.
34. The question of minimum age of marriage has been prevalent in debates about women's rights and Islam. In 1979, the minimum age of marriage was lowered from 20 to 15 for boys and from 16 to 9 for girls (the 1967/75 Family Protection Law). During the presidency of Khatami, the minimum age for girls was increased to 13. The legal age of marriage does not, however, reflect the social realities in Iran, as statistics show that in 1966 the average age of marriage for women was 22.4 and for men 25.6 (Moghadam 2011: 119). Nonetheless, the minimum age of marriage has been an issue of debate.
35. 'Absence of marriage portion in the fact of a temporary marriage will under the contract be void.' (Article 1095 of the Iranian Civil Code)
36. 'The death of the wife in a temporary marriage during the period of marriage will not cause the forfeiture of the marriage portion; the same will be true if the husband did not have any relations with her up to the end of the period of marriage.' (Article 1096 of the Iranian Civil Code)
37. 'If the husband waives his rights to the whole period of marriage in a temporary marriage before having any relations with the wife, he must pay half of the marriage portion.' (Article 1097 of the Iranian Civil Code)
38. 'If the marriage, whether temporary or permanent, was void, and there has not been any matrimonial relations, the wife will not be entitled to any marriage portion and the husband can demand the refund of the marriage portion if it has been settled.' (Article 1098 of the Iranian Civil Code)
39. 'If there be more than one wife, the fourth or eighth part, which belongs to the wife, will be divided equally among them.' (Article 942 of the Iranian Civil Code)
40. The 1931 Marriage Law did, however, demand the registration of all marriages and divorces (Mir-Hosseini 1996: 145). Still, the Law contained no specific reference to temporary marriage.

Chapter 3 The Family Protection Bill

1. Other European-based law codes enacted in Iran at the time made no reference to Shari'a, such as the Codes of Commercial Law (1932) and Civil Procedure (1939), Criminal Law (1912, 1926, 1940) and Criminal Procedure (1911, 1932) (Mir-Hosseini 2010: 327). Since 1979, however, new codes based on *fiqh* have gradually replaced European-based ones as a means of conforming the judiciary to Shi'a Islamic legal norms under the slogan 'return to Shari'a' (op. cit.: 333).
2. A *mujtahid* is an *'alim* (Islamic scholar) who is qualified to perform *ijtihad* (independent reasoning).
3. *Ezdevaj-e movaqat* is the term used in Article 22 of the 2007 Family Protection Bill. *Nekah movaqat* is the term used in Article 22 of the 2010 Family Protection Bill. *Sighe* and *mut'a* are frequently used in the debates on the 2007 and 2010 Family Protection Bill.
4. *Ta'adod-e ezdevaj* is the term used in Article 23 of the 2007 Family Protection Bill. *Ezdevaj-e mujadad-e dayem* is the term used in Article 23 of the 2010 Family Protection Bill. *Ezdevaj-e mut'aded* is the correct legal term for polygyny according to Mir-Hosseini (March 2011). *Chandzani* is the term frequently used in the public debates on the 2007 and 2010 Bills.
5. *Mehrieh* is the term used in Article 25 of the 2007 Family Protection Bill, and Article 24 of the 2010 Family Protection Bill. *Mahr* is the Arabic term used in the Iranian Civil Code, and sometimes in the debate on the 2007 and 2010 Bills.
6. The Constitutional article states: 'The government must ensure the rights of women in all respects, in conformity with Islamic criteria, and accomplish the following goals: (1) To create a favourable environment for the growth of woman's personality and the restoration of her rights, both the material and intellectual; (2) The protection of mothers, particularly during pregnancy and child-rearing, and the protection of children without guardians; (3) Establishing competent courts to protect and preserve the family; (4) The provision of special insurance for widows, aged women and women without support; (5) The awarding of guardianship of children to worthy mothers, in order to protect the interests of the children, in the absence of a legal guardian' (Article 21 in the 1979 Constitution of the Islamic Republic of Iran).
7. The Constitutional article states: 'The Head of Judiciary is responsible for the following: (1) Establishment of structure necessary for the justice commensurate with mentioned under Article 156; (2) Drafting judicial bills appropriate for the Islamic Republic; (3) Employment of just and worthy judges, their dismissal, appointment, transfer, assignment to particular duties, promotions, and carrying out similar administrative duties, in accordance with the law.' (Article 158 of the 1979 Constitution of the Islamic Republic of Iran)
8. The 2007 Family Protection Bill is said to replace the following laws if ratified: (1) Law on Marriage approved 14 August 1931; (2) Law on Denial of Marital

Relationship, approved 11 March 1933; (3) Law Mandating Presentation of Medical Certificate prior to Marriage approved 4 December 1938; (4) Family Protection Law approved 4 February 1975; (5) Law on Right of Custody approved 13 July 1986; (6) Law Mandating Anti-Tetanus Immunisation for Ladies prior to Marriage approved 12 April 1988; (7) Law of Amendment to Divorce Regulations, approved 12 March 1992; (8) Law for Assignment of a number of existing courts to perform as courts of subject of Article 21 of the Constitution, 30th July 1997; (9) Law for Period of Validity of Certificate of Impossibility of Reconciliation, approved 2 November 1997; (10) Islamic Penal Code, Articles 645 and 646, approved 22 May 1996 (Article 53 of the 2007 Family Protection Bill).

9. The Iranian Civil Code was drafted in three volumes between 1927 and 1935 by a commission appointed by the Ministry of Justice (*Vezarat-e Dadgostari*). The Civil Code was based mainly on three authoritative Shi'ite legal texts of Najm al-Din Mohaqqeq Helli, Zayn al-Din 'Ameli Sahid-al-Tani and Sheikh Morteza Ansari. Moreover, the Belgian, French, and Swiss Codes were used as models of the new Codification (Mir-Hosseini 2010: 327). The second volume dealt with personal statue and family law and was ratified by the Majles in 1935. The latter introduced few changes and was mostly based on classical Shi'i Shari'a. The only exceptions were adopted from other schools of law in order to extend the grounds for women's access to divorce (Article 1129 and 1130). Also, Article 1041 prohibited the marriage of girls under 13 (op. cit.: 351).
10. 'The Family Court shall convene with the President or the alternate judge and two advisers in attendance, where possible one of the two assessors being a lady with judicial rank. The sitting and the judgement shall be valid with a majority.' (Article 2 of the Family Protection Bill 2007)
11. According to the One Million Signatures Campaign website the following groups are part of the initiative: Change for Equality, the One Million Signatures Campaign, Women's Organization of Iran, Feminist School, Women's Field, Organisation of Female Journalists, Organisation of Human Rights Defenders, the Mothers Committee of the One Million Signatures Campaign, the Public Relations Committee of the One Million Signatures Campaign, the Workshop Committee of the Campaign, The One Million Signatures Campaign in California, The Human Rights Committee of the Organisation of Iranian Alumni (ADVAR), Hastia Andish NGO, Mothers for Peace, Assembly of Reformist Women, Human Rights Organisation of Kurdistan, Independent Organisation of Students and Alumni of Qazvin, Iranian Cultural Network in Europe, Cultural Research Organisation of Iran–Sweden, Student Committee for Defence of Political Prisoners, The site of the People's Voice (We Change website, 18 August 2008).
12. The article states: 'In the event that only the husband is applying for divorce, a petition for issuance of a certificate of impossibility of reconciliation shall be submitted to the court. However, if the wife is applying for divorce, the court

shall be petitioned for a judgement to mandate divorce or to ascertain the conditions for exercise of representation in divorce, as the case may be.' (Article 28 of the Family Protection Bill 2007)

13. The article states: 'Any foreign national who marries an Iranian woman without obtaining the permit mentioned under Article 1060 of the Civil Code, shall be sentenced from 91 days to one year's imprisonment. In that case, the woman, if she got married of her free will, the girl's father, if the marriage has taken place with his permission, and the marriage solemniser shall be sentenced as accomplices to the offence.' (Article 46 of the Family Protection Bill 2007)
14. According to Ziba Mir-Hosseini, Article 24 of the 2007 Family Protection Bill was one of the articles added by Ahmadinejad's cabinet (conversation at SOAS, London in March 2011).
15. Mousavi is a former prime minister of Iran (1981–9), and was a reformist candidate in the 2009 presidential election. Since the 2009 election, he has also become known as the leader of the so-called Green Movement of Iran (*Jombesh-e Sabz-e Iran*).

Chapter 4 Conceptions of Shari'a and Family Law

1. Generally, Shi'a and Sunni Islam share beliefs in the main doctrines of monotheism (*tawhid*), prophethood (*nabuwwa*) and resurrection (*ma'ad*). In addition, Shi'ism adheres to the doctrines of the Imamate (*imama*) and justice (*'adl* or *'edalat*). The latter refers to God's divine justice and is a central part of Shi'i faith (Moomen 1985: 176–7). In terms of *fiqh*, however, there are some significant differences. For instance, Shi'i *fiqh* has different categories of *ijtihad* from Sunni *fiqh*. In the *usuli* branch of Shi'i *fiqh*, there is a clear hierarchy of *ulama* often described as a hierarchy of deference (op. cit.: 204). In general, Shi'ism has had a more open approach towards the principle for *ijtihad* for this reason. Whereas Sunni schools of law have dealt with a debate on whether the 'closing of the door of *ijtihad*' took place or not, a similar discussion has not been prevalent in Shi'ism (Hallaq 2009: 113–17).

Chapter 5 Conceptions of Dower, Polygyny and Temporary Marriage

1. The Council is also called the Women's Information and Statistics Centre (*Markaz-e Ettela'-e va Amar-e Zanan*).
2. The second article of the Family Protection Bill mentioned by the interviewee was Article 25 regarding dower (*mehrieh*).
3. The press conference of the Women's Coalition opposing the Family Protection Bill was held on 25 April 2009 in connection with the opening of the election campaigns of presidential candidates. The participants included Simin

Behbahani, Shirin 'Ebadi, A'zam Taleqani, Elaheh Kolai'i, Shahla Lahiji, Farzaneh Taheri and Shahla E'zazi.

4. It should be added that the word used for temporary marriage is *sighe*, which literally means 'concubine' and refers to the type of marriage contract in use (Haeri 1989: 50). *Sighe* is, however, never used for a man. 'A man does *sighe*, whereas a woman either becomes a *sighe* or is a *sighe*.' (op. cit.: 51) There are also differences in terms used for 'wife' in the two forms of marriage. A wife in a permanent marriage is referred to as *zawjih*, but a wife in a temporary marriage is simply called *sighe* (ibid.).
5. According to Haeri, temporary marriage is from one hour to 99 years (1989: 2), and not one second as the interviewee explained.
6. Sherkat was the editor of the former women's journal *Zanan*.

Chapter 6 Women's Rights Activism in Iran Since 1900

1. Ebrahim Yazdi, The Islamic Republic's first foreign minister, introduced the division of the history of the Islamic Republic of Iran into three different phases after 1979 (Buchta 2005: 2–3). The first phase refers to the decade under Ayatollah Ruhollah Khomeini (1979–89); the second phase to the period under the leadership of Ayatollah 'Ali Hossein Khamenei and President Ayatollah Akbar Hashemi Rafsanjani (1990–96); and the third phase was initiated with the election of President Muhammad Khatami in 1997. Each of these periods has its own characteristics. Correspondingly, I have labelled the phase of Mahmoud Ahmadinejad's presidency as the 'Fourth' Islamic Republic (2005– 13). For a more detailed presentation of the history of the Islamic Republic, see Keddie 2003, Buchta 2005 and Paidar 1995.
2. Studies on women's rights activism during the Safavid and Qajar periods and generally before the Constitutional Revolution have been limited. Women's roles as scholars, teachers and in transmitting religious knowledge have been overlooked in most research on this era, although there are some exceptions (see for example Babayan 1999). Even though studies are limited, Keddie asserts that the role of women varied considerably according to class and status during Qajar rule (Keddie 2003: 30). Some women from the elite class enjoyed influence derived from the position of their male relatives, and there were some female mullas who dealt with women's religious activities in particular by reading and commenting on the Qur'an and the lives of the Imams (op. cit.: 29). It is not known whether there was any political participation of lower class women, or men for that matter, before the Constitutional Revolution.
3. Among these were the boycott of foreign goods and the assassination of constitutionalists conducted by women (Sanasarian 1982: 19).
4. Sanasarian presents some common features of the contributors to the early Iranian women's movement. She analyses the involvement of 12 women based on the city of their activities, their socioeconomic status, type of work and educational background. She concludes that all 12 members belonged to

affluent Iranian families, represented high socioeconomic groups and were well-educated (1982: 42–3).

5. For accounts of the Egyptian women's movement see Badran 1995 and Baron 2005, and for Turkey, Arat 1998 and Al-Ali 2000, 2002 and 2004.
6. After 1979, however, links to neighbouring countries were again established.
7. Ayatollah Taleqani (1911–79) was a high-ranking Shi'i *'alim*. Together with 'Ali Shari'ati and Mehdi Bazarga, among others, he founded Nehzat-e Azadi-ye Iran (Freedom Movement of Iran). Taleqani was also a symbol of the opposition movement to the Shah. Prior to the 1979 Revolution, he was closely associated with Ayatollah Khomeini and a supporter of the Islamic Revolution. Ayatollah Taleqani died in September 1979.
8. The People's Mujahedin of Iran (*Sazeman-e Mujahedin-e Khalq-e Iran*) was established in 1965. The movement initially had an Islamic and communist orientation, and fought an armed struggle against the Shah, capitalism and imperialism. It is still active today, although its ideological basis has undergone significant changes since the 1960s.
9. After 1979 there were some attempts to rebuild the women's organisations in the country and hundreds of small organisations were founded (for a complete list see Yeganeh and Tabari 1982: 201–30). Attempts to form a broad women's association was made in 1979 and 1980 with the Women's Solidarity Committee, but as a result of the political differences among women's rights activists at the time it was hard to unite. A range of other women's organisations did, however, also exist at the time (a chronology of various events related to women's rights (speeches, resolutions, legislations, demonstrations) taking place between 1905 and 1981 can be found in Yeganeh and Tabari 1982: 23–39.
10. Azar Tabari is the pseudonym of Afsaneh Najmabadi, and Nahid Yeganeh the one of Parvin Paidar.
11. Zeynab is the daughter of Fatemeh and 'Ali, and the grand-daughter of the Prophet Muhammad. She is often referred to as a pious, caring, strong and an outspoken role model for women in Shi'i Islamic movements (Deeb 2006: 153).
12. Among other affiliated members of WSIR were Zahra Rahnavard, Monir Gorji and Shahin Tabatabai.
13. In the 1980 Majles election, three among 270 representatives were women. The third female representative was Goharolsharieh Dastgheib (Paidar 1995: 309).
14. Khomeini introduced the position of *velayat-e faqih* in 1979. It forms the basis of the Constitution of the Islamic Republic and exemplifies the transformations that Shi'a religious authorities faced after the establishment of the Republic. Khomeini's time as *velayat-e faqih* was fairly unproblematic, as he was already an acknowledged *marja'-e taqlid* (source of emulation), which indicates the highest rank of Shi'a *ulama*. After Khomeini's death, however, Ayatollah Khamenei was appointed the new *velayat-e faqih*. He was not a recognised *marja'*, and thus the conflict between Shi'a religious and political authorities increased (Keddie 2003: 260–2 and Vali Nasr 2007: 125–6).

15. Perhaps the most important move towards the international community was Iran's attendance at the sixth Organisation of the Islamic Conference (OIC) in Senegal in 1991. After this meeting, more than ten countries decided to renew their diplomatic relations with Iran – broken off because of the Iran–Iraq war – and thus reopened for business with Iran (Ehteshami and Zweiri 2007: xiii–xiv).
16. The 'new religious thinking' gradually emerged during the 1990s and regained a foothold after the rise of the Iranian reform movement in 1997 (Mir-Hosseini 2006: 636).
17. *Fiqh-e sunnati* (traditional jurisprudence) represents the opposite view and projects a stricter view of jurisprudence.
18. Mir-Hosseini has accused 'Abdolkarim Soroush in particular of being reluctant to address the topic of women's rights. She says that the general debate on women's rights is dependent on the political climate in Iran, as evidenced both during the reformist era of the 1990s and after the 2004 parliamentary elections which led to a conservative turn in the gender debate (Mir-Hosseini 2006: 636).
19. In 1964, the journal reflected the view of reformist religious scholars and supported the Family Protection Law in 1967 (Mir-Hosseini 2002: 75). In 1979, it was taken over by the Islamic Republican Party and adopted an Islamically defined point of view on women's issues. *Zan-e Ruz* is still published and sold in newsstands in Iran today. Articles now deal, for example, with the work of the Centre for Women and Family Affairs, the relationship between men and women, recipes and handicrafts (examples from *Zan-e Ruz*, 31 Farvardin 1387/ 19 April 2008). Thus, *Zan-e Ruz* has moved away from involvement in contemporary legal discussions.
20. The representatives elected were Fakhr Taj Amir Shaqaqi (Tabriz), Fatemeh Homayun (Tabriz), Maryam Behrouzi (Tehran), Parvin Salehi (Tehran), Nafiseh Faiyaz Bakhsh (Tehran), Manijeh Nobakht (Tehran), Marzieh Vahid-Dastjerdi (Tehran), Akhtar Derakhshandeh (Kermanshah) and Qadiseh 'Alavi (Mashhad) (Gheytanchi 2001).
21. In addition to Faezeh Hashemi (Tehran), Fatemeh Ramazanzadeh (Tehran), Soheila Jelodarzadeh (Tehran), Fatemeh Karrubi (Tehran), Marzieh Vahid-Dastjerdi (Tehran), Nafiseh Faiyaz Bakhsh (Tehran), Qadsleh 'Alavi (Mashhad), Elaheh Rastgoo (Malayer), Shahrbanu Amani-Anganeh (Orumieh), Marzieh Dabagh (Hamadan), Zahra Pishgahi-Fard (Esfahan), Nayereh Akhavan-Bitarf (Esfahan) and Monir Nobakht (Tehran) were elected (Gheytanchi 2001).
22. In addition, Faezeh Hashemi was the managing director of a communications network of women's NGOs. This functioned as a kind of umbrella organisation for these NGOs and was based in Tehran.
23. The Guardian Council consists of 12 members that have the power to approve all candidates for elections, to interpret the Constitution, and to veto any proposed bill from the Majles if the Council finds that it contradicts Islam.
24. The Centre for Women's Participation (*Markaz-e Mosharekat-e Zanan*) was established by President Khatami in 1997. After the election of Ahmadinejad

in 2005, however, it was renamed the Centre for Women's and Family Affairs (*Markaz-e Umur-e Zanan va Khanevadeh*).

25. During the late 1990s and early 2000s there was an increase in women's NGOs in Iran. Their number rose from 13 in 1976–7 to 137 in 2001–2 (Povey 2004: 257).
26. The Guardian Council approved a total of eight candidates for the 2005 presidential election. Rafsanjani gained the second highest number of votes, 35.9 per cent (Ehteshami and Zweiri 2007: 45).
27. Also, the neoconservative turn in politics has brought a more confrontational tone in foreign policies, especially towards the United States and Israel. Although Ahmadinejad, in the opinion of many Iranians, crossed a line, for example by rejecting the Holocaust, it seems that he has the support of most Iranians when arguing for Iran's right to develop a nuclear capability.
28. For instance, in June 2006 women's rights activists were beaten and arrested for demonstrating for women's rights in the centre of Tehran (Harrison, 12 June 2006). And in March 2007, 33 were arrested (BBC, 4 March 2007). After the 2009 presidential election, women's rights activists have been arrested on different occasions (Feminist School website, 01 August 2009) and in January 2010, 19 of them were arrested (Payvand, 14 January 2010).
29. *Basij* (literally: mobilisation) is a paramilitary volunteer group of private soldiers that was founded by Khomeini in 1979. More recently, though, *Basij* involves larger groups of volunteers who are organised, for instance, in the Student *Basij* (*Basij-e Daneshjui-ye*) or the Public Service *Basij* (*Basij-e Edari*).
30. The campaign is also known as the One Million Signatures Campaign Demanding Changes to Discriminatory Laws and Change for Equality.
31. Pictures from the 8 March 2006 demonstration can be seen at: http://www.youtube.com/watch?v=kxLWXVRZhr0.
32. I have reports of the demonstrations from interviewees who were there as eyewitnesses.
33. The website of the One Million Signatures campaign: http://www.onemillionsigns.info/english/. The website is filtered from time to time and consequently the url address may change.
34. Hastia Andish is a women's NGO working in particular on women's education, violence against women and the HIV/AIDS problem.
35. In addition, rulings about who can be elected President of Iran, the prescribed dress codes for women, social security laws and the stoning as a penalty that is usually inflicted on women are being addressed (Tohidi, 12 December 2007).
36. Interviews of and presentations by more members of the OMSC can be found here: http://www.sign4change.info/english/spip.php?rubrique14.
37. The website of the Feminist School can be found at: http://www.iranfemschool.com/english/.
38. The website of the initiative is http://fairfamilylaw.info/.

Chapter 7 Shifting Paradigms on Gender and Sexuality

1. The Constitutional Revolution in 1905/06 culminated in the draft of the first Constitution of Iran and the establishment of the first Majles in 1906. In 1925, the Constitutional Revolution also ended to the Qajar period (1794–1925). In 1928 a new Civil Code was drafted, and in the years that followed Reza Shah Pahlavi (reigned 1925–41) a period of socioeconomic reforms was instigated that brought major changes to the country.
2. The gender-undifferentiated ideals of beauty are related to two types of pleasure that are believed to await Muslim men in the afterlife – the eternally young and female virgins called *hur* (popular), and the beautiful young and beardless men referred to as *ghilman* (i.e. servant) or more commonly *amrad* (hairless, smooth) (Najmabadi 2005: 59). These ideals thus draw on the distinction between adult manhood and young manhood (*amradhood*). An *amrad* signifies an adolescent beardless man. Adult men who shaved their beards, however, were called *amrad numa* (looking like an *amrad*) and not *zan numa* (looking like a woman) (op. cit.: 16). Being a woman and an *amrad* both signified demarcation from manhood. The *amrad* was thus considered something of a liminal role before entering manhood.
3. *Bazari* refers to a group of merchants in the Iranian bazars. *Bazaris* represent a significant economic force in Iran as they engage in international trade and organise into guilds. Traditionally, they have also had a special link to *ulama*. Often they belonged to the same families, and *bazaris* provided income for *ulama* and observed a high degree of religious piety (Keddie 2003: 30).
4. In Article 83 in the Islamic Penal Code of Iran from 1991, the punishment for homosexuality is equal to that for adultery (*zina*), which is *hudud* (a limit or restriction) and punished by stoning or flogging. The whole of Chapter Three of the Penal Code is dedicated to defining punishments for adultery. Chapter Two deals with ways to prove adultery in court and Chapter One elaborates on definitions of adultery.
5. The day of 'Ashura' commemorates the martyrdom of Hussein, grandson of the Prophet, and his companions and family who were killed in the battle of Karbala' on 10 *Muharram* 61 / 2 October 680.
6. Ayatollah Rafsanjani was President of Iran from 1989 to 1997. In the 1980s, however, he was Chairman and Speaker of the Majles (1980–9). In 2007, Rafsanjani was elected Chairman of the Assembly of Experts (*Majles-e Khobregan or Majles-e Khobregan-e Rahbari*), which is in charge of appointing the Supreme Leader of Iran (*velayat-e faqih*). Also in 2007, Rafsanjani was elected Chairman of the Expediency Council (Majma'-ye Tashkhis Maslahat-e Nezam), an assembly appointed by the *velayat-e faqih* that gives guidance to the *velayat-e faqih* and resolves differences between the Majles and the Guardian Council (*Shura-ye Negahban*).

7. Iran's population has experienced increased access to education, health care, electricity and mass media alongside a larger process of urbanisation. Concurrently, the Total Fertility Rate (TFR) has decreased from 7.0 children per woman in 1980 to 2.2 children in 2000, which can be seen as a direct outcome of the changes in family planning policies from 1989 (Abbasi-Shavazi et al. 2008: 217).
8. Molkara was born a man, but wanted a surgery that could transform her into a woman. In 1975 she started writing letters to Khomeini, asking him to authorise a sex reassignment surgery, and in 1987 Khomeini issued a fatwa allowing the surgery to take place (Tait, 28 July 2005).
9. *'Alim* is the singular of *ulama*.
10. In the late 1990s, the right wing of Iranian politics suffered many defeats. In the seventh and eighth presidential elections in 1997 and 2001 the reformist candidate Khatami gained the most votes, and in the 1999 local elections the reformist camp won more than 80 per cent of the votes (Ehteshami and Zweiri 2007: 35). Again, in the elections for the sixth Majles in 2000, reformists won a secure victory. Still, the traditional conservative forces maintained control over the armed forces, the media, the judiciary and major economic organisations during this period, and thus restricted the influence of reformists because of the organisation of the political system in Iran. This was primarily due to the Guardian Council's right to veto any decision made by the president or the Majles.

Chapter 8 Sources of Legitimacy

1. Holliday addresses identity formation in Iran during the presidential periods of Khatami (1997–2005) and Ahmadinejad (2005–13) (2011). In the analysis, she refers to 'Abdolkarim Soroush's definition of the cultural heritage of Iran, which she claims draw on three kinds of culture, namely Iranian culture, Islamic culture and western culture.
2. Eftekhari's speech was held at the Inter-Parliamentary Union of Islamic Countries' Female Deputies in Damascus in 2011.
3. The book is called *Senator: Mehrangiz Manoochehrian's activities on the Foundation of the Legal Struggles of Women in Iran* (*Senator: Mehrangiz Manoochehrian bar Bestar Mebarzat-e Hoqoq-e Zanan-e Iran*) (2003).
4. The original title in Persian is *Vaziat-e Hoqoq-e Zanan dar Javan* and it was published by the Association for Women Lawyers in Iran (*Dokhtaran-e Sangeman-e dar Iran*) in February 1963.
5. Manoochehrian pushed for the elimination of husbands' permission for women to obtain a passport and to travel abroad. Because of her resistance to this law, Manoochehrian lost her seat in the Senate (Afkhami 2004: 126).
6. Article 1133 states that 'A man can divorce his wife whenever he wishes to do so.' (1928 Iranian Civil Code)

7. The conditions for divorce stated are: (1) Adultery; (2) Incurable mental illness; (3) Physical abuse; (4) Incurable diseases; (5) Infertility after 15 years of marriage; (6) Absence of six months; (7) Husband's refusal to pay alimony (*nafaqa*) (Article 1133, Manoochehrian 1963/64).
8. Nowruz is the name of the Iranian New Year (literally: 'new day'). It marks the first day of the Iranian calendar and also the first day of spring. Nowruz is originally a Zoroastrian ritual but is still celebrated in Iran. It is often seen as representing Iran's ancient heritage of Persian culture.
9. In 1955 Farrokhzad published her first collection of poetry, *Asir* (*The Captive*). Soon after, the collections *Divar* (*The Wall*) and *Osian* (*Rebellion*) came out. Farrokhzad studied cinematography in Italy during the late 1950s, which resulted in the documentary film *Khane-ye Siyah ast* (*The House is Black*), among others (Javadi 2010: xi). In 1967 she died in a car accident at the age of 32.
10. Badran notes, however, that not all Egyptian women's rights activists were feminists, or secular-oriented for that matter (2005: 9).

BIBLIOGRAPHY

List of interviews and interviewees

Interview with Afsaneh, professor, in April 2008 [in English].

Interview with Afsaneh, professor, in May 2008 [in English].

Interview with Afsaneh, professor, in February 2009 [in English].

Interview with 'Ali, Shahla and Roya, members of the One Million Signatures Campaign and Feminist School, in February 2009 [in English and Persian, partly with translator].

Interview with Arezoo, director of a women's rights organisation, in November 2002 [in English and Persian. with translator].

Interview with Arezoo, director of a women's rights organisation, in May 2008 [in English and Persian with translator].

Interview with A'zam Taleqani, previous Member of Parliament, editor of *Payam-e Hajar* (Hagar's Message) and director of the Women's Society of the Islamic Revolution (*Jam'e-ye Zanan-e Enghelab-e Eslami*), in May 2008 [in English and Persian, partly with translator].

Interview with Bahareh, journalist and a former employee at a women's rights organisation, in November 2002 [in English].

Interview with Elham, previously director of a women's rights organisation and editor of a women's journal, in November 2002 [in English].

Interview with Faezeh Hashemi, former member of parliament, editor of *Zan* (Woman) and current president of the Islamic Countries Women's Sports Solidarity Council, in May 2008 [in English and Persian, partly with translator].

Interview with Leyli, member of the One Million Signatures Campaign (*Yek Milyun Emza-ye Baraye Taghir-e Qavanin-e Tab'iz Amiz*), in May 2008 [in Persian with translator].

Interview with Leyla, director of a women's rights organisation, in May 2008 [in English].

Interview with Leyli, member of the One Million Signatures Campaign, in February 2009 [in Persian with translator].

Interview with Maryam, professor, in March 2009 [in English].

Interview with Minoo, former employee at the Centre for Women's Participation (*Markaz-e Mosharekat-e Zanan*), in May 2008 [in English].
Interview with Parisa, a lawyer and former director of a women's rights organisation, in November 2002 [in English].
Interview with Parisa, lawyer and previous director of a women's rights organisation, in October 2010 [in English and Persian, partly with translator].
Interview with Parvin, a former employee at the Centre for Women's Participation (*Markaz-e Mosharekat-e Zanan*), in November 2002 [in English].
Interview with Shahla, member of Feminist School (*Madrese-ye Feministi*), in May 2008 [in English].
Interview with Shahla, member of Feminist School in March 2009 [in English].
Interview with Touran and Zohreh, writer and lawyer, in August 2011 [in Persian and English without translator].
Interview with Ziba, student in women's studies, in March 2009 [in English].

Books and articles

Abbasgholizadeh, Mahboobeh. (2000). 'The Experience of Islamic Feminism in Iran'. *Farzaneh*, vol. 5, no. 1.
Abbasi-Shavazi, Muhammad J., McDonald, Peter, and Hossein-Chavoshi, Meimanat. (2008). 'The Family and Social Change in Post-Revolutionary Iran'. In *Family in the Middle East: Ideational Change in Egypt, Iran and Tunisia*, K. M. Yount and H. Rashad (eds). New York, London: Routledge.
Abu-Lughod, Lila and Rao, Anupama. (eds). (2011). 'Women's Rights, Muslim Family Law, and the Politics of Consent'. Collection of Working Papers. *Social Difference Online*, vol. 1, December. Center for the Critical Analysis of Social Difference, Columbia University. Available at: http://socialdifference.columbia.edu/files/socialdiff/publications/SocDifOnline-Vol12012.pdf, accessed 22 September 2013.
Afary, Janet. (1989). 'On the Origins of Feminism in Early 20th-Century Iran'. *Journal of Women's History*, vol. 1, no. 2. pp. 65–87.
———. (2009). *Sexual Politics in Modern Iran*. Cambridge, UK: Cambridge University Press.
Afkhami, Mahnaz. (2004). 'The Women's Organization of Iran: Evolutionary Politics and Revolutionary Change'. In *Women in Iran from 1800 to the Islamic Republic*, L. Beck and G. Nashat (eds). Champaign, IL: University of Illinois Press.
Ahmadi, Fereshteh. (2006). 'Islamic Feminism in Iran: Feminism in a New Islamic Context'. *Journal of Feminist Studies in Religion*, vol. 22, no. 2. pp. 33–53.
Al-Ali, Nadje. (2000). *Secularism, Gender and the State in the Middle East: The Egyptian Women's Movement*. Cambridge, UK: Cambridge University Press.
———. (2002). 'The Women's Movement in Egypt, with Selected References to Turkey'. Civil Society and Social Movements Programme Paper, no. 5. *United Nations Research Institute for Social Development*. Available at: http://kms1.isn.ethz.ch/serviceengine/Files/ISN/102668/ipublicationdocument_singledocument/d9d5c414-c0b6–40a9–86c0-b19b61ffabd9/en/5.pdf, accessed 6 January 2012.

———. (2004). 'Secular Women's Activism in Contemporary Egypt'. In *Warning Signs of Fundamentalisms*, A. Imam, J. Morgan and N. Yuval Davis (eds). London: Women Living Under Muslim Law, pp. 144–57.

Amin, Sonia Nishat. (1996). *The World of Muslim Women in Colonial Bengal 1876–1939*. Leiden: Brill.

Appelros, Erica. (2007). 'Religious Proximity. A Tool for Intersectional Analyses Involving Religion'. Unpublished paper presented at the Conference: 'Religion on the Borders: New challenges in the Academic Study of Religion'. Södertörn: Södertörn University College.

Arat, Yesim. (1998). 'Feminists, Islamists, and Political Change in Turkey'. *Political Psychology*, vol. 19, no. 1. pp. 117–31. Available at: http://onlinelibrary.wiley.com/doi/10.1111/0162–895X.00095/pdf, accessed 6 January 2012.

Arjomand, Said Amir. (ed.). (1988). *Authority and Political Culture in Shi'ism*. Albany: State University of New York Press.

Asad, Talal. (1986). 'The Idea of an Anthropology of Islam'. *Occasional Papers Series*. Washington, DC: Institute for Contemporary Arab Studies at Georgetown University.

Babayan, Kathryn. (1999). '*The 'Aqa'id al-Nisa*: A Glimpse at Safavid Women in Local Isfahani Culture'. In *Women in the Medieval Islamic World: Power, Patronage, and Piety*, G.R.G. Hambly (ed.). New York: St Martin's Press.

Badran, Margot. (1995). *Feminists, Islam, and Nation: Gender and the Making of Modern Egypt*. Princeton, NJ: Princeton University Press.

———. (2011). 'From Islamic Feminism to a Muslim Holistic Feminism'. *Institute of Development Studies Bulletin*, vol. 42, no. 1. pp. 78–87.

Bangstad, Sindre. (2007). *Global Flows, Local Appropriations: Facets of Secularisation and Re-Islamization Among Contemporary Cape Muslims*. ISIM dissertations. ISIM/Leiden: Amsterdam University Press.

———. (2009). 'Contesting Secularism/s: Secularism and Islam in the Work of Talal Asad'. *Anthropological Theory*, vol. 9, no. 2. pp. 188–208. Available at: http://ant.sagepub.com/content/9/2/188, accessed 11 February 2012.

Bargach, Jamila. (2005). 'An Ambiguous Discourse of Rights: the 2004 Family Law Reform in Morocco'. *Hawwa*: Journal of Women of the Middle East and the Islamic world, vol. 3, no. 2. pp. 245–66.

Baron, Beth. (2005). *Egypt as a Woman: Nationalism, Gender, and Politics*. Berkeley: University of California Press.

Basu, Amrita. (ed.). (2010). *Women's Movements in the Global Era: The Power of Local Feminisms*. New York: Westview Press.

Berger, Maurits and Sonneveld, Nadia. (2010). 'Shari'a and national law in Egypt'. In *Shari'a Incorporated: A Comparative Overview of the Legal Systems of Twelve Muslim Countries in Past and Present*, J.M. Otto (ed.). Leiden: Leiden University Press.

Bowen, John R. (2003). *Islam, Law, and Equality in Indonesia: Anthropology of Public Reasoning*. Cambridge, UK: Cambridge University Press.

Buchta, Wilfred. (2005). 'Taking Stock of a Quarter Century of the Islamic Republic of Iran'. *Islamic Legal Studies Programme, Harvard School of Law* (ILSP). Occasional publications 5 June. Available at: http://www.law.harvard.edu/programs/ilsp/publications/buchta.pdf, accessed 4 February 2010.

Buskens, Léon. (2003). 'Recent Debates on Family Law Reform in Morocco: Islamic Law as Politics in an Emerging Public Sphere'. *Islamic Law and Society*, vol. 10, no. 1. pp. 70–130.

———. (2010). 'Shari'a and National Law in Morocco'. In *Shari'a Incorporated: A Comparative Overview of the Legal Systems of Twelve Muslim Countries in Past and Present*, J.M. Otto (ed.). Leiden: Leiden University Press.

Bøe, Marianne. (2012). 'Fornying og videreføring av midlertidig ekteskap i sjia-muslimske minoritets og majoritetsposisjoner'. *DIN, Tidsskrift for religion og kultur*, no. 1–2.

——— and Tønnessen, Liv. (2011). 'Nye utfordringer til islamsk feminisme: Kvinneaktivismens mange ansikter i Sudan og Iran'. *Tidsskrift for Kjønnsforskning*, vol. 4, no. 11, pp. 327–51.

Carlisle, Jessica. (2008). 'From Behind the Door: A Damascus Court Copes with an Alleged Out of Court Marriage'. In *Les Metamorphoses du Mariage au Moyen-Orient*, B. Drieskens (ed.). L'Institut Français du Proche-Orient. Available at: http://ifpo.revues.org/454, accessed 10 August 2011.

Coulson, Noel J. (1964). *A History of Islamic Law*. Edinburgh: Edinburgh University Press.

Dabashi, Hamid. (2011) *Shi'ism: A Religion of Protest*. Harvard, MA: Harvard University Press.

Dahlgren, Susanne. (2008). 'The Incomplete Family: Ethnographic Explorations on Domestic Relations in Aden'. *Hawwa*: Journal of Women of the Middle East and the Islamic world, vol. 6, no. 1. pp. 75–101.

Deeb, Lara. (2006). *An Enchanted Modern: Gender and Public Piety in Shi'i Lebanon*. Princeton and Oxford: Princeton University Press.

DeLong-Bas, Natana, J. and Esposito, John, L. (2001). *Family Law*. 2nd edition. Syracuse, NY: Syracuse University Press.

Ehteshami, Anoushiravan and Zweiri, Mahjoob. (2007). *Iran and the Rise of its Neoconservatives: The Politics of Tehran's Silent Revolution*. London: I.B.Tauris.

Eickelman, Dale F. and Anderson, John W. (2003). *New Media in the Muslim World: The Emerging Public Sphere*. Bloomington, Indianapolis: Indiana University Press.

———. and Piscatori, James. (2004). *Muslim Politics*. New Edition. Princeton, NJ: Princeton University Press.

Fakhro, Munira. (1996). 'Gulf Women and Islamic Law'. In *Feminism and Islam: Legal and Literary Perspectives*. M. Yamani (ed.). Reading, NY: Ithaca Press. pp. 251–26.

Farhi, Farideh. (2001). 'Religious Intellectuals, the "Woman Question", and the Struggle for the Creation of a Democratic Public Sphere in Iran'. *International Journal of Politics, Culture, and Society*, vol. 15, no. 2.

Ferdows, Adele, K. (1985). 'The Status and Rights of Women in Ithna 'Ashari Shi'i Islam'. In *Women and the Family in Iran*, A. Fathi (ed.). Leiden: Brill.

Fischer, Michael M. (2003). *Iran: From Religious Dispute to Revolution*. Wisconsin: University of Wisconsin Press.

Garthwaite, Gene R. (2005). *The Persians*. Oxford: Blackwell Publishers.

Geertz, Clifford. (1973). *The Interpretation of Cultures*. New York: Basic Books.

Gerami, Shahin. (2003). 'Mullahs, Martyrs and men: Conceptualizing Masculinity in the Islamic Republic of Iran'. *Men and Masculinities*, vol. 5, no. 3. pp. 257–95.

Gheytanchi, Elham. (2001). 'Civil Society in Iran: Politics of Motherhood and the Public Sphere'. *International Sociology*, vol. 16, no. 4. pp. 557–76.

Gleave, Robert. (2007). *Scripturalist Islam: The History and Doctrines of Akhbari Shi'i School*. Leiden: Brill.

Gorji, Monir and Ebtekar, Massoumeh. (1997). 'The Life and Status of Fatima Zahra: A Woman's Image of Excellence'. *Farzaneh*, vol. 3, no. 8. Available at: http://www.iiav.nl/ezines/web/Farzaneh/1997/Vol2Nr8/farzanehjournal/arti2n8.doc, accessed 4 January 2012.

Habermas, Jürgen. (1991). *The Structural Transformation of the Public Sphere: An Inquiry into a Bourgeois Society*. Translated by T. Burger, assisted by F. Lawrence. Massachusetts: Massachusetts Institute of Technology.

Haeri, Shahla. (1989). *Law of Desire: Temporary Marriage in Iran*. London: I.B. Tauris.

Hakken, David. (1999). *Cyborgs@Cyberspace*. New York: Routledge.

Hallaq, Wael B. (2001). *Authority, Continuity, and Change in Islamic Law*. Cambridge, UK: Cambridge University Press.

———. (2009). *Shari'a: Theory, Practice, Transformations*. New York: Cambridge University Press.

Halper, Louise. (2005). 'Law and Women's Agency in Post-revolutionary Iran'. *Harvard Journal of Law and Gender*, vol. 28. pp. 85–142.

———. (2007). 'Law, Authority, and Gender in Post-Revolutionary Iran'. *Buffalo Law Review*, vol. 54. pp. 1137–90.

Harding, Andrew. (2010). 'Shari'a and National Law in Malaysia'. In *Shari'a Incorporated: A Comparative Overview of the Legal Systems of Twelve Muslim Countries in Past and Present*, J.M. Otto (ed.). Leiden. Leiden University Press.

Hélie-Lucas, Marie-Aimée. (1994). 'The Preferential Symbol for Islamic Identity: Women in Muslim Personal Laws'. In *Identity Politics and Women: Cultural Reassertions and Feminisms in International Perspective*, V.M. Moghadam (ed.). Boulder, CO: Westview Press.

Hermansen, Marcia. (1983). 'Fatima as a Role Model in the Work of Ali Shari'ati'. In *Women and Revolution in Iran*, G. Neshat (ed.). Boulder, CO: Westview.

Hinchcliffe, Doreen. (1968). 'The Family Protection Act'. *International and Comparative Law Quarterly*, vol. 17. pp. 516–21.

Holliday, Shabnam. (2011). *Defining Iran: Politics of Resistance*. Farnham, England and Burlington, USA: Ashgate.

Hoodfar, Homa. (1999). 'The Women's Movement in Iran: Women at the Crossroads of Secularization and Islamization'. *Women Living Under Muslim Laws – The Women's Movement Series*, no. 1. Grabels, France.

———. (2008). 'Family Law and Family Planning Policy in Pre- and Post-Revolutionary Iran'. In *Family in the Middle East: Ideational Change in Egypt, Iran and Tunisia*, K.M. Yount and H. Rashad (eds). London, New York: Routledge.

———. (2009). 'Against All Odds: The building of a Women's Movement in the Islamic Republic of Iran'. *Women's United Nations Report Network* (WUNRN). Available at: http://www.wemc.com.hk/web/rf/Hoodfar_Against_All_Odds_Iran.pdf, 6 January 2012.

Ismail, Salwa. (2004). 'Being Muslim: Islam, Islamism and Identity Politics'. *Government and Opposition*, vol. 39, no. 4. pp. 614–31.

Javadi, Hasan. (2010). *Another Birth and Other Poems*. Washington: Mage Publishers.

Joseph, Suad (ed.). (2000). *Gender and Citizenship in the Middle East*. Syracuse, NY: Syracuse University Press.

Kalinock, Sabine. (2003). 'Between Party and Devotion: Mowludi of Teheran Women'. *Critique: Critical Middle Eastern Studies*, vol. 12, no. 2. pp. 173–87.

Kamalkhani, Zahra. (1996). *Women's Islam: Religious Practice among Women in Today's Iran*. PhD Dissertation. Bergen: University of Bergen.

Keddie, Nikki R. (2003). *Modern Iran: Roots and Results of Revolution*. New Haven and London: Yale University Press.

Khan, Muhammad M. (2010). *Encyclopaedia of Islamic law and Jurisprudence*. New Delhi: Discovery Publishing House.

Kian-Thiébaut, Azadeh. (2000). 'Women's Religious Seminaries in Iran'. *ISIM Newsletter*, vol. 6, no. 23. Leiden: Institute for the Study of Islam in the Modern World. Available at: https://openaccess.leidenuniv.nl/bitstream/handle/1887/17451/ISIM_6_Women-s_Religious_Seminaries_in_Iran.pdf?sequence=1, accessed. 6 January 2012.

———. (2002). 'Women and the Making of Civil Society in Post-Islamist Iran'. In *Twenty Years of Islamic Revolution: Political and Social Transition in Iran since 1979*, E. Hooglund (ed.). Syracuse, NY: Syracuse University Press.

Kinninmont, Jane. (2011). 'Framing the Family Law: A Case Study of Bahrain's Identity Politics'. *Journal of Arabian Studies*, vol. 1, no. 1. pp. 53–68. Available at: http://dx.doi.org/10.1080/21534764.2011.576048, accessed 6 January 2012.

Künkler, Mirjam and Fazaeli, Roja. (2012). 'The life of two *mujtahidahs*: Female Religious Authority in 20th century Iran'. In *Women, Leadership and Mosques: Changes in Contemporary Islamic Authority*, M. Bano and H. Kalmbach (eds). Leiden: Brill.

Labidi, Lila. (2005). 'Human Rights in North Africa'. In *Encyclopedia of Women and Islamic Cultures*, S. Joseph and A. Najmabadi (eds). *Family Law and Politics*, vol. 2. Leiden: Brill.

Layish, Aron. (2006). *Women and Islamic Law in a Non-Muslim State: A Study Based on Decisions of Shari'a Courts in Israel*. New Brunswick, NJ: Transaction Publishers.

Mahmood, Saba. (2005). *Politics of Piety: The Islamic Revival and the Feminist Subject*. Princeton, NJ: Princeton University Press.

Mehran, Golnar. (2003). 'The Paradox of Tradition and Modernity in Female Education in the Islamic Republic of Iran'. *Comparative Education Review*, vol. 47, no. 3. pp. 26–86. Available at: http://www.jstor.org/stable/3542220, accessed 3 May 2010.

Meyer, Birgit, and Moors, Annelies. (eds). (2006). *Religion, Media, and the Public Sphere*. Bloomington and Indianapolis: Indiana University Press.

Mir-Hosseini, Ziba. (1996). 'Women and Politics in Post-Khomeini Iran: Divorce, Veiling, and Emerging Feminist Voices'. In *Women and Politics in the Third World*, H. Afshar (ed.). London: Routledge.

———. (2000a). *Marriage on Trial: A Study of Islamic Family Law*. London: I.B. Tauris.

———. (2000b). *Islam and Gender: The Religious Debate in Contemporary Iran*. London, New York: I.B. Tauris.

———. (2002). 'Religious Modernists and "the Woman Question"'. In *Twenty Years of Islamic Revolution: Political and Social Transitions in Iran from 1979*, E. Hooglund (ed.). Syracuse, NY: Syracuse University Press.

———. (2003). 'The Construction of Gender in Islamic Legal Thought and Strategies for Reform'. *Hawwa*: Journal of Women of the Middle East and the Islamic World. no.1, pp. 1–25.

———. (2006). 'Muslim Women's Quest for Equality: Between Islamic Law and Feminism'. *Critical Inquiry*, vol. 32, no. 4. pp. 629–45. Available at: http://www.jstor.org/stable/10.1086/508085, accessed 4 January 2011.

———. (2007). 'Negotiating the Forbidden: On Women and Sexual Love in Iranian Cinema'. *Comparative Study of South Asia, Africa, and the Middle East*, vol. 27, no. 3. pp. 673–9.

———. (2010). 'Shari'a and National Law in Iran'. In *Shari'a Incorporated: A Comparative Overview of the Legal Systems of Twelve Muslim Countries in Past and Present*, J.M. Otto (ed.). Leiden: Leiden University Press.

Moallem, Minoo (2005). *Between Warrior Brother and Veiled Sister: Islamic Fundamentalism and the Politics of Patriarchy in Iran*. California: University of California Press.

Moghadam, Valentine M. (2003). *Modernizing Women: Gender and Social Change in the Middle East*. Boulder, CO: Lynne Rienner Publishers.

———. (2011). 'Feminism and Family Law in Iran: The Struggle for Women's Economic Citizenship in the Islamic Republic of Iran'. In *Women and the Middle East and North Africa: Agents of Change*, F. Sadiqi and M. Ennaji (eds). New York: Routledge.

———. (2013a). *Globalization and Social Movements: Islamism, Feminism, and the Global Justice Movement*. 2nd edition. Lanham, MD.: Rowman & Littlefield.

———. (2013b). *Modernizing Women: Gender and Social Change in the Middle East*. 3rd edition. Boulder, CO, London: Lynne Rienner Publishers.

Momen, Moojan. (1985). *An Introduction to Shi'i Islam: The History and Doctrines of Twelver Shi'ism*. New Haven and London: Yale University Press.

Moors, Annelies. (1995). *Women, Property, and Islam: Palestinian Experiences 1920–1990*. Cambridge, UK: Cambridge University Press.

———. (2003). 'Public Debates on Family Law Reform. Participants, Positions, and Styles of Argumentation in the 1990s'. In *Islamic Law and Society*, vol. 10, no. 1. pp. 1–11.

———. (2006). 'Representing Family Law Debates in Palestine: Gender and the Politics of Presence'. In *Religion, Media, and the Public Sphere*, B. Meyer and A. Moors (eds). Bloomington and Indianapolis: Indiana University Press. pp. 115–31.

———. (2008). 'Registering a token dower: The multiple meanings of a legal practice'. In *Narratives of Truth in Islamic Law*, B. Dupret, B. Drieskens and A. Moors (eds). London: I.B. Taurus.

Nagar, Richa. (2000). 'Religion, Race and the Debate over Mut'a in Dar Es Salam'. *Feminist Studies*, vol. 26, no. 3. pp. 661–90. Available at: http://www.jstor.org/stable/3178645, accessed 14 September 2010.

Najmabadi, Afsaneh. (1998). 'Feminism in an Islamic Republic: Years of Hardship, Years of Growth'. In *Islam, Gender and Political Change*, Y.Y. Haddad and J. Esposito (eds). Oxford: Oxford University Press.

———. (2005). *Women with Mustaches and Men without Beards: Gender and Sexual Anxieties of Iranian Modernity*. Berkeley: University of California Press.

Osiek. Carolyn. (1985). 'The Feminist and the Bible: Hermeneutical Alternatives'. In *Feminist Perspectives on Biblical Scholarship*, A.Y. Collins (ed.). Society of Biblical Literature: Centennial Publications. California: Scholars Press.

Otto, Jan Michiel. (2010). 'Shari'a and National Law in Indonesia'. In *Shari'a Incorporated: A Comparative Overview of the Legal Systems of Twelve Muslim Countries in Past and Present*, J.M. Otto (ed.). Leiden. Leiden University Press.

Paidar, Parvin. (1995). *Women and the Political Process in Twentieth-Century Iran*. Cambridge, UK: Cambridge University Press.

Povey, Elaheh Rostami. (2004). 'Trade Unions and Women's NGOs: Diverse Civil Society Organisations in Iran'. *Development in Practice*, vol. 14, no. 1–2. pp. 254–66. Available at: http://www.jstor.org/stable/4030131, accessed: 27 January 2010.

Rabo, Annika. (2011). 'Syrian Transnational Families and Family Law'. In *From Transnational Relations to Transnational Laws: Northern European Laws at the Crossroads*, A. Hellum, S.S. Ali, and A. Griffiths (eds). Aldershot: Ashgate.

Repstad, Pål. (2007). *Mellom Nærhet og Distanse: Kvalitative Metoder i Samfunnsfag*. Oslo: Universitetsforlaget.

Rezai-Rashti, Goli, M. (2011). 'Exploring Women's Experience with Higher Education and the Changing Nature of Gender Relations in Iran'. In *Gender in Contemporary Iran: Pushing the Boundaries*, R. Bahramitash and E. Hooglund (eds). Oxford: Routledge.

Rosen, Lawrence. (1989). *The Anthropology of Justice: Law as Culture in Islamic Society*. Cambridge, UK: Cambridge University Press.

Salime, Zakie. (2009). 'Revisiting the Debate on Family Law in Morocco: Context, Actors, and Discourses'. In *Family, Gender, and Law in a Globalizing Middle East and South Asia*, K. M. Cuno and M. Desai (eds). Syracuse, NY: Syracuse University Press.

Salvatore, Armando. (2007). *The Public Sphere: Liberal Modernity, Catholicism, Islam*. New York, NY: Palgrave Macmillan.

Sanasarian, Eliz. (1982). *The Women's Rights Movement in Iran*. New York: Praeger.

Schielke, Samuli. (2010). 'Second Thoughts about the Anthropology of Islam, or How to Make Sense of Grand Schemes in Everyday life'. *ZMO Working Paper*. vol. 2. Available at: http://www.zmo.de/publikationen/WorkingPapers/schielke_2010.pdf, accessed 31 January 2012.

Schulz, Dorothea, E. (2003). 'Political Factions, Ideological Fictions: The Controversy over Family Law Reform in Democratic Mali'. *Islamic Law and Society*, vol. 10, issue 1. pp. 132–64. Available at: http://heinonline.org/HOL/Page?handle=hein.journals/islamls10&div=11&g_sent=1&collection=journals, accessed 5 January 12.

Selvik, Kjetil and Shahibzadeh, Yadollah. (2003). 'Islam og menneskerettigheter: Mojtahed Shabestaris postislamisme'. In *Babylon: Nordisk Tidsskrift for Midtøstenstudier*, vol. 1, no. 2. pp. 42–52. Available at: http://www.tidsskriftet-babylon.com/Sharia%20og%20menneskerettigheter.pdf, accessed 22 September 2013.

Shaham, Ron. (1997). *Family and the Courts in Modern Egypt: A Study Based on Decisions by Shari'a Courts, 1900–1955*. Studies in Islamic Law and Society. Leiden: Brill.

Shahd, Laila. (2003). *An Investigation of the Phenomenon of Polygyny in Rural Egypt*. Cairo Papers in Social Science, vol. 24, no. 3.

Shahidian, Hammed. (1994). 'The Iranian Left and the "Woman Question" in the Revolution of 1978–79'. *International Journal of Middle East Studies*, vol. 26, issue 2. pp. 223–47.

Shari'ati, 'Ali. (1980). *Fatima is Fatima*. Translated by L. Bakhtiar. Iran: The Shari'ati Foundation.

Sharma, Arvind and Young, Katherine K. (1999). *Feminism and World Religion*. Albany: State University of New York Press.

Shehada, Nahda Younis. (2005). 'Justice without Drama: Observations from Gaza City Shari'a Courts'. In *Gender, Religion, and Change in the Middle East: Two Hundred Years of History*. I. Flaskerud and I.M. Okkenhaug (eds). Oxford: Berg.

Singerman, Diane. (2010). 'The Economic Imperatives of Marriage: Emerging Practices and Identities Among Youth in the Middle East'. Working Paper. *Middle East Youth Initiative*. Available at: http://www.shababinclusion.org/files/559_file_Singerman_Paper_11_6_07.pdf, accessed 6 January 12.

Soares, Benjamin, F. (2009). 'The Attempt to Reform Family Law in Mali'. *Die Welt des Islams*, vol. 49, no. 3–4. pp. 398–428.

Sonneveld, Nadia. (2009). '"Khul" Divorce in Egypt Public Debates: Judicial Practices, and Everyday Life'. PhD Dissertation. Amsterdam: University of Amsterdam. Available at: http://dare.uva.nl/document/129513, accessed 5 November 2011.

Souaiaia, Ahmed E. (2008). *Contesting Justice: Women, Islam, Law, and Society*. Albany: State University of New York Press.

Tabari, Azar and Yeganeh, Nahid. (1982). *In the Shadow of Islam*. London: Zed.

Tajali, Mona. (2011). 'Notions of Female Authority in Modern Shi'i Thought'. *Religions*, vol. 2. pp. 449–68. Available at: http://www.mdpi.com/2077–1444/2/3/449/pdf, accessed 4 January 2012.

Taleqani, A'zam. (1997/1367). 'Why I can be a Presidential Candidate in the Republic?/ *Chera Kandidai-ye Riasat-e Jomhuri-ye Shodam?*'. *Payam-e Hajar*, no. 227. pp. 2–4.

Tohidi, Nayereh. (2002). 'Islamic Feminism: Perils and Promises'. *Middle East Women's Studies Review*, vol. 16, no. 3 and 4. Available at: http://www.nayerehtohidi.com/wp-content/uploads/docs/tohidi-article-2001-abstract-islamic-feminism-perils-promises.pdf, accessed 22 September 2013.

Tucker, Judith E. (2008). *Women, Family, and Gender in Islamic Law*. Cambridge, UK: Cambridge University Press.

Tønnessen, Liv. (2011). 'The Many Faces of Political Islam in Sudan: Muslim Women's Activism For and Against the State'. PhD Dissertation. Bergen: University of Bergen.

Umar, Muhammad S. (2004). 'Mass Islamic Education and Emergence of Female 'ulama' in Northern Nigeria: Background, Trends, and Consequences'. In *The Transmission of Learning in Islamic Africa*, S.S. Reese (ed.). Leiden: Brill.

Vali Nasr, Seyyed Vali Reza Nasr. (2007). *The Shi'a Revival: How Conflicts within Islam will Shape the Future*. New York: Norton.

Varisco, Daniel. (2000). 'Slamming Islam: Participant Webservation with a Web of Meanings to Boot. Working Papers from the MES'. Available at: http://www.aaanet.org/mes/lectvar1.htm, accessed 10 November 2011.

———. (2002). 'September 11: Participant Webservation of the "War on Terrorism"'. *American Anthropologist*, vol. 104, no. 3. pp. 934–8. Available at: http://www.jstor.org/stable/3567268, accessed 5 January 2012.

Vikør, Knut S. (2003). *Mellom Gud og Stat: Ei historie om islamsk lov og rettsvesen*. Oslo: Spartacus Forlag.

Weber, Max. (1964). *The Theory of Social and Economic Organization*. New York: The Free Press.

Welchman, Lynn. (2000a). 'Palestine: Pre-State Positioning on Family Law'. *International Survey of Family Law*. pp. 289–307. Available at: http://eprints.soas.ac.uk/2822/, accessed 6 January 2012.

———. (2000b). *Beyond the Code: Muslim Family Law and the Shari Judiciary in the Palestinian West Bank*. The Hague: Kluwer Law International.

———. (2007). *Women and Muslim Family Laws in Arab States: A Comparative Overview of Textual development and Advocacy*. ISIM Series on Contemporary Muslim Societies. ISIM/Leiden: Amsterdam University Press.

Würth, Anna. (2003). 'Stalled Reform: Family Law in Post-Unification Yemen'. *Islamic Law and Society*, vol. 10, no. 1. pp. 12–33. Available at: http://www.jstor.org/stable/3399218, accessed 6 January 2012.

Yamani, Maha, A.Z. (2008). *Polygamy and Law in Contemporary Saudi Arabia*. Reading: Ithaca Press.

Yassari, Nadjma and Saboory, Mohammed Hamid. (2010). 'Shari'a and National Law in Afghanistan'. In *Shari'a Incorporated: A Comparative Overview of the Legal Systems of Twelve Muslim Countries in Past and Present*, J.M. Otto (ed.). Leiden: Leiden University Press.

Young, Iris M. (1997). *Intersecting Voices: Dilemmas of Gender, Political Philosophy, and Policy*. Princeton, NJ: Princeton University Press.

Zeitzen. Miriam K. (2008). *Polygamy: A Cross Cultural Analysis*. Oxford, New York: Berg.

Zubizarreta, John. (1992). 'The Woman Who Sings No, No, No: Love, Freedom, and Rebellion in the Poetry of Forugh Farrokhzad'. *World Literature Today*, vol. 66, no. 3. pp. 421–6. Available at: http://www.jstor.org/stable/40148358, accessed 23 May 2011.

Legal Codes, Bills and Drafts

1928 Iranian Civil Code. 2002/1380. *The Civil Code of Iran / Qanun-e Madani*. English-Persian translation by F. Badrian. *Entesharat-e Daneshvar*, Tehran.

1967/75 Family Protection Law /*Qanun-e Hemayat-e Khanevadeh 1345/53*. Full text is available at: http://fis-iran.org/en/women/laws/family, accessed 31 December 2011.

1979 Constitution of the Islamic Republic of Iran. Full- text is available at: http://www.iranonline.com/iran/iran-info/government/constitution.html, accessed 31 December 2011.

1991 Islamic Penal Code of Iran. Full text in English is available at: http://www.unhcr.org/refworld/pdfid/4d384ae32.pdf, accessed 4 January 2012.

2007 Family Protection Bill / *Layehe-ye Hemayat-e az Khanevadeh 1386*. Full text in Persian is available at: http://fairfamilylaw.org/spip.php?article4, accessed 30.12.11. Full text in English is available at: http://meydaan.org/english/ShowArticle.aspx?arid=375, accessed 30 December 2011.

2010 Family Protection Bill / *Layehe-ye Hemayat-e az Khanevadeh 1389*. Full text in Persian is available at: http://familylaw.irangenderequality.com/spip.php?article1053, accessed 30 December 2011.

Convention on the Elimination of all Discrimination Against Women (CEDAW). 1979. The full text is available at: http://www.un.org/womenwatch/daw/cedaw/cedaw.htm, accessed 30 December 2011.

Mehrangiz Manoochehrian's Alternative Draft of Family Law 1963/64 / *Layehe-ye Pishnahadi az Mehrangiz Manoochehrian dar mord-e Qavanin-e Khanevadeh dar 1342*. Full text in Persian is available at: http://iranianfeministschool.com/spip.php?page=print&id_article=1218, and at: http://fairfamilylaw.info/spip.php?article1, accessed 30 December 2011.

Films and documentaries

Be Like Others. 2008. Directed by Tanaz Eshaghian. Iran and Canada.

Divorce Iranian Style. 1998. Directed by Kim Longinotto and Ziba Mir-Hosseini. Iran and England.

Hemlock / Showkaran. 2000. Directed by Behrouz Afkhami. Iran.

Letters to the President. 2009. Directed by Petr Lom. Iran, Canada and France.

Websites

ABC Science. 30 July 2003. 'Divorce via SMS approved by Malaysian court'. Available at: http://www.abc.net.au/science/articles/2003/07/30/913433.htm, accessed 8 January 2012.

Aftab News. 30 May 2007. 'I will not have us Join the Convention on Women's Rights / *Nemi Kozaram be Konvension-e Hoqoq-e Zanan-e Bepivandim*'. Available at: http://aftabnews.ir/fa/news/47049/-بپیوندیم-زنان-حقوق-کنوانسیون-به-گذارم-نمی, accessed 22 September 2013.

Amani, Elah. 2008. 'Widespread Opposition to Iran's "Family Protection Bill"'. Available at http://www.wunrn.com/news/2008/08_08/08_11_08/081108_iran.htm, accessed 21 April 2010.

Arjomand, Said Amir. 2010. 'The Iranian Revolution in the New Era'. Available at: http://www.currenttrends.org/research/detail/the-iranian-revolution-in-the-new-era, accessed 23 September 2013.

Ayoubi, Roula. 26 January 2011. 'Iraq toys with Polygamy as Solution for War Widows'. Available at: http://www.bbc.co.uk/news/world-middle-east-12266986, accessed 8 January 2012.

BBC. 4 March 2007. 'Iran Women Arrested over Protests'. Available at: http://news.bbc.co.uk/2/hi/6416789.stm, accessed 23 February 2012.

———. 3 March 2008. 'Iranian to Pay 124,000 Rose-Dowry'. Available at: http://news.bbc.co.uk/2/hi/middle_east/7275506.stm, accessed 8 January 2012.

BBC Persian. 3 December 2003. 'Perspective on Senator's Book / *Negahi-ye be Ketab-e Senator*'. Available at http://www.bbc.co.uk/persian/arts/story/2003/12/031202_pm-senator.shtml, accessed 6 June 2011.

———. 30 July 2011. 'Elimination of "Renewed Marriage" from Family Protection Bill: Your Opinions / *Hazf-e 'Ezdevaj-e Mujadad' az Layehe-ye Hemayat-e az Khanevadeh: Nazerat-e Shoma*'. Available at: http://newsforums.bbc.co.uk/ws/fa/thread.jspa?forumID=14327, accessed 8 January 2012.

Boghrati, Niusha. 2 May 2006. 'Islamic Dress Code to be Strictly Enforced'. Available at: http://www.worldpress.org/Mideast/2334.cfm, accessed 22 May 2010.

British Museum website. 'Cyrus Cylinder'. Available at: http://www.britishmuseum.org/explore/highlights/highlight_objects/me/c/cyrus_cylinder.aspx, accessed 8 January 2012.

Bøe, Marianne. 25 June 2009. 'Symbolsk Makt / Symbolic Power'. Available at: http://www.aftenposten.no/meninger/article3140246.ece, 8 January 2012.

Campaign for Equality website. 7 November 2010. 'Article of 24 of Family Protection Bill May Be Eliminated'. Available at: http://www.campaignforequality.info/english/spip.php?article786, accessed 10 March 2011.

———. 29 November 2010. 'The Family Protection Bill hurts not only Women, but Men and Children too'. Available at: http://www.campaignforequality.info/english/spip.php?article792, accessed 29 November 2010.

———. 27 December 2007. '"Family Protection Act" and the Future of our Daughters'. Available at: http://www.sign4change.info/english/spip.php?article195, accessed 8 Janyary 2012.

'Ebadi, Shirin. 10 December 2003. 'Nobel Lecture'. Available at: http://nobelpeaceprize.org/en_GB/laureates/laureates-2003/ebadi-lecture/, accessed 22 September 2013.

Erdbrink, Thomas and Branigin, William. 27 June 2009. 'Iranian Cleric Says Protesters Wage War Against God'. Available at: http://www.boston.com/news/world/middleeast/articles/2009/06/27/iranian_cleric_says_protesters_wage_war_against_god//, accessed 8 January 2012.

Fair Family Law website. 9 September 2007. 'Over 2000 Equal Rights Defenders Object to Proposed 'Family Support' Legislation'. Available at: http://www.fairfamilylaw.info/spip.php?article407, accessed 22 September 2013.

———. 16 February 2008. 'Ayatollah Sane'i: Polygamy without Consent of First Wife is not Permissible in Islam'. Available at: http://www.fairfamilylaw.info/spip.php?article405, accessed 22 September 2013.

———. 26 July 2008. 'Gity Porfazel: Family Protection Bill is Inconsistent with the Structure of Human Rights / *Gity Porfazel: Layehe-ye Hemayat-e Khanevadeh ba Sakhtar Hoqoq-e Bashar Moghayerat Darad*'. Available at: http://www.fairfamilylaw.info/spip.php?article153, accessed 30 December 2011.

———. 4 August 2008. 'Conversation with Sadeqi Vasmaqi: Male Bill for Women / *Goftego-ye ba Sadeqi Vasmaqi: Layehe-ye Mardaneh baraye Zanan*'. Available at: http://www.fairfamilylaw.info/spip.php?article187, accessed 30 December 2011.

———. 23 August 2008. 'Opposing the Family Protection Bill: Statement of the Coalition of Women's Rights Activists and Groups Against the "Family Protection Bill"'. Available at: http://www.fairfamilylaw.info/spip.php?article410, accessed 22 September 2013.

———. 31 August 2008. 'Some women rights activists, such as Shirin 'Ebadi and Simin Behbahani met and talked with some MPs about the Family Protection Bill'. Available at http://familylaw.irangenderequality.com/spip.php?article424 (read on 10 March 2011).

———. 15 January 2010. 'Overview of the Family Support Act Article 25: Men who Don't Pay Dower will be Imprisoned /*Morori-ye bar Madeh 25 Layehe-ye Hemayat-e az Khanevadeh: Mardani-ye ke Mehrieh Nemi Dahand Zendani Nemi*

Shavand'. Available at: http://fairfamilylaw.info/spip.php?article281, accessed 29 November 2010.

———. 24 April 2010. 'Take a Dowry: the Divine Gift of a Social Dilemma / *Negahi-ye be Mehrieh: Az 'Atieh Elahi-ye ta Mo'zul-e Ejtema'i-ye*'. Available at: http://fairfamilylaw.info/spip.php?article650, accessed 1 December 2010.

———. 7 May 2010. 'Legislator Must not be Able to Determine the Rate for Dower / *Qanungezar Nabayad Varud Muzu'-ye Ta'iyn Mizan Mehrieh Shod*'. Available at: http://fairfamilylaw.info/spip.php?article1469, accessed 1 December 2010.

———. 8 May 2010. 'Towards an Alternative Family Law/ *Be Sevi-ye Qanun-e Khanevadeh-ye Jayigozin*'. Available at: http://fairfamilylaw.info/spip.php?article732, accessed 8 January 2012.

———. 8 May 2010a. 'Alternative Propositions of Women from Different Iranian cities – Polygyny / *Pishnahadha-ye Zanan Irani dar Sharha-ye Mokhtalef – Chandhamsari/ta'adod-e Zujat*'. Available at: http://www.fairfamilylaw.info/spip.php?article736, accessed 22 September 2013.

———. 8 May 2010b. 'Alternative Propositions of Women from Different Iranian cities – Temporary Marriage / *Pishnahadha-ye Zanan Irani dar Sharha-ye Mokhtalef – Ezdevaj-e Movaqat* (*sighe*)'. Available at: http://www.fairfamilylaw.info/spip.php?article735, accessed 22 September 2013.

———. 8 May 2010c. 'Alternative Propositions of Women from Different Iranian cities – Dower / *Pishnahadha-ye Zanan Irani dar Sharha-ye Mokhtalef – Mehrieh*'. Available at: http://www.fairfamilylaw.info/spip.php?article737, accessed 22 September 2013.

———. 19 May 2010. 'Based on Current Law any Man can have a Small Harem/ *Bar Esas Qanun F'eli har Mard mitavanad yek Haremsari-ye Kochek dashte bashad*'. Available at: http://fairfamilylaw.info/spip.php?article793, accessed 1 December 2010.

———. 23 September 2010. 'A Statement by Equal Rights Defenders in Protest against Article 23 of Family Protection Bill: "Prohibit Polygamy!"'. Available at: http://fairfamilylaw.info/spip.php?article1538, accessed 29 June 2011.

———. 15 October 2010. 'Maryam Behrouzi: Some of the Articles 22 and 23 are in Opposition to the bill / *Bar Khi Chun Khodeshan Mesdaq Madeha-ye 22 va 23 Hastand ba Hamleh be Mokhalefin Layehe Fera Fekoni Mikonand*'. Available at: http://fairfamilylaw.info/spip.php?article1508, accessed 22 September 2013.

———. 19 October 2010. 'Zohreh Elaheyian: Family Protection Bill is Women's best Option against CEDAW / *Zohreh Elaheyian: Layehe-ye Hemayat-e az Khanevadeh Behtarin Gozineh dar Moqabel CEDAW Ast*'. Available at: http://fairfamilylaw.info/spip.php?article1671, accessed 30 December 2011.

———. 12 November 2010. 'Overview of Events Related to the Family Protection Bill in 1389 / *Moror bar Etefaqat-e Mortebat-e ba Layehe-ye Hemayat-e az Khanevadeh dar Sal-e 1389*'. Available at http://fairfamilylaw.info/spip.php?article1815, accessed 10 March 2011.

———. 1 December 2010. 'Ten Thousand Signatures Against Polygamy' Available at: http://fairfamilylaw.info/spip.php?article1948, accessed 30 December 2011.

———. 21 June 2011. 'Does Doctor Shari'ati Have anything to Say to Today's Woman? / *Aya Doktor Shari'ati baraye Zan-e Emruz harfi baraye Goftan Darad?*'. Available at: http://fairfamilylaw.info/spip.php?article3195, accessed 22 September 2013.

———. 29 July 2011. 'Policy of "this Column is the Final Column" of Iranian Majles and the Fate of the Family Law Article 23/ *Siasat-e az "in Sutun be an Sutun-e Farj Ast" Majles-e Iran va Sarnevesht Madeh 23 dar Layehe-ye Khanevadeh*'. Available at: http://www.fairfamilylaw.info/spip.php?article3646, accessed 22 September 2013.

———. 4 August 2011. 'Deletion of Article 23 is Equal to Bringing Silence to Polygyny/ *Hazf-e Madeh 23 Sukut Qanun-e Gozar dar Barabar Chandhamsari ast*'. Available at: http://www.fairfamilylaw.info/spip.php?article3718, accessed 22 September 2013.

———. 16 August 2011. 'Divorce Rights are not Enough: Single Men have Permission to Temporary Marriage / *Hoq-e Talaq Kafi nist: Mardan Mojarad Ejaze-ye Ezdevaj-e Movaqat-e Dashte Bashand*'. Available at: http://www.fairfamilylaw.info/spip.php?article3864, accessed 22 September 2013.

Farda News. 13 August 2011. 'The Legal Right to Divorce for Women / *Hoq-e Talaq Baraye Zanan Qanuni-ye Mishod*'. Available at: www.fardanews.com/fa/news/158148/حق-طلاق-برای-زنان-قانونی-می-شود, accessed 16 August 2011.

Farsinet website. 'Cyrus: First Charter of Human Rights'. Available at: http://www.farsinet.com/cyrus/index.html, accessed 8 January 2012.

Feminist School website. 18 August 2008. 'From Bad to Worse'. Available at: http://www.iranianfeministschool.info/english/spip.php?page=print&id_article=123, accessed 8 January 2012.

———. 25 August 2008. 'Mehrangiz Manoochehrian's Alternative Draft of Family Law 1963/64 / *Layehe-ye Pishnahadi-ye az Mehrangiz Manoochehrian dar mord-e Qavanin-e Khanevadeh dar 1342*'. Available at: www.iranfeministschool.info/spip.php?article1218&var_recherche=پیشنهادی, accessed 8 January 2012.

———. 10 June 2009. 'The Coalition of Women's Movement in Election: Press Conference'. Available at: http://feministschool.com/english/spip.php?article304, accessed 8 January 2012.

———. 1 August 2009. 'Women's Movement Activists in Detention in Iran". Available at: http://www.feministschool.com/english/spip.php?article324, accessed 23 February 2012.

———. 12 February 2010. 'Family law Rules: Reproducing the Structural Violence Against Women. Interview with Doctor Shahla E'zazi/ *Qvanin-e Marbut-e be Khanevadeh: Baztolid-e Khoshvenat-e Sakhtari-ye 'Ali-ye Zanan Ast. Goftego ba Doktor Shahla E'zazi*'. Available at: http://www.feministschool.com/spip.php?article4226, accessed 22 September 2013.

———. 3 March 2010. 'Stop Iran's Parliament from Ratifying an Anti-Family Bill'. Available at: http://www.feministschool.com/english/spip.php?article369, accessed 22 September 2013.

———. 21 April 2010. 'Interview with Faezeh Hashemi: How Can a Woman Become a Lawyer and a Minister but be Secondary Gender and Minor in Family? /*Dar Goftego ba Faezeh Hashemi: Chetor Ast ke Zan Mitavanad Vakil va Ozir Bashad amma dar Khanevadeh Seghir ast va Jens-e Dovvom?*'. Available at: http://www.feministschool.com/spip.php?article4689, accessed 22 September 2013.

———. 29 December 2010. 'For Forough was Another Voice: Protest Voice / *Baraye Forough Sedai-ye Digar Bud: Seda-ye Motarez*'. Available at: http://www.feministschool.org/spip.php?article6519, accessed 8 January 2012.

———. 31 July 2011. 'We Have Abolished Polygyny or Have We Collected a Vote for the Majles Representatives? / *Ma Chandhamsari Laqy-e Kardim ya Baraye Majlesi-yan Ray-e Jam'e Kardim?*'. Available at: https://www.facebook.com/notes/the-feminist-school--را-چندهمسری-ما/فمینیستی-مدرسه-سام-نازنین
لغو-کردیم-یا-برای-مجلسیان-رای-جمع-کردیم, accessed 8 January 2012.

Forough Farrokhzad website. 'The Authenticity of Forough Farrokhzad'. Available at: http://www.forughfarrokhzad.org/papers/papers4.htm, accessed 8 January 2012.

Gooch, Liz. 5 January 2010. 'Malaysian Polygamy Club Draws Criticism'. Available at: http://www.nytimes.com/2010/01/06/world/asia/06malaysia.html?_r=1, accessed 8 January 2012.

Hamza, Masjaliza and Othman, Norami. 14 January 2010. 'Stress, Quarrels, and Neglect: The "Normal" Polygamous Family'. Available at: http://www.opendemocracy.net/5050/masjaliza-hamzah-norami-othman/stress-quarrels-and-neglect-normal-polygamous-family, accessed 8 January 2012.

Harrison, Frances. 12 June 2006. 'Iran Police Beat Women Activists'. Available at: http://news.bbc.co.uk/2/hi/5073328.stm, accessed 23 March 2012.

———. 2 June 2007. 'Iran Talks up Temporary Marriage'. Available at: http://news.bbc.co.uk/2/hi/6714885.stm, accessed 8 January 2012.

Icana News. 13 August 2011. 'Added Divorce Right for Women in the Family Protection Bill / *Ezaf-e Shod Hoq-e Talaq Baray-e Zanan dar Layeh-ye Hemayat-e az Khanevadeh*'. Available at: http://www.icana.ir/NewsPage.aspx?NewsID=174800, accessed 16 August 2011.

Iranian Labour News Agency website. 24 August 2010. 'Elahe Rastgoo: "The Representatives have Promised Not to Vote in Favour of Article 22, 23 and 24" / *Elahe Rastgoo: "Nemaiyandgan Qul-e Dadeand-e be Mavad 22, 23, va 24 Rai-ye Movafaq-e Nadahand*"'. Available at: www.aftabir.com/news/view/2010/aug/24/c4c1282634017_social_family_home_family.php/-مواد۲۲-اند-به-قول-داده
الهه-راستگو-نمایندگان, accessed 22 September 2013.

———. 25 August 2010. 'Opponents of Family Protection Act want to Join Convention for Elimination of Discrimination Against Women / *Makhalefan Layehe-ye Hemayat-e az Khanevadeh mikhahand be Konvension-e Raf'e-ye Tab'iz-e 'Alieh-ye Zanan-e Bepivandim*'. Available at: www.aftabir.com/news/view/2010/aug/25/c4c1282719771_social_family_home_family.php/
الهیان-مخالفان-لایحه-حمایت-از-خانواده-می-خواهند, accessed 22 September 2013.

Iran Daily. 30 December 2005. 'Women *Basij* Nationwide'. Available at: http://www.iran-daily.com/1384/2464/html/national.htm, accessed 9 April 2010.

Islamic Republic News Agency. 26 November 2007. 'Supreme Leader inspects *Basij* Units'. Available at: http://www.turkishweekly.net/news/50644/ayatollah-khamenei-inspects-basij.html, accessed 9 January 2012.

Karmand News. 13 August 2011. 'Article 23 Deleted from Family Protection Bill / *Madeh 23 Hafz-e az layehe-ye Hemayat-e az Khanevadeh*'. Available at: http://www.karmandnews.ir/shownews.aspx?ID_News=20332, accessed 3 September 2011.

Knickmeyer, Ellen. 2008. 'A New text in Islamic Law'. Available at: http://www.washingtonpost.com/wp-dyn/content/article/2008/01/18/AR2008011803628.html, accessed 22 September 2013.

Learning Partnership website. 8 February 2008. 'Zanan, Iran's Leading Women's Magazine, Shut Down by Government'. Available at: http://play.learningpartnership.org/en/advocacy/alerts/zanan0208, accessed 8 January 2012.

Mardomak News. 26 July 2011. 'Majles Vote: Polygyny of Men Eliminated from the Family Protection Bill / *Ra-ye Majles, Hazf-e Chandhamsari-ye Mardan dar Layehe-ye Hemayat-e az Khanevadeh*'. Available at: http://www.mardomak.org/story/63838, accessed 8 January 2012.

Meydan website. 10 August 2008. 'Why Protest the Tax, Not the Original Dower? / *Chera E'teraz-e be Vaze'-ye Maliyat-e bar Mehrieh Na be Asl Mehrieh?*'. Available at: http://meydaan.info/ShowArticle.aspx?arid=632, accessed 29 November 2010.

Musawah website. 'Morocco'. Available at: http://www.musawah.org/spotlight-morocco, accessed 22 September 2013.

Nobel Peace Prize website. 10 December 2003. 'Nobel Peace Prize 2003'. Available at: http://nobelpeaceprize.org/nb_NO/laureates/laureates-2003/, accessed 8 January 2012.

Norwegian Broadcasting Association (NRK). 6 July 2010. 'Hestehale er uislamsk / Ponytale is un-Islamic'. Available at: http://www.nrk.no/nyheter/verden/1.7198736, accessed 8 January 2012.

Payvand. 28 September 2002. 'Women's Divorce Right is Rejected by Iran's Guardians Council'. Available at: http://www.netnative.com/news/02/sep/1102.html, accessed 8 January 2012.

———. 13 June 2006. 'Iranian Police Forcibly Disperse Women's Rights Protest in Tehran"'. Available at: http://www.payvand.com/news/06/jun/1126.html, accessed 9 January 2012.

———. 18 August 2008. "'Iran: Ayatollah Support Women's Right to Inheritance and Abortion"'. Available at: http://www.payvand.com/news/08/feb/1170.html, accessed 9 January 2012.

———. 14 January 2010. 'Iran: Arrest of 19 Activists from the Women's Movement, Women Journalists and Civil Activists'. Available at: http://www.payvand.com/news/10/jan/1131.html, accessed 9 January 2012.

———. 18 September 2010. 'Iranian MP criticizes Ahmadinejad for praising Cyrus the Great'. Available at: http://www.payvand.com/news/10/sep/1173.html, accessed 8 January 2012.

Press TV. 29 August 2010. 'Judiciary Issues Statement on Ashtiani'. Available at: http://www.presstv.ir/detail/140508.html, accessed 9 January 2012.

———. 12 September 2010. 'Ahmadinejad Hails Cyrus Cylinder'. Available at: http://edition.presstv.ir/detail/142251.html, accessed 22 September 2013.

Qantara. 28 October 2010. 'We Need to Rethink Old Dogmas: Interview with Ziba Mir-Hosseini'. Available at: http://en.qantara.de/We-Need-to-Rethink-Old-Dogmas/9555c9654i1p660/index.html, accessed 4 December 2011.

Radio Zamaneh. 17 November 2010. 'Iran Opposition Insists on Gender Equality'. Available at: http://www.zamaaneh.com/enzam/2010/11/iranian-opposition-insist.html, accessed 8 January 2012.

Rahnavard, Zahra. 21 August 2010. 'Calling of the Family Protection Bill is a Symbol of National Demand / *Kharej-e Kardan Layehe be Estelah-e Hemayat-e az Khanevadeh Nemad Khavasti Mely ast*'. Available at: http://www.facebook.com/note.php?note_id=433598777611, accessed 1 December 2010.

Rohama. 6 April 2011. 'Hazrat Zeinab (AS) is the Paradigms for all Muslim women'. Available at: http://www.rohama.org/en/news/4482/hazrat-zeinabas-is-the-paradigms-for-all-muslim-women, accessed 8 January 2012.

Roozonline. 18 August 2008. 'More Women-only Universities in Provinces'. Available at: http://www.roozonline.com/english/news3/newsitem/article/more-women-only-universities-in-provinces.html, accessed 22 September 2013.

Sadr, Shadi. 2007. 'Stop Stoning Campaign; An Unfinished Story'. Available at: http ://goo.gl/yLVfOF, accessed 22 September 2013.

———. 2010. 'Stones Aimed at Us: An Overview of the Discourse and Strategies of the Stop Stoning Forever Campaign'. *AWID*. Available at: http://www.awid.org/Media/Files/CF_CaseStudy_Iran, accessed 22 September 2013.

Scioloino, Elaine. 4 October 2000. 'Love finds a way'. Available at: http://www.nytimes.com/2000/10/04/world/love-finds-a-way-in-iran-temporary-marriage.html?pagewanted=1, accessed 14 April 2010.

Schulz, Matthias. 15 July 2008. 'Falling for Ancient Propaganda'. Available at: http ://www.spiegel.de/international/world/0,1518,566027,00.html, accessed 17 January 2011.

Siddiqui, Pervez Iqual. 27 October 2010. 'Talaq Joke on Skype Ends Marriage'. Available at: http://articles.timesofindia.indiatimes.com/2010–10–27/lucknow/28230688_1_talaq-three-times-dar-ul-ifta-iddat-period#ixzz13dRRqAED, accessed 8 January 2012.

Sign 4 Change website, 28 August 2006. 'The Effect of Laws on Women's Rights'. English and Persian version of text available at: http://www.sign4change.info/english/spip.php?article41, accessed 8 January 2012.

Sisters in Islam. 16 March 2003. 'Campaign for Monogamy'. Available at: http://www.sistersinislam.org.my/news.php?item.833.8, accessed 22 September 2013.

———. 28 December 2006. '"Polygamy's Effect on Muslim Families"'. Available at: http://www.sistersinislam.org.my/print.php?news.76, accessed 8 January 2012.

Strobel-Dahan, Antoine. 23 June 2009. 'Neda, une Histoire qui Synthétise la Complexité du Conflit / Neda, a Story that Sums up the Complexities of the Conlict'. Available at: http://www.lemonde.fr/proche-orient/article/2009/06/23/neda-icone-de-la-revolte-iranienne_1210120_3218.html, accessed 8 January 2012.

Tabnak. 24 April 2008. 'Ahmadinejad: The Culture of Martyrdom as a Solution to Economic Problems / *Ahmadinejad: Farhang-e Shahadat Baraye Hall-e Moshkelat-e Eqtesadi*'. Available at: http://www.tabnak.ir/pages/?cid=9559, accessed 20 May 2010.

Taheri, Amir. 8 January 2011. 'Cyrus the Great Cylinder and Ahmadinejad's Quest for legitimacy'. Available at: http://www.cais-soas.com/news/index.php?option=com_content&view=article&id=330:cyrus-the-great-cylinder-a-ahmadinejads-quest-for-legitimacy&catid=50, accessed 8 January 2012.

Tait, Robert. 28 July 2005. 'A Fatwa for Transsexuals'. Available at: http://www.salon.com/2005/07/28/iran_transsexuals/, accessed 8 January 2012.

Telegraph. 21 June 2009. 'Iran's *Basij* Force: The Shock Troops Terrorising Protesters'. Available at: http://www.telegraph.co.uk/news/worldnews/middleeast/iran/5588291/Irans-Basij-force-the-shock-troops-terrorising-protesters.html, accessed 8 April 2010.

Tohidi, Nayereh. 2006. 'Iran's Women's Rights Movement and the One Million Signatures Campaign'. Available in English at: http://www.payvand.com/news/06/dec/1174.html, accessed 7 January 2012. Available in Persian at: http://www.we-change.org/spip.php?article137, accessed 7 January 2012.

———. 12 December 2007. 'Iran's Women's Rights Movement and the One Million Signatures Campaign'. Available at: http://www.we-change.org/spip.php?article208, accessed 8 January 2012.

United Nations website. 'Reservations to CEDAW'. Available at: http://www.un.org/womenwatch/daw/cedaw/reservations.htm, accessed 8 January 2012.

Vaswani, Karishma. 17 December 2009. 'Club Promotes Polygamy in Malaysia'. Available at: http://news.bbc.co.uk/2/hi/8412496.stm, accessed 8 January 2012.

We Change website. 26 August 2006. 'About One Million Signatures Campaign Demanding Changes to Discriminatory Laws'. Available at: http://www.we-change.org/spip.php?article18, accessed 8 January 2012.

———. 16 February 2008. 'Ayatollah Sane'i Issues Fatwa in Support of Women's Inheritance'. Available at: http://we-change.org/english/spip.php?article217, accessed 8 January 2012.

———. 18 August 2008. 'Opposing the Family Protection Bill: Statement of the Coalition of Women's Rights Activists and Groups against the Family Protection Bill'. Available at: http://www.we-change.org/english/spip.php?article324, accessed 1 December 2010.

———. 7 November 2010. 'Article 24 of Family Protection Bill may be Eliminated'. Available at: http://we-change.org/english/spip.php?article786, accessed 26 November 2010.

———. 28 July 2011. 'Iranian Parliament Omits Controversial Family Law Bill'. Available at: http://www.we-change.org/english/spip.php?article925, accessed 8 January 2012.

WLUML website. 'Polygamy in Central Asia'. Available at: http://www.wluml.org/node/1204, accessed 8 January 2012.

Worth, Robert F. 20 November 2008. 'Hezbollah Seeks to Marshal the Piety of the Young'. Available at: http://www.nytimes.com/2008/11/21/world/middleeast/21lebanon.html?_r=1, accessed 10 October 2010.

Zan-e Farda website. 30 October 2010. 'Problem in the Name of Dowers are Big and Strange / *Moshgel-e dar Nam-e Mehrieh Sangin va 'Ajib Hastand*'. Available at: http://zanefarda.ir/1389/08/, accessed 1 December 2010, and at: http://fairfamilylaw.info/spip.php?article1735, accessed 22 September 2013.

INDEX

www.ingramcontent.com/pod-product-compliance
Ingram Content Group UK Ltd.
Pitfield, Milton Keynes, MK11 3LW, UK
UKHW020206290926
15470UKWH00001B/25

9 781780 769004